THE
National ⟨SABR⟩ Pastime

SABR 51
Heart of the Midwest

Edited by Cecilia M. Tan

 ⟨SABR⟩ **Published by The Society for American Baseball Research**

THE NATIONAL PASTIME – 2023 EDITION

Copyright © 2023 The Society for American Baseball Research

Editor: Cecilia M. Tan
Design and production: Lisa Hochstein
Cover design: Lisa Hochstein
Fact checker: Clifford Blau
Proofreader: Jason Nielsen, Keith R.A. DeCandido

ISBN 978-1-970159-94-3 print edition
ISBN 978-1-970159-93-6 ebook edition

Society for American Baseball Research, Inc.
Cronkite School at ASU
555 N. Central Ave. #406C
Phoenix, AZ 85004

Web: www.sabr.org
Phone: (602) 496–1460

CONTENTS

From the Editor   Cecilia M. Tan   5

The Empire of Freeport
Base Ball in Northern Illinois and Iowa in 1865   Jim Leeke   7

Did Bud Fowler Almost Break the Major-League Color Line In 1888?
A Midwestern Memoir of John T. Brush and Guy M. Smith   David Kathman   11

Exit Stage Left
The Sad Farewell of Cap Anson   Michael Haupert   18

Boodle and Barnstorming
When Politics and the National Pastime Convened in Dwight, Illinois   Bill Pearch   22

The 1906 World Series
The First World Series with Umpire Hand Signals   R.A.R. Edwards   27

The Chicago Green Sox   Steven M. Glassman   32

For Whom the Ballgame Tolls
Ernest Hemingway Attends a White Sox Game Before Shipping Off to War   Sean Kolodziej   36

The White Stockings' Fleet-Footed Preacher
Billy Sunday vs. the Alcohol Machine   Joseph L. Thompson   38

Guilty as Charged
Buck Weaver and the 1919 World Series Fix   Bill Lamb   41

The Endurance of Black Sox Mythology
Narrative Conventions and Poetic Form   Bill Savage and S.P. Donohue   53

Which Manager Knew First That the 1919 World Series Was Fixed?   Tim Newman   58

Major League Baseball in Iowa
Iowa's History of Hosting Negro League Contests   John Shorey and Kevin Warneke   63

Chicago, Latina Culture, and Community of Women's Baseball   Emalee Nelson   69

Hack Wilson: A Pugilist   John Racanelli   73

Stan Hack
Leadoff Batter Extraordinaire   Herm Krabbenhoft   78

Handy Andy Pafko
A Wisconsin-Born Player Succeeds In Chicago And Milwaukee   Steve Krevisky   89

A Fox in White Sox — Joseph Wancho — 91

The Path to the Cubs and White Sox from the Negro Leagues
17 Barrier Breakers — Alan Cohen — 93

The Michigan City White Caps — Bob Webster — 98

1967: A Perfect Season for Ken Holtzman
A Weekend Wonder in the Summer of Love — Jeff Allan Howard — 101

The South Side's First Home Run King: Bill Melton — Joseph Wancho — 103

Bill Veeck
The Second Time Around — Dan Helpingstine — 106

Belle of the Ballclub
Marla Collins's Unusual Path from Cubs Ballgirl to Playboy Model — Dan VanDeMortel — 110

Field of Hollywood Dreams
Actors and Their Baseball Roles Beyond the World's Most Famous Cornfield — David Krell — 116

Larry Fritsch, Card King
First Full-time Dealer's Legacy Continues After 53 Years — Tom Alesia — 119

Reborn at 111
Wausau Wisconsin's Athletic Park Plays with History — Tom Alesia — 122

Contributors — 126

FROM THE EDITOR

Welcome, my friends, not just to the Windy City, but to the windswept plains, lakeshores, towns, and church ballfields in the heart of the Midwest. In this issue of *The National Pastime*, we will barnstorm through Indiana, Iowa, and Wisconsin, as well as several stops in Illinois, both in Chicago and in towns just a train ride away.

The last time the SABR convention was in Chicago, in 2015, we featured a map of the city on the cover, and photos of one White Sox star and one Cubs star (Minnie Miñoso and Ernie Banks). The focus was very much on the urban center. So when we found out SABR would be returning to Chicago for the 2023 summer convention, I wanted to broaden the horizon of the publication to see what interesting stories could be discovered if we included not just Illinois but its bordering states.

SABR members responded, as they always do, with a plethora of tales. Some of them do concern favorite Chicago topics like beloved Bill Veeck and bedeviled Buck Weaver, and both Smiling Stan Hack and Hack Wilson, Cap Anson and Ken Holtzman, but we'll also meet a Mexican women's baseball team based in East Chicago (Indiana), minor league teams from Michigan City (also Indiana) and Wausau, Wisconsin, some baseball-savvy politicians, a card-collecting magnate, and hear all about the Negro Leagues teams who barnstormed through Iowa on a regular basis—often facing each other in league play.

And much more. So grab some peanuts and Cracker Jack—a local snack made famous at the 1893 World's Columbian Exhibition in Chicago—and watch our "SABR All-Stars" take the field.

– Cecilia M. Tan
July 2023

2023 Jerry Malloy Negro League Conference
July 20-23 | Detroit, MI

Featuring research presentations, panels, discussions and a banquet with prominent African American players from different eras, the Jerry Malloy Negro League Conference is the only symposium dedicated to preserving and promoting Black baseball history.

Black baseball has a long history in Michigan, especially centered in the Motor City. Among the original entrants to the Negro National League in 1920 was Tenny Blount's Detroit Stars, managed by Pete Hill and anchored by Big Bill Gatewood on the mound. The Detroit Wolves and Motor City Giants also played in Mack Park and Hamtramck Stadium. In addition to the well-known Turkey Stearnes (pictured), other star players included catcher Bruce Petway, the speedy Jimmie Lyons and the powerful Edgar Wesley.

This year's event will be hosted at various venues throughout Detroit, including Wayne State University, Hamtramck Stadium, Comerica Park, and the Detroit Historical Museum.

Register today at sabr.org/malloy

The Empire of Freeport

Base Ball in Northern Illinois and Iowa in 1865

Jim Leeke

The Empire Base Ball Club of Freeport, Illinois, began its 1865 season by lamenting "the melancholy and terrible blow which has fallen upon this country by the untimely death of President Lincoln."[1] The assassination of "Father Abraham" only days after the surrender of the rebel Army of Northern Virginia especially distressed the residents of Freeport, site of a Lincoln-Douglas debate in 1858. Within hours of the president's passing on April 15, the town's ballplayers resolved to drape their club rooms in black and wear badges of mourning for thirty days.

Formed three years earlier, the Empire club never had enjoyed a peacetime season. As noted in the Freeport press, when the club was founded, "it was the only Base Ball Club in the State, with the exception, perhaps, of a club in Chicago."[2] (The big city, in fact, had fielded at least 18 clubs by 1861, but the sport there had "rather fallen into the background since the commencement of the war.") With many area men away fighting in the Union Army, the Empire club did little during 1862 except practice the game and learn its rules. The following year, it searched in vain for contests in Illinois, Iowa, and Wisconsin, before finally arranging three games with the Garden City club of Chicago. Two wins at home after an opening loss in Chicago prompted the prairie upstarts to declare themselves state champions.

"In 1864 the club continued its organization and its practice," as reported in the *Freeport Journal*, "but the war thinned out its ranks, and, although holding itself ready to play any aspiring club, it sought no contest, and the year passed without any match game of importance."[4] (The unimportant contests, however, included a "most exciting and entertaining game" in August with the fledgling Grant Base Ball Club, also of Freeport.[5] Empire lost by a score typical for the era, 31–19.)

The townsfolk saw their next baseball six weeks following Lincoln's assassination. Empire and Grant had since merged, but briefly separated again to play an intrasquad game June 1. "The lovers of Base Ball play, will have a rare treat on Thursday," reported the *Freeport Weekly Journal*, "as the Empire have divided into equal sides...for a complete game of nine innings, 'Home and Home Game,' on Thursday at 2 o'clock."[6] Empire beat Grant, 46–33, in four hours on its field near the fairgrounds. Both sides exhibited "great energy and skill...although the heat was intense and labor hard."[7]

The next week Empire issued a general challenge to all baseball clubs in the West (what is considered the Midwest today) for a series of games. An established club in St. Louis—also named Empire—earlier had challenged its Freeport counterpart to a game in Chicago; the smaller club had declined, claiming a challenged team's right to select the ground. The two Empires now agreed to play at Freeport on the Fourth of July. "We understand there will be quite a number of the friends of the game," a St. Louis newspaper noted, "who will take advantage of the opportunity and will accompany the club on their excursion."[8]

The contest seemed a mismatch. St. Louis boasted a population of 160,000, while Freeport had fewer than 5,400. But talent is where you find it, and the underdogs were optimistic. The challengers arrived in town following a grueling twenty-five hour, 320-mile journey north on the St. Louis Alton and Terre Haute Railroad. They were "warmly received by the Freeport club at the depot and thence escorted to their hotel. ... After supper [the St. Louis visitors] strolled through the town, and were agreeably surprised to find it not only a brisk business city but also an exceedingly beautiful one."[9]

The national holiday dawned under a scorching sun and grew progressively hotter. "I was awakened of an early hour this morning, not by the ringing of bells or the booming of cannon, but by the excessive oppressiveness of the atmosphere," a *Chicago Tribune* correspondent wrote. "It was as if red hot stoves had been suspended in the air, and placed by a lavish hand upon every available spot of ground in the town and the adjoining country."[10] Six thousand spectators turned out from as far away as Iowa to see the game at the local ballfield.

The Sporting News decades later called Empire-versus-Empire the "first fly ball match west of the Alleghenies." In the past, both fair and foul balls caught on one bounce had been outs. A rule change in December 1864 meant fair balls were now outs only if caught on the fly. The switch took time to take hold, however, and the teams meeting at Freeport hadn't decided whether to play under bounder or fly rules. "Just as you please," the St. Louis skipper said when asked which it should be. Freeport's captain then promptly chose the latter, since "the 'fly' game was still quite a novelty, and though some of the St. Louis boys felt a little weak over the chances of winning."[11]

Play again lasted four hours, "and though the heat was intense, nearly all who were present were so deeply interested in the contest they remained until the close," said the *Freeport Weekly Journal*.[12] The St. Louis club's experience was evident during most of the game. At the bottom of the ninth inning the Mound City men led, 27–13, but "really fine batting done by Freeport, and the poor fielding of St. Louis," let the home team score seven runs before the visitors snuffed the rally.[13] A New York newspaper said the 27–20 victory gave St. Louis the "Championship of the West."[14]

"The St. Louis Club is unquestionably one of the best in the whole country, and the boys of the [Freeport] 'Empire' lost no laurels in being defeated by so close a margin by them," the *Weekly Journal* said proudly. "Had they done as well throughout the game as they did near its close, St. Louis would have gone home vanquished. Both parties did nobly. Both gained in reputation."[15] The visiting team caught an evening train home and had to decline the hospitality offered by Col. John W. Shaffer, a political supporter and friend of the late president's. Shaffer had gotten involved in Freeport baseball since his return from the war and his presence would be felt later in the season.

By midsummer, Freeport was fielding four baseball teams: "one old men's—one young men's—and two boys' clubs."[16] Empire, Empire Jr., Union, and Atlantic played each other until the senior Empires traveled a couple of dozen miles east for a July 30 game at Rockford, Illinois. Empire easily beat the local Forest City club, 55–21, at the slightly larger town in Winnebago County. That game concluded baseball on the prairie for a while. "During the hot month of August the club took a breathing spell, and gathered strength for the fall contests."[17]

Despite the summer's heat, the Winnebago County Agricultural Society glimpsed possibilities in the new sport. It organized a state championship tournament to be played September 19 and 20 at its county fairgrounds.

FREEPORT WEEKLY JOURNAL

Here the dispute arose that terminated the game; the Excelsior claiming that Cavanagh was fairly put out, which Cavanagh himself and the spectators in the immediate vicinity of the base, emphatically denied. The umpire, Mr. Marshal, of the Capital City Club of Madison, Wis., decided at first in favor of the Excelsior, but, after a patient hearing of both sides, and becoming convinced that his decision was not justified by the facts, reversed it; whereupon the Excelsior Club withdrew from the field and abandoned the contest; thus leaving the umpire no other alternative but to declare the Empire Club the winners of the ball and bat. The following is the score, as it stood at the termination of the match:

EXCELSIOR.	O.	R.	EMPIRE.	O.	R.
J. W. Sterns, c.	1	4	Buckman, 1st b.	1	4
Smith, l. f.	4	1	Cavanagh, s. s.	3	1
Malcomb, 2d b.	1	4	Deifendorf, c. f.	3	2
Kennedy, p	2	1	Thomas, c.	0	3
Goodrich, l. f.	4	1	Lighthart, r. f.	1	2
Mackey, s. s.	3	0	Lebkicker, l. f.	3	1
Foley, 3d b.	3	2	Best, p.	3	1
Gillespie, 1st b.	1	2	Brewster, 3d b.	2	0
Quick, r. f.	3	1	Stoskopf, 2d b.	3	1
	21	16		19	15

Excerpt from the September 27, 1865, newspaper account of how the Empires came to win the match following a disputed umpire's call.

"We trust this favorable opportunity will be taken advantage [of] by the Base Ball Clubs of this city to measure batting, &c., with their Rockford friends, and mark the improvement each has made since last they met to contest for superiority in this manly game," the *Freeport North-West* said.[18]

Empire entered the tournament, as did Freeport's latest team, the Shaffer Base Ball Club, also known as Shaffer's Nine. Filling out the slate were Forest City plus two clubs from Chicago, old rivals Atlantic and Excelsior. The championship trophy was a silver ball and rosewood bat. "All lovers of this truly exciting and beautiful game are invited to be on hand to witness some spirited contests," the *North-West* said.[19]

Atlantic beat Forest City, 26–20, in the opening game on Tuesday morning. That afternoon Excelsior easily topped Shaffer, 37–8. The winner of the Atlantic-Empire game Wednesday morning was then supposed to play Excelsior for the title. "A large crowd assembled at the appointed time, eager to witness the sport," the *Freeport Weekly Journal* said, "but, a dispute arising as to whether the Atlantic should be allowed to substitute two men in place of two of the players of the previous day, and add one man to make up their full nine, a long controversy ensued, which terminated in the withdrawal of the Atlantic from the contest."[20] The championship game thus became Empire's only appearance in the tournament.

Empire and Excelsior met at two o'clock before a sea of spectators. Crowd estimates were as large as ten thousand. "Excelsior played *beautifully*; they showed that they had an easy job, and were in great glee," the *North-West* reported.[21] But betting was heavy as Empire rallied to trail by one run, 16–15, during the seventh inning. With one out and runners at the corners, the game then descended into chaos as St. Louis attempted a pickoff at third base. The umpire—a Mr. Marshal from the Capital City Club of Madison, Wisconsin—initially called an out, but reversed his ruling after outcries from the runner and fans nearest the base.

A Chicago newspaper later charged that Marshal had been "afraid to decide against several thousand for fear of a *coup d'etat* from unlucky countrymen who had bet and lost; therefore, from the first to the last, he decided against the Excelsiors."[22] Their outraged opponents, however, suspected the Chicagoans of trying to delay play until the game was called for darkness, securing victory. "The Excelsiors refused to play further unless that man [at third] was held to be out, whereupon Captain [R.M.] Buckman of the Empire told the Umpire to 'declare the man out for the sake of going on with the game.' He did so but still the Excelsiors refused to play."[23]

Marshal declared Empire the winner. Threats flew both ways over possession of the championship silver ball and rosewood bat. Only the host Winnebago County Agricultural Society emerged with its reputation intact. A Chicago newspaper later called Empire-Excelsior "an unwise rivalry, and it is to be hoped that in their future matches they will study to cultivate a more gentlemanly bearing towards each other."[24]

Empire's final tournament of 1865 came September 29 at Dubuque, Iowa, for what was billed as the championship of the Northwest. Dubuque lay sixty-five miles to the west on the opposite bank of the Mississippi River. Empire's morning opponent was again Empire of St. Louis. The second Empire-versus-Empire matchup was a gem. The *Freeport Journal* later called it "the best match game played that year in the United States."[25]

The big city again bested the prairie town in a low-scoring, 12–5 affair that took three and a half hours to play. Unlike at Rockford, everyone at Dubuque exhibited good behavior. "The game was conducted in a most friendly and gentlemanly manner from beginning to end, no controversies of any kind arising."[26] Empire

This article is already to long, but we cannot close without adding a word in praise to the honorable manner in which all the clubs were treated by the Officers of the Agricultural Society and the citizens of Rockford, and will say that any time the Excelsior Club think they can beat the Empire, for the championship (the Empire Club will *not* play for money) or for *fun*, they need give but five minutes notice, to be accommodated with all they want *after the fourth inning*.

EMPIRE.	H. L.	R	EXCELSIOR.	H. L.	R
Buckman, R. 1st b	1	4	Stearns, J. W. c	1	4
Cavagagh, E. s s	8	1	Smith, J. H. c f	4	1
Delfendorf, J. c f	8	8	Mulcom, J. 2d b	1	4
Thomas, W. c	0	8	Kennedy A. p	2	1
Lighthart, W. r f	1	2	Goodrich, A. c f	4	1
Lebkicker, S. l f	8	1	Mackey, B. s s	8	0
Best, Jas. p	8	1	Foley, T. 3d b	2	2
Brewster, A. W. 3d b	2	0	Gillispie J. 1st b	1	2
Stoskopf, Louis, 2d b	8	1	Quick, L. r f	8	1
Total	27	15	Total	27	16

The newspaper *The North-West* bore the tagline "Independent in Everything—Neutral in Nothing," and they certainly let their feelings be known in their September 28, 1864, game recap.

of Freeport then played the Julian club of Dubuque for second place during the afternoon, pulling out a 27–26 win despite its players' weariness from the morning's game.

The northwestern Illinois baseball clubs continued playing into the autumn. Shaffer's Nine fell to Forest City, 31–23, October 20 at Freeport. "Some fine playing was exhibited on both sides. In the evening the members of the Forest City, Shaffer and Empire Clubs and a few of their friends met at Col. Shaffer's, where a bountiful repast was served up and an hour or two passed in friendly intercourse, singing and having a good time generally."[27]

The senior Empire club expected to end its season six days later, at home versus Excelsior of Chicago. "This game will be for the championship of the State, and will be well worth the attention of all who can attend upon the match," the *Weekly Journal* proclaimed.[28] But wet grounds and foul conditions thwarted the eagerly awaited finale, which "failed to come off on account of the weather. The Chicago men were on hand, but were compelled to return home with the question of State championship undecided."[29]

Empire hadn't quite concluded its first peacetime season. "The club rested from base ball during the winter, of course, excepting one game which was played among themselves on Skates in Stephenson Park," the *Freeport Journal* said of a January 31 event. Despite the late October rainout, the newspaper added that the squad was "still the champion club of the State, and must be prepared every year to earn the honor of that position."[30] Empire's players reemerged in the early spring of 1866, resembling Union artillery officers in their club uniforms of blue pantaloons with red stripes. "The sunny days have come," said the *North-West*, "and with them we will have a renewal of this healthful out door sport. Freeport stumps the world on Base Ball playing."[31] ■

Notes

1. "The Empire Club on the Death of the President," *Freeport* (Illinois) *Weekly Journal*, April 19, 1865, 5. (The paper later switch to daily publication as the *Freeport Journal*.)
2. "Empire Base Ball Club," *Freeport Journal*, June 6, 1866, 5.
3. Chicago, IL at Protoball.org: https://protoball.org/Chicago,_IL; "The City: Amusements," *Chicago Tribune*, June 3, 1865, 4.
4. "Empire Base Ball Club."
5. "That Base Ball Match," *Freeport Weekly Journal*, August 10, 1864, 3.
6. "Base Ball Sport," *Freeport Weekly Journal*, May 31, 1865, 3.
7. "Base Ball," *Freeport Weekly Journal*, June 7, 1865, 3.
8. "Base Ball Match Game," *St. Louis Missouri Republican*, June 26, 1865, 3.
9. "Base Ball Match at Freeport, Ill., July 4," *St. Louis Missouri Democrat*, July 8, 1865, 4.
10. "Freeport," *Chicago Tribune*, July 7, 1865, 2.
11. "Back in 1865," *The Sporting News*, November 9, 1895: 5.
12. "The Champion Base Ball Match," *Freeport Weekly Journal*, July 12, 1865, 3.
13. "Base Ball Match at Freeport."
14. "Ball Championship of the West," *New York Clipper*, July 22, 1865, 116.
15. "The Champion Base Ball Match."
16. "Base Ball," *Freeport Weekly Journal*, August 2, 1865, 3.
17. "Empire Base Ball Club."
18. "Base Ball Championship," *Freeport* (Illinois) *North-West*, August 31, 1865, 5.
19. "Local Matters," *Freeport North-West*, September 7, 1865, 5.
20. "Base Ball Tournament at Rockford," *Freeport Weekly Journal*, September 27, 1865, 2.
21. "Base Ball Tournament at Rockford; Second Day," *Freeport North-West*, September 28, 1865, 1. Published a day later, the *North-West* occasionally ran a headline that was similar or identical to one in the earlier *Weekly Journal*.
22. *Chicago Times*, reprinted in "Truth Versus the *Chicago Times*," *Freeport Weekly Journal*, September 27, 1865, 3.
23. "Base Ball Tournament at Rockford; Second Day."
24. *Chicago Journal*, reprinted in "The Base Ball Tournament at Rockford," *Freeport Weekly Journal*, October 4, 1865, 3.
25. "Empire Base Ball Club."
26. "Base Ball Match at Dubuque," *Freeport Weekly Journal*, October 4, 1865, 3.
27. "Local Items of Interest," *Freeport Weekly Journal*, October 25, 1865, 3.
28. "Base Ball Match," *Freeport Weekly Journal*, October 25, 1865, 3.
29. "Base Ball Match," *Freeport Weekly Journal*, November 1, 1865, 3.
30. "Empire Base Ball Club."
31. "Local Matters," *Freeport North-West*, April 19, 1866, 5.

Did Bud Fowler Almost Break the Major-League Color Line in 1888?

A Midwestern Memoir of John T. Brush and Guy M. Smith

David Kathman

Bud Fowler's election to the National Baseball Hall of Fame in December 2021 has brought new attention to this Black baseball pioneer of the nineteenth century. Fowler was one of the first Black players to make a living in so-called "Organized Baseball," playing for a series of otherwise all-white teams between 1878 and 1895 before helping organize the Page Fence Giants, a pioneering Black professional team, in the 1890s.[1] The teams that Fowler played for in his prime were all in circuits such as the Northwestern League, the Illinois-Iowa League, and the Nebraska State League, all minor leagues or independent leagues. He never played in any one place for very long, both because of the financial instability of these leagues, and because of the racism that faced him everywhere he went.

Some tantalizing evidence suggests that in 1888, Fowler was almost signed to a major-league contract by John T. Brush of the Indianapolis Hoosiers (then in the National League), but that racist objections by the Hoosier players sabotaged the idea. This story appears in several modern accounts of Brush's life, including his Wikipedia entry, but these all ultimately derive from the same source: a typescript in the Giamatti Research Center (GRC) at the National Baseball Hall of Fame and Museum in Cooperstown, New York.[2] According to the typescript (henceforth the "Brush typescript"), the incident happened after the Crawfordsville, Indiana, franchise in the Central Interstate League collapsed. Brush, who "had been keeping his optics closely trained on her star second baseman, a negro—J.W. (Bud) Fowler," arranged to bring Fowler to Indianapolis (about 50 miles from Crawfordsville) for a tryout. But the Indianapolis roster was full of Irish players whose strong objections caused Brush to drop the plan.[3]

The typescript is not in Fowler's file at the GRC, but in the file for Brush, a baseball magnate who began his career in Indianapolis in the 1880s and eventually owned the New York Giants in their glory years of the early 1900s. The 20-page document is apparently a transcription of a handwritten original, consisting of an account of Brush's early baseball career in

Indianapolis, including the Fowler incident. The account was written by Guy M. Smith, whose name appears at the end, and may have been transcribed by sportswriter Dan Daniel, whose name is written in felt-tip pen at the top of the first page. It can be dated between 1937 and 1940 on internal evidence: Smith refers to "the late Harry S. New," who died May 9, 1937, but refers to Joe Quinn, who died in 1940, as "now a St. Louis mortician."[4] In 1941, Smith said that he had almost finished writing a book called *Across the Years in Baseball*, and that if he couldn't afford to get it published, "I'll just hand along all of my records and data to the Cooperstown shrine." Presumably this typescript (or the manuscript it is based on) was part of the materials for that never-published book, helping explain how it got to the Hall of Fame.[5]

At first glance, this does not appear to be a very reliable source: a typed transcription of a lost original, written 50 years after the events it describes. However, there are reasons to take this account seriously, starting with the author, Guy M. Smith. Smith was a very interesting character who was in a good position to know about the events in question. His published writings from the same time period are generally reliable in their broad strokes, if not in every detail, and the same is true of things in the Brush typescript that can be checked against the documentary record. In order to properly evaluate Smith's account of Brush and Fowler, it will be helpful to explore Smith and his career in some detail.

GUY M. SMITH, INDIANAPOLIS BASEBALL HISTORIAN

Guy McIlvaine Smith was born in Indianapolis on December 2, 1870 (possibly), and grew up there as a rabid baseball fan, around the time of the events described in the typescript.[6] Indianapolis nearly always had a professional baseball team during Smith's youth, including three that briefly achieved major-league status (in 1878, 1884, and 1887–89). Smith regularly attended games and got to know some of the players and executives, especially on the 1887–89 team, of which John T. Brush was president. Smith attended

DePauw University and worked as a newspaperman from 1889 to 1895, after which he moved to Danville, Illinois, and took a series of railroad jobs. In 1936 he retired after 34 years as a railroad mail clerk and became a full-time writer, mostly about baseball.[7]

By the 1930s, Smith had become well-known to sportswriters as a source of information about nineteenth-century baseball, especially if it involved Indianapolis. In 1935 he wrote his first baseball history article for *The Sporting News*, an obituary of Paul Hines, and over the next decade he wrote frequently for that publication, and occasionally for others. His memory appears to have been quite good well into his seventies, and he also had a formidable library of baseball books and publications. A 1941 profile of Smith in *The Sporting News* calls him "a veritable encyclopedia of the game," and says that "if Brother Smith tells you something happened at 4 o'clock in the afternoon of Thursday, July 7, 1889, or August 11, 1886, put it down as correct."[8] This is undoubtedly an exaggeration, but many of the events Smith describes in his published articles (or in articles that quote him) can be at least partially confirmed in the historical record.

For example, in that 1941 *Sporting News* profile, Smith recalled how, as a child in 1876, he and his older brother "went to the Indianapolis park, where the famed Chicago White Stockings were to play an Indianapolis team that included such stars as Silver Flint and Mike Golden. Through a hole in the fence, young Guy and his brother saw Al Spalding pitch and Deacon White catch for Chicago." Indianapolis did not have a National League team in 1876, but in fact the White Stockings did play exhibition games there on July 31 and August 4, 1876, against the local semi-pro team. In both games Silver Flint and Mike Golden played for Indianapolis, and Spalding pitched and Deacon White caught for Chicago.[9] The newspaper account of the July 31 game describes the many people who watched the game without paying, including dozens on surrounding rooftops and boys who climbed telegraph poles.[10]

In that same 1941 profile, Smith recalled seeing Deacon White, now with Cincinnati, catching his brother Will White in 1878 while wearing an improved catcher's mask he had invented. "As a boy, I saw Deacon wear the mask for the first time that year and it attracted much attention. At the close of the game, White explained its merits to a crowd that had gathered around. Silver Flint, who caught for Indianapolis that day, wore the old rubber face protector."[11] Two games in Indianapolis's 1878 schedule fit Smith's description: June 4 and June 6, in both of which

Bud Fowler

Cincinnati was in town, with Deacon White catching and Will White pitching, and Silver Flint catching for Indianapolis.[12] Existing (short) biographies of White do not mention the mask story, but it is consistent with what we know. After a decade as a star catcher, White had switched to first base and the outfield in 1877, in order to save his body from the punishing abuse that catchers of the day had to endure. But 1877 was also the year that catcher's masks began to be widely adopted, and in 1878 White went back to catching full-time.[13]

Smith wrote most often about the National League team Indianapolis had from 1887 through 1889, with John T. Brush as team president.[14] He personally knew Brush and many of the players, and witnessed many of the things he wrote about. For example, Smith wrote a long article about Jack Glasscock, star shortstop of the 1887–89 Hoosiers, for the July 9, 1939, edition of the *News-Register* of Wheeling, West Virginia (Glasscock's hometown), in honor of Glasscock's 80th birthday.[15] Smith interviewed Glasscock for the article, which included Glasscock's opinions on baseball in 1939 as well as Smith's firsthand recollections of Glasscock's fielding skill as a shortstop. The 1941 *Sporting News* profile of Guy Smith cites his 1939 interview with Glasscock and describes how Smith brought out a glove that he said Glasscock had given to him during the 1889 season after replacing it with a new one.

Much of the Brush typescript deals with Indianapolis baseball during the same period (1887–89), and it can be a valuable complement to Smith's articles, as long as its limitations are kept in mind.[16] For example, in his 1935 *Sporting News* obituary of Paul Hines, Smith wrote about an incident that he witnessed in 1889, when Amos Rusie was a rookie pitcher for the Hoosiers.[17] After being sent to the minors for seasoning, Rusie was recalled to the big club in August, by Smith's account, with his first start coming against Boston. In the third inning, manager Jack Glasscock almost pulled him from the game after the rookie issued a couple of walks, but "Rusie, humiliated by the presence of 200 South Side friends" who had come to watch him pitch, pleaded to be allowed to stay in. Paul Hines came over from first base and convinced Glasscock to keep Rusie in, whereupon "Hines, placing his arm around the youthful hurler, walked back with him to the box. The writer witnessed this act and it was the finest example of graciousness he has ever seen upon the diamond."

The typescript gives a more detailed account of Rusie's return to the Hoosiers in August 1889, though without mentioning the Hines anecdote. "Rusie went into action August 20 against Chicago with Ad Gumbert and gave the 'Ruby One' a run for his money but lost by 'one' run. Three days later he defeated Cleveland with Enoch Bakely—one hundred Grand Avenue rooters cheering him to the skies and his father and mother guests of Brush in the private loge."[18] Rusie's first start after his return was indeed against Chicago (not Boston, as in the 1935 article), but it was a 12–6 loss on August 21 against Frank Dwyer, not a one-run loss on August 20 against Ad Gumbert (who had pitched on August 19). The typescript is correct that Rusie beat Cleveland in his next start on August 23, though the opposing pitcher was Henry Gruber, not Enoch Bakley (who had pitched the day before).[19] This August 23, 1889, game against Cleveland is probably the one where Smith saw Hines comfort Rusie. Rusie did get into trouble in the third inning, but not by issuing two walks; rather, Paul Radford singled, went to second on an error by center fielder Ed Andrews, and scored on two sacrifice hits.[20]

This tendency to get small details *almost* right, but not quite, is a notable feature of the Brush typescript. When it came to filling in details that he had not personally witnessed or couldn't remember, Smith relied on his reference library, which, while impressive for the time, was not always reliable by modern standards. Smith apparently had a list of all the games Amos Rusie had pitched, since he said in 1941 that "by careful checking he had established that Rusie never was taken out of a game for ineffectiveness during his National League career."[21] But this list must have had some mistakes that made their way into the Brush typescript, not surprising given that it had to have been compiled by hand in the days before spreadsheets and easily accessible online newspapers.

THE BRUSH TYPESCRIPT AND BUD FOWLER

With all this as background, we can take a closer look at Guy Smith's account in the typescript of John T. Brush's attempt to sign Bud Fowler. Unlike the Rusie material, this story does not appear in any of Smith's published writings, nor is it described in any contemporary sources that I can find. Even so, it is detailed enough to be worth examining closely. The passage is short enough to quote in full. I have corrected a few obvious typos, but have kept Smith's run-on writing style intact.

Crawfordsville, Indiana passed up her franchise in the Central Interstate in '87. Brush had been keeping his optics closely trained on her star second baseman, a negro—J.W. (Bud) Fowler who was a member of the Keokuk Iowa Western League team of '84 and pastimed there with such later day as D.C. Dugdale, "Mit" Kennedy and Nate Hudson. Brush arranged to bring Fowler to Indianapolis but it so happened that names like Boyle, Cahill, Daily, Denny, McGeachy and Seery formed on the club's roster and in the minds of Indianapolis ball lovers, as well. A delegation from the foregoing group waited on Brush and informed him that there was positively nothing doing in connection with Fowler and both Brush and the colored star opined that it was best to avoid a collision with the Celtic temperament and Fowler joined Binghamton where he continued to star for several seasons. In 1892 he organized and managed the famous Page Fence Giants who were sponsored by the Page Mfg. Co. of Adrian, Michigan and who traveled the country in their palace on wheels built by the Pullman Co.[22]

The first two sentences are mostly accurate, except that the dates are off by one year, similar to the discrepancies we saw in Smith's Amos Rusie story. Bud Fowler played for the Crawfordsville, Indiana, team of the Central Interstate League not in 1887, but in 1888; also, Fowler had starred for Keokuk of the Western League not in 1884, but in 1885. The Keokuk teammates listed by Smith were in fact with the team in 1885, as long as we assume that "Mit" Kennedy is a mistranscription for "Ted" Kennedy. Keokuk's opening day lineup on April 8, 1885, included Fowler at second base, Dan Dugdale at catcher, and Ted Kennedy pitching; by mid-May, Nat Hudson, who would pitch for the St. Louis Browns the following year, had joined Keokuk as a second pitcher.[23]

John T. Brush may well have become aware of Bud Fowler in 1885 when the Black star played for Keokuk, and Indianapolis was one of the six founding members of the new Western League. Keokuk was initially an "alliance club," meaning that they were officially independent but each Western League team agreed to play five games at Keokuk.[24] Indianapolis traveled to Keokuk for games on April 30, May 7, and May 8, losing the first one, 12–6, and winning the next two, 10–4 and 8–4.[25] Keokuk was admitted as a full member of the Western League in early June after the Omaha club collapsed, but less than two weeks later, the entire league imploded, and the Indianapolis directors sold their franchise and players to Detroit of the National League for a reported $5,000.[26] Keokuk tried to continue as an independent team for a few more weeks before finally disbanding in July. Soon afterward, on July 22, 1885, *Sporting Life* wrote: "Fowler, the crack colored player…is one of the best general players in the country, and if he had a White face he would be playing with the best of them."[27]

Three years later, when Brush was president of the Indianapolis franchise in the National League, he and Bud Fowler came into each other's orbits once again. In the early part of 1888, Fowler played for Crawfordsville, Indiana, in the Central Interstate League, and quickly became the star of the team.[29] On May 9, a writer going by "Punch" wrote in *Sporting Life*: "Fowler is playing a great game at second, and it is a very unusual thing for a ball to get by him. I shall be very much surprised if the 'coon,' as he is called, does not have a record equal to any in our League in his position."[29] Under the circumstances, it makes sense that Brush would "have his optics closely trained on" Fowler, as Smith wrote. Crawfordsville was only about 50 miles northwest of Indianapolis, with a rail line connecting the two. More significantly, one of the Hoosier players in 1888, Otto Schomberg, had been Fowler's teammate at Stillwater, Minnesota, in 1884 and at Keokuk in 1885, and could have alerted Brush to Fowler.[30]

The Central Interstate League of 1888, like the Western League of 1885, was unstable due to financial difficulties. The Crawfordsville franchise moved to Terre Haute in early July, then disbanded on the morning of Monday, July 23, after which the players became free agents.[31] That same day, Indianapolis was at home to open a three-game series against the Chicago White Stockings. The Indianapolis *News* reported Terre Haute's demise in a small item on its front page on that evening.[32] Brush could have read this item or a similar one and telegraphed Fowler an offer,

intending to bring him with the team on the road trip they were due to depart for on July 25 if a deal was reached. Of course, this did not happen. On Wednesday, July 25, Fowler was in Terre Haute playing in a benefit game against a "picked nine" to raise money for the players, and two days later the Terre Haute *Express* was reporting that he had secured a position with Santa Fe, New Mexico.[33]

THE COLOR LINE IN 1888

According to Guy Smith's account, racism by the team's many Irish players was the reason Brush did not sign Fowler. This would not be surprising, given that the color line in the affiliated professional leagues was in the process of being drawn at this time. Numerous Black players had played on minor league teams over the previous few years, but a racist backlash had made it increasingly difficult for White teams to hire them. In 1887 more than a dozen Black players had played on affiliated minor league teams, including Bud Fowler, who played for Binghamton in the International Association. He put up outstanding numbers, batting .350 in 34 games with 30 stolen bases, but he and his Black teammate William Renfro faced relentless racism. In late June, nine White Binghamton players signed a petition refusing to play with Fowler and Renfro, just after two teammates had quit the team for the same reason. Fowler resigned from the team and eventually joined Montpelier in the Northeastern League.[34]

The most famous incident in the drawing of baseball's color line happened shortly after Fowler's resignation from Binghamton. Before the 1887 season, Newark (also in the International Association) had signed a Black battery, pitcher George Stovey and catcher Fleet Walker, who were quite successful. Stovey would win more than 30 games for Newark that year, while Walker was a top-notch catcher who is best known today as the first openly Black player in a segregated major league, playing in 1884 with Toledo in the American Association. (William Edward White, who had a White father and a Black mother, played in one game for the National League's Providence Grays in 1879, but he "passed" as White.)[35] On July 14, 1887, Newark was scheduled to play an exhibition game against Cap Anson and the Chicago White Stockings, but Anson announced that his team would not take the field if Stovey pitched. He had tried this tactic in 1883 when Walker was with Toledo, but Toledo had not backed down, and Walker played in the game (in right field). By 1887, though, the tide was turning, and Stovey did not play against the White Stockings,

John T. Brush, shown here in 1911, when he was owner of the New York Giants. He was in ill health and died in 1912.

ostensibly because he was not feeling well. The same day, the International Association directors met to discuss "the question of colored players," and decided that no more Black players could sign contracts to play in the league, though existing contracts would be honored.[36]

Before this infamous incident, Cap Anson had already derailed two attempts by the New York Giants to sign George Stovey. In 1886 Stovey was pitching for Jersey City in the Eastern League and doing an excellent job, compiling a 16–15 record with a 1.13 ERA despite deliberately poor support from some of his teammates.[37] The September 8, 1886, *Sporting Life* reported: "New York has been seriously considering the engagement of Stovey, Jersey City's fine colored pitcher. The question is would the League permit his appearance in League championship games?"[38] Manager Pat Powers recalled several years later that the Giants were in a pennant race with Chicago at the time, and that team executive Walter Appleton wanted Stovey to join the Giants for a crucial four-game series in Chicago. "In fact, a deal was fixed between Appleton, the Jersey club, and Stovey to this end. Stovey had his grip packed and awaited the word, but he was not called owing to the fact that Anson had refused to play in a game with colored catcher Walker at Toledo and the same result was feared."[39]

On April 7, 1887, the Giants played a preseason exhibition against Newark, for whom George Stovey and Fleet Walker were now playing. The Giants won in a squeaker, 3–2, with Hall of Famer Tim Keefe barely outdueling Stovey, and Walker threw out New York

captain John Montgomery Ward trying to steal.[40] The Giants were so impressed that the Newark *Daily Journal* reported on April 9 that New York manager Jim Mutrie had offered to buy the contracts of Stovey and Walker from Newark, but that "Manager Hackett informed him they were not on sale."[41] Twenty years later Sol White, a historian of early Black baseball, gave a fuller and slightly different version of the story. According to White, it was Ward who wanted to sign Stovey, "and arrangements were just about completed for his transfer from the Newark club, when a brawl was heard from Chicago to New York. The same Anson, with all the venom of hate which would be worthy of a Tillman or Vardaman of the present day, made strenuous and fruitful opposition to any proposition looking to the admittance of a colored man into the National League."[42]

Given this history, it may not be a coincidence that Anson and his White Stockings were in Indianapolis at the same time that John T. Brush was (apparently) thinking about signing Bud Fowler in late July 1888. This is not to say that Brush's plan would have succeeded if Anson had not been in town, but his presence nearby could have been a factor in the way things played out (as described by Guy Smith). As Sol White later wrote, "[Anson's] repugnant feeling, shown at every opportunity, toward colored ball players, was a source of comment through every league in the country, and his opposition, with his great popularity and power in base ball circles, hastened the exclusion to the Black man from the White leagues."[43]

Later in 1888 Anson again refused to play against Fleet Walker, who was now the popular starting catcher for the Syracuse Stars. When the team was celebrated at a banquet on September 22 after winning the International Association pennant, *Sporting Life* reported that "Catcher Moses Walker, of the Star team, returned thanks to the directors and citizens on behalf of himself and fellow players and everybody was happy."[44] However, when Anson and the White Stockings stopped in Syracuse for an exhibition game on September 27, Anson refused to let his team play if Walker was in the lineup. The team caved, no doubt fearful of losing the gate receipts (a large crowd of 4,000 was on hand), and Chicago won the game, 3–0.[45] We only know about Anson's demands from a couple of African-American newspapers, the *Indianapolis World* and the *New York Age*. Apparently, behavior like Anson's had become so normalized by this time, and the color line so established, that the White press saw no need to mention it.[46] This may also be one reason why no newspapers mentioned the Brush-Fowler incident at the time, leaving it to Guy Smith to describe it decades later.

A handful of Black players hung on in the minor leagues for a few years after 1888, but they continued to face enormous obstacles. Fleet Walker returned to Syracuse in 1889, but he was released in August and retired.[47] Bud Fowler and George Stovey played for integrated minor league teams in 1889 and 1890, but after that, such opportunities almost entirely dried up, as the color line became entrenched throughout the minor leagues. Stovey played for the Cuban Giants and other all-Black teams until his retirement in 1897.[48] Fowler managed to play partial seasons in two minor leagues that briefly integrated, the Nebraska State League (1892) and the Michigan State League (1895), but his major achievements were as an organizer, owner, and manager of Black baseball teams, most notably the Page Fence Giants.[49] It is primarily thanks to this work as a pioneering organizer of Black baseball that Fowler was inducted into the National Baseball Hall of Fame.

Did John T. Brush almost sign Bud Fowler to a National League contract in 1888? The answer depends on how much we trust the Brush typescript and its author, Guy M. Smith. The evidence laid out in the preceding pages shows that Smith was quite a reliable witness, albeit one prone to confusing minor details. Although the typescript (or the manuscript underlying it) was written about fifty years after the events it describes, Smith retained a sharp memory, such that many of his eyewitness accounts can be confirmed by the documentary record. Furthermore, although his account of Brush and Fowler has some minor errors, it meshes remarkably well with the events of one specific week in central Indiana in late July 1888, when Fowler's Terre Haute team folded just as Brush and his Hoosiers were preparing to leave on a long road trip. More broadly, the story is consistent with the state of race relations in professional baseball in the summer of 1888, when some Black players remained but the color line was rapidly being established.

If we accept that Smith's account is accurate at its core, how much does it matter? Even if Brush had somehow succeeded in his plan, and Fowler had played in at least one major league game, the forces that were excluding Black players from all of affiliated baseball would undoubtedly have continued. Fowler might have joined William Edward White, Bumpus Jones, Fleet Walker, and Fleet's brother Welday as Black players who played major league baseball in the late 1800s, but the color line would have still been established. Even if that's the case, however, the Brush-Fowler incident is worth having as part of the historical record. It adds another piece to the story of how baseball's color line came about, and it provides an important detail for the biographies of both Brush and Fowler, two men who were both baseball pioneers in their own ways. ∎

Notes

1. Jeffrey Michael Laing, *Bud Fowler: Baseball's First Black Professional* (Jefferson, NC: McFarland & Co., 2013).
2. Guy M. Smith, "John T. Brush," typescript in the John T. Brush file at the Giamatti Research Center in the National Baseball Hall of Fame and Museum, Cooperstown, New York, pp. 5–6. Brush's Wikipedia entry (https://en.wikipedia.org/wiki/John_T._Brush; accessed September 10, 2022) does not have a specific citation for the Fowler story, but among the sources it lists is *Baseball: The Biographical Encyclopedia* (2000), which also includes the story in its entry on Brush (138–9). That book does not include source citations, but it is apparent that one of its main sources for Brush was Richard R. Johnson's "The Forgotten Indiana Architect of Baseball," in the May 4, 1975, *Indianapolis Star Magazine*. This article uses the Guy M. Smith typescript as a primary source, supplemented with the reminiscences of Brush's younger daughter Natalie.
3. The typescript actually has "colfesion" where my quotation says "collision;" this is one of many obvious mistranscriptions in the typescript, which I have silently corrected here and elsewhere.
4. Smith, "John T. Brush," 4, 6. Harry S. New was later a US Senator from Indiana and US Postmaster General.
5. Dick Farrington, "Guy Smith, Diamond Historian, Keeps Young By Romancing of Game's Early Days," *The Sporting News*, May 1, 1941, 5.
6. Farrington, "Guy Smith," gives his birthdate as December 2, 1870, but various census data disagree. The 1880 census lists him as seven years old, while in the 1900 U.S. Census he gave his birthdate as December 1869.
7. Farrington, "Guy Smith."
8. Farrington, "Guy Smith."
9. Farrington, "Guy Smith."
10. "Chicago vs. Indianapolis," *Indianapolis News*, August 1, 1876, 1; "Chicago vs. Indianapolis," *Indianapolis News*, August 5, 1876, 4.
11. Farrington, "Guy Smith." According to Smith, "Deacon White, following the close of the 1877 season, worked out a blueprint for an improved mask and took it to a Boston wire worker, who fashioned a mask very much like the one in use today."
12. "Nolan's Day," *Indianapolis News*, June 5, 1878, 1; "White Wins," *Indianapolis News*, June 7, 1878, 4. Indianapolis also played home games against Cincinnati on June 26, 27, 28, and 29, but Flint played left field in those games, and with manager John Clapp at catcher.
13. Peter Morris, *Catcher* (Chicago: Ivan R. Dee, 2009), 123–27.
14. Technically, Brush did not become team president until July 1, 1887, after a scandal that led to the resignation of the previous president, Louis Newberger. See David Kathman, "John T. Brush: The Early Years, 1845–1888," *Base Ball: New Research on the Early Game* 11 (2019), 118–39.
15. Guy M. Smith, "Play of Shortstop's Position Revolutionized by Jack Glasscock," *Wheeling News-Register*, July 9, 1939, part V, 2, 5.
16. The typescript was never edited, as Smith's newspaper articles were, and sometimes it is rather hard to read. The fact that it is a transcription also means that there are errors and typos that were (probably) not in the handwritten original.
17. Guy M. Smith, "Passing of Hines Finds Few Players of His Period Among the Survivors," *The Sporting News*, July 25, 1935, 3.
18. Smith, "John T. Brush," 9–10.
19. See the 1889 Indianapolis game log at Retrosheet (https://www.retrosheet.org/boxesetc/1889/VIN301889.htm).

20. "Double-Umpire System," Indianapolis *Journal*, August 24, 1889, 5.
21. Farrington, "Guy Smith."
22. Smith, "John T. Brush," 5–6.
23. Laing, *Bud Fowler*, 83–85; *Sporting Life*, April 22, 1885, 4; *Sporting Life*, June 3, 1885, 7; Sporting Life, June 24, 1885, 2.
24. Laing, *Bud Fowler*, 84; Indianapolis *Journal*, "Western League Affairs," April 3, 1885, 8.
25. Indianapolis *Sentinel*, May 1, 1885, 4; Indianapolis *Journal*, May 8, 1885, 4; Indianapolis *Sentinel*, May 9, 1885, 4.
26. Indianapolis *Journal*, "The Ball Club Disbands," June 16, 1885, 8.
27. *Sporting Life*, July 22, 1885, 4.
28. Laing, *Bud Fowler*, 98–99.
29. *Sporting Life*, "Crawfordsville Chips," May 9, 1888, 9.
30. See Laing, *Bud Fowler*, 78–83; https://sabr.org/bioproj/person/Bud-Fowler; and https://sabr.org/bioproj/person/otto-schomberg.
31. Terre Haute *Express*, July 4, 1888, 1; Terre Haute *Express*, July 5, 1888, 1; Terre Haute *Express*, July 24, 1888, 1.
32. Indianapolis *News*, "Terre Haute Base Ball Club No More," July 23, 1888, 1.
33. Terre Haute *Express*, July 26, 1888, 1; Terre Haute Express, July 27, 1888, 1.
34. Laing, *Bud Fowler*, 89–92. Note that Smith's account says that Fowler starred for Binghamton after the Brush incident, rather than before, but this is obviously another example of Smith confusing details.
35. Stefan Fatsis, "Mystery of Baseball: Was William White Game's First Black?" *Wall Street Journal*, January 30, 2004; Peter Morris and Stefan Fatsis, "Baseball's Secret Pioneer," *Slate*, February 4, 2014 (https://slate.com/culture/2014/02/william-edward-white-the-firstblack-player-in-major-league-baseball-history-lived-his-life-as-a-white-man).
36. The best account of these events is still Jerry Malloy, "Out At Home: Baseball Draws the Color Line, 1887," *The National Pastime* (SABR), 2 (1983); 14–28, reprinted in *The Armchair Book of Baseball II*, ed. John Thorn (Charles Scribner's Sons, 1987), 267.
37. Brian McKenna, "George Stovey," SABR BioProject, https://sabr.org/bioproj/person/George-Stovey.
38. *Sporting Life*, September 8, 1886, 5.
39. "Stovey, the Pitcher and his Experience in Jersey City – Anson's Prejudice," *Cleveland Gazette*, February 13, 1892; reprinted in Jerry Malloy, ed., *Sol White's History of Colored Base Ball, With Other Documents on the Early Black Game, 1886–1935* (Bison Books, 1996), 141–2.
40. *Sporting Life*, April 8, 1887, 9; David W. Zang, *Fleet Walker's Divided Heart: The Life of Baseball's First Black Major Leaguer* (Bison Books, 1998), 55.
41. Malloy, ed., *Sol White's History of Colored Base Ball*, lvii.
42. Malloy, ed., *Sol White's History of Colored Base Ball*, 76. White's book was published in 1907. Benjamin Tillman was a violently racist US Senator from South Carolina; James Kimble Vardaman was the racist governor of Mississippi from 1904 to 1908, and later a US Senator. Both were White supremacists who openly advocated lynching Blacks.
43. Malloy, ed., *Sol White's History of Colored Base Ball*, 76–77.
44. "Syracuse Champions," *Sporting Life*, October 3, 1888, 1.
45. *Sporting Life*, October 3, 1888, 1 (a separate item after the column cited above).
46. The *Indianapolis World* account is described by Malloy, "Out At Home" (p. 241 in the 1988 edition), and the *New York Age* account (from the October 13, 1888 edition) is cited by Zang, *Fleet Walker's Divided Heart*, 141n47.
47. Zang, *Fleet Walker's Divided Heart*, 61.
48. "George Stovey," SABR BioProject.
49. Laing, *Bud Fowler*, 126–34.

Exit Stage Left

The Sad Farewell of Cap Anson

Michael Haupert

Adrian "Cap" Anson was one of a handful of players whom William Hulbert pilfered from eastern clubs before the 1876 season.[1] In a storied White Stockings career, Anson managed the team for 19 years, capturing five titles, becoming the first member of the 3,000 hit club, being elected to the Hall of Fame in 1939, and even becoming part owner of the White Stockings. But there is one goal he did not achieve, and it ultimately led to his exit from the team on terms very different than his career should have dictated. In turn, that exit led Anson to an ending hardly becoming of the man the *Chicago Tribune* once called "the most conspicuous ballplayer in the nation."[2]

IN THE BEGINNING

Adrian Constantine Anson was born in Marshall (present-day Marshalltown), Iowa, on April 17, 1852. By his own admission, he was a lackluster student, but when it came to baseball, he practiced diligently until he mastered the game. At age 15 he earned a spot on the town team. At age 19 he signed his first professional contract with Rockford in the National Association for the princely sum of $66.66 per month.[3]

Rockford lasted only one season, but Anson outlasted the organization. He starred for the Athletics for the next four years, and then jumped from the National Association to the National League's Chicago White Stockings, where he would remain for the final 22 seasons of his career.

Albert Spalding retired from his managerial and playing duties after the 1877 season, and took over the presidency of the Chicago White Stockings. He named Anson manager for the 1879 season. There he remained, as "Cap" for the rest of his career.

Anson opened the 1880 season with another title to add to his player-manager status: stockholder. On April 1, he purchased five shares of the team.[4] This ownership of stock was credited as a powerful influence in keeping him from absconding to the Players' League a decade later.[5]

The Players' League was formed in 1890, competing head-to-head with the National League in seven of eight NL cities. By this time Anson was a 20-year veteran and had been a part-owner for half of that time. As such, he was not going to bolt to a new league, but he was severely critical of those who did. With Spalding working behind the scenes, Anson served as a foghorn, blasting the "traitors" who jumped to the new league. The PL lasted only one season, but the enmity Anson sowed amongst the players who returned lingered on.

While Anson was hailed in the press as "the man who saved the National League," he was not viewed so gallantly by his former teammates. Stars Hugh Duffy and George Van Haltren refused to return to Chicago, crippling the White Stockings during the 1891 season. In September the White Stockings held first place, but a late-season surge by Boston gave them the flag. Anson blamed his detractors from the PL for easing up when they played Boston, allowing them to overtake his club down the stretch.[6]

In April 1891, after an exhausting but successful battle to defeat the PL, Albert Spalding resigned his club presidency in order to devote more time to his sporting goods business. He recommended club secretary James Hart for the position, who was unanimously elected by the board. He retained stock in the ballclub, and expressed his confidence in Hart, "a man thoroughly competent and well qualified."[7]

The transition was not a smooth one. Anson was not happy to have been passed over for the presidency. Despite conciliatory words from Spalding, who assured him that Hart was merely a figurehead, the incident opened a rift between Spalding and Anson.[8] Anson also had problems with Hart, and the two began to butt heads almost immediately. "Hart regarded Anson as a relic of the past who was unwilling to change with the times. Anson countered by calling Hart a usurper who undermined his authority by encouraging rebellion among the players."[9]

In the fall of 1892 Spalding and Hart reorganized the club as part of a sale that would eventually result in Hart owning a majority of the shares. The new corporation was chartered by Hart and two associates, but the original stockholders had the opportunity to buy into the new corporation. Spalding and Anson took advantage of the opportunity, and Anson stayed on as field manager. Anson signed a new contract with the newly formed corporation, but it was for one year less than the ten-year pact he had signed three years earlier. Anson would later claim that he was unaware of this detail, and it would prove to be a costly oversight on his part.

The performance of the team fell off dramatically after Hart became president. Over the final six seasons of his tenure with the club, Anson's Colts, as the press dubbed them, experienced four losing seasons, and never finished higher than fourth place. During his first 13 seasons at the helm, Anson had never experienced a losing season, compiling a .632 winning average and claiming five pennants. Anson publicly blamed Hart for the team's struggles on the field, complaining that he was miserly and refused to obtain good players because he didn't want to pay the salaries they would command.

1897 was a dismal season for Anson and the White Stockings. The team plunged to ninth place, 34 games out of first. Only once before during Anson's tenure had they fallen so low and finished so far behind. Their .447 winning average was the third lowest in Anson's 19 years at the helm. Anson's on-field performance also fell short of his career standards. His RBI total fell for the third straight year, and his batting and slugging averages were below the league average. At 45, he was the oldest player in the league by five years, and it was starting to show.

The decision of whether or not to retire was not left up to Anson. His long-term contract expired in January of 1898 (one year earlier than originally negotiated) and Hart did not renew it, almost certainly with the blessing of Spalding (even though, as president, Hart did not need Spalding's approval). The following month, perhaps as a consolation after his dismissal, Spalding offered Anson a 60-day window to purchase controlling interest in the team. But by the April 15 deadline, Anson did not have the money and the deal fell through. An incensed Anson accused Spalding of duplicity, charging, "there was never any intention on the part of A.G. Spalding and his *confrères* to let me get possession of the club."[10] Anson was probably right, in that Spalding certainly realized he was highly unlikely to be able to come up with that kind of cash in such a short period of time.

Hart explained that the decision to let Anson go was made by the stockholders, who felt the fans desired a change of management. He praised Anson's long and

Adrian "Cap" Anson's 1888 tobacco card.

faithful service to the club, wishing him the best in his future endeavors. "There is not now, and never has been, friction between Captain Anson and myself."[11] Both parties belied this lack of friction in a contentious exchange of letters published in the *Chicago Tribune* later that year.

Seeking to defend his motives, Hart explained Anson's financial connections to the White Stockings. His contract called for a fixed salary plus a percentage of net profits each year. According to Hart there were no profits in any year from 1890–93. Nevertheless, in two of those years Anson was paid a sum "nearly double that called for in his contract." And in a third a debt to the club in the amount of $2,600 for previously purchased shares of stock was forgiven. In 1897, Anson once again took an advance from the club, this time in the amount of $2,400, "which at the present time stands charged to him on the books of the club, and it has never been paid."[12]

Anson rebutted, claiming that Hart overstated losses and denied, "emphatically that I owe the club $2,400…I worked for the club for a period of time extending over twenty-two years, my contract calling for a stated salary and 10 per cent of the net profits…but I have never been allowed to see [the books], and whether I have had all that was coming to me or not is an open question in my mind."[13]

The end of the Anson era in Chicago was bitter and ugly, hardly becoming the career of a legend. After 27 seasons, Cap Anson's playing career was over. He retired as baseball's winningest manager, and its all-time leader in games played, at-bats, runs, RBIs, doubles,

The 1885 champion White Stockings baseball club, Cap Anson in the center with bat.

and hits. He was the first member of the 3,000 hit club, and its only member until 1914. The *Chicago Tribune* estimated that since he began playing ball as a teenager in Marshalltown, Iowa, he had piled up more than 7,000 hits.[14] There would be no more.

Spalding planned a testimonial dinner for Anson, raising $50,000 for a tribute to the long-time star. "It seems a pity," said Spalding, "that a man like Anson should be allowed to drop from sight without the people being given a chance to show their high esteem of him."[15]

Anson refused the honor, saying "I don't know as I am yet ready to say that I am out of baseball. I am neither a pauper nor a rich man, and prefer to decline. The public owes me nothing...the kind offer to raise a large public subscription for me...is an honor and compliment I duly appreciate... At this hour I deem it both unwise and inexpedient to accept the generosity so considerately offered."[16]

Anson retired as a player, but returned to the bench in 1898, replacing Bill Joyce as manager of the New York Giants. He lasted only as many games as years he spent in Chicago. After going 9–13, he was fired, and Joyce was reinstated. It was his last official association with major-league baseball, though not due to lack of effort.

After his exit from the Giants, Anson tried to obtain a Western League franchise and move it to the South Side of Chicago, but Spalding, whose approval for the move was necessary under rules of the National Agreement, refused permission. For a third time, Spalding spiked his former teammate's desire to move into the front office of a professional ballclub. Later, Anson served as president of an ill-fated revival of the American Association, which attempted to play in 1900, but folded due to financial pressures.[17]

BEYOND BASEBALL

In the summer of 1901 rumors abounded that Cap Anson was on the verge of making a comeback in Chicago by purchasing his old team.[18] But the rumors proved unfounded. Instead, it was his nemesis, Jim Hart, who took over majority control.

Cap Anson was finished with baseball. He lived out the final two decades of his life in the entertainment industry, but not as a ballplayer. Anson opened a bowling and billiards parlor in downtown Chicago in 1899. He served as a vice-president of the new American Bowling Congress. He then turned to politics, serving one term as Chicago city clerk. In late 1905 Anson sold his stock in the Chicago ballclub and expanded his business.

He invested the remaining funds from his stock sale in semipro ball, purchasing a team (called Anson's Colts) and constructing his own ballpark. He even occasionally donned a uniform and took the field, but the Colts never achieved more than mediocrity and Anson sold the team after three years.[19]

This was the latest in a string of failures for Anson. He had mortgaged his home to buoy his business ventures, and he lost it, leaving him penniless, homeless, and unemployed. He and his wife, Virginia, moved in with their daughter. In 1916, after a long illness, Virginia died. Though broke, Anson was still wildly popular in Chicago and his reputation as a ballplaying legend extended across the country. He thus began the final chapter of his career by hitting the boards and travelling the vaudeville circuits. Though he eventually reached the big time, he did not grow rich.[20]

In January 1922, Anson was hired to manage the new Dixmoor Golf Club, set to open later that year. He actively promoted the club and took enthusiastically to his new calling. But it did not last long. While taking a walk near his home, he collapsed and was rushed to the hospital, where he died a few days later, on April 15, 1922, just two days shy of his 70th birthday.

His death was front page news. The *Chicago Tribune* lauded him as an honest, temperate, and dignified gentleman as well as a model husband and ballplayer.[21] Hugh Fullerton gushed that Anson was, "the greatest man in the history of baseball...what Ruth is to baseball today is but a small comparison to what Capt. Anson was when he led his White Stockings onto the field."[22]

The baseball fraternity mourned Anson. His funeral was attended by hundreds, ranging from baseball fans to political and business dignitaries. The overflow crowd spilled onto Michigan Avenue, snarling traffic. The White Sox game that day was delayed until late afternoon to allow time for the players of both teams to attend the funeral, where Judge Landis delivered the eulogy.[23]

Anson did not leave an estate, and the National League paid for his hospital and funeral expenses. They also arranged to have his wife's remains relocated from Philadelphia to lie alongside Anson in Chicago, and erected a tombstone at his gravesite. On it was inscribed the simple but certain epitaph, "He played the game."[24] ■

Notes

1. For a full discussion of Hulbert's machinations, see Michael Haupert, William Hulbert SABR bio and Michael Haupert, SABR Chicago Cubs club bio.
2. "Capt. Anson, Baseball Hero, Dies at 70," *Chicago Tribune*, April 15, 1922, 1.
3. Thorn, John, "Anson's First Baseball Contract," May 1, 2019, https://ourgame.mlblogs.com/ansons-firstbaseball-contract-4c73bdb3ddef.
4. *Cash Book 1876–1881*, Chicago Cubs Collection, 223–24.
5. Harold Seymour, *Baseball: The Early Years* (New York: Oxford University Press, 1960), 330, 331.
6. David Fleitz, "Cap Anson," SABR bio project https://6 sabr.org/bioproj/person/cap-anson.
7. "Hart is President Now," *Chicago Tribune*, April 15, 1891, 5.
8. "Anson Replies to Hart," *Chicago Tribune*, January 7, 1900, 17.
9. Art Ahrens, "Chicago Cubs: Sic Transit Gloria Mundi," In Peter C. Bjarkman, ed., *Encyclopedia of Major League Baseball Team Histories: National League* (Westport: Meckler Publishing, 1991), 137–80.
10. David Porter, "Cap Anson of Marshalltown: Baseball's First Superstar," *The Palimpsest* 61, no 4 (July/August 1980): 98-107.
11. "Good-By to Anson," *Chicago Tribune*, February 2, 1898, 4.
12. "Hart Writes of Anson," *Chicago Tribune*, December 31, 1899, 18.
13. "Anson Replies to Hart," *Chicago Tribune*, January 7, 1900, 17.
14. "Played 3000 Games," *Chicago Tribune*, February 1, 1898, 4.
15. "Tribute to Anson," *Chicago Tribune*, February 4, 1898, 4.
16. "Anson Won't Take It," *Chicago Tribune*, February 6, 1898, 7.
17. Fleitz, David, "Cap Anson," SABR bio project https://sabr.org/bioproj/person/cap-anson.
18. "Anson May Get in Games," *Chicago Tribune*, July 15, 1901, 2.
19. Fleitz, David, "Cap Anson," SABR bio project https://sabr.org/bioproj/person/cap-anson.
20. Robert H. Schaefer, "Anson in Greasepaint: The Vaudeville Career of Adrian C. Anson," *The National Pastime*, Vol 28, 2008.
21. "Capt. Anson, Baseball Hero, Dies at 70," *Chicago Tribune*, April 15, 1922, 1.
22. Hugh Fullerton, "Even Ruth Unable to Touch Anson's Role," *Chicago Tribune*, April 15, 1922, 15.
23. "Notes," *Chicago Tribune*, April 16, 1922, 26.
24. Hugh Fullerton, "Unveil Monument to 'Cap' Anson Today," *Chicago Tribune*, September 16, 1923, 26.

Boodle and Barnstorming

When Politics and the National Pastime Convened in Dwight, Illinois

Bill Pearch

Col. Frank Leslie Smith (1867–1950) was a banker, real estate dealer, congressman, and baseball fan. A slender, self-made man, Smith adhered to a simple doctrine that empowered his rise from humble roots into the political sphere: the end justifies the means.[1] This motto helped forge formidable business connections and amass political clout on local, regional, and national stages. Smith also used any means necessary to construct a winning team for Dwight, Illinois, a strategy that paralleled his rise to national prominence and his ultimate downfall.

While Smith lacked talent to play professional ball, he gained status within the Illinois Republican party and weaved the game into his lifelong pursuit of elected office. Despite repeated efforts to secure office, he only made it to Congress twice. He claimed to stand "for the honest conduct of political office and public trust."[2] But when Smith died in 1950, the *Chicago Sun-Times* mentioned his scandalous pursuits of a US Senate seat, acknowledging defeat "by only 11,000 votes," and ultimately, being "beaten by $285,000."[3]

The town of Dwight today remains best known as the former headquarters of the Keeley Institute and its unorthodox alcoholism treatments. At the time of Col. Smith's birth there, approximately 70 miles southwest of Chicago, Dwight was a community of about a thousand residents. Rockford's *Register-Gazette* suggested in 1892 that Dwight was a first-class community devoid of any amusement, making it ideal for a minor league team in the Illinois-Iowa League.[4]

Dwight's earliest documented baseball reference appeared in June 1868, when Willie Gardner, captain of the Pony Club of Dwight, challenged "any Base Ball Club in the City of Wilmington which has no member over 14 years of age" to a game.[5] Later that summer, a scathing editorial shamed locals and asked, "What has become of the Base Ballists?" and questioned their desire "for allowing other towns of less magnitude to excel in the national game."[6] No local ordinances prohibited baseball, so perhaps "the young men are either too lazy or do not wish to run the risk of having broken fingers."[7] Perhaps the editorial prompted the 1871

formation of the Dwight Renfrews, named after Lord Renfrew, the Prince of Wales' alias used during a local hunting expedition in 1860.[8]

While details of Smith's childhood remain sparse, baseball proved formative. Smith was known locally as an expert ballplayer "playing just about as good ball as anyone" and "making good stops and placed the ball well when batting."[9,10,11] Many of the traits that defined his professional career—aggressiveness and a will to dominate—manifested themselves during juvenile sandlot games.[12]

Smith was likely too young to witness one of Dwight's earliest organized games against Broughton Township in June 1871, but perhaps an 1874 military display sparked his passion.[13,14] Prior to a game between the Renfrews and Pontiac Athletics, a steam engine exploded and injured several onlookers. Simultaneously a gentleman named Slane Turner suffered arm injuries when a cannon prematurely fired. Explosions aside, nearly 3,000 people watched Dwight win, 20–13.[15]

Smith's rise to political prominence began in 1895 when he became the junior partner at Romberger & Smith, a real estate and private banking firm.[16] After hours, he managed the firm's semiprofessional baseball team—the Dwight R&S, named after his partner and himself.

Smith organized schedules against town teams and semipros from neighboring locales. He demonstrated a knack for securing elite homegrown talent and distinguished newcomers. Most of Smith's players never advanced beyond the semiprofessional level, but several local players—Burt Keeley, George Cutshaw, and Bud Clancy—donned local jerseys before jumping to the majors. The roster included one Dwight native, Eddie Higgins, who briefly pitched for the St. Louis Cardinals. Smith even signed major league stars for short stints, including "Turkey" Mike Donlin and Bill Sherdel.

As Smith's team gained notoriety for playing fast and dynamic games, he opted to test their mettle—and simultaneously shine a light on his burgeoning political aspirations—by attracting barnstormers and novelty acts to Dwight. He also arranged a handful of games against American, National, and Federal League teams on his home field.

One thousand fans traveled to Dwight on August 27, 1901, to witness the community's most significant baseball game to date.[17] Smith organized a contest against the traveling Nebraska Indians and granted Dr. Herbert Lehr—a recent transplant and University of Michigan three-sport star[18]—pitching honors. The Dwight R&S plated four runs in the bottom of the first inning as Lehr was unhittable until the third when the floodgates opened. The game ended in 16–6 onslaught in favor of the barnstormers. Despite the final score, Smith had established a standard for competition and a vehicle for self-promotion.[19]

In 1902, Smith gained control of his partner's portion of the firm.[20] With new business arrangements, he rebranded both the firm and baseball team. The Dwight R&S became the Frank L. Smiths.[21]

During the ensuing years, Smith's political aspirations grew as did the quality of his team's competition. He suffered an unsuccessful run for Illinois lieutenant governor opening in 1904, as the Smiths began challenging teams from Chicago's semipro circuit and several Black baseball teams at Dwight's West Side Park.[22]

Captivated by the Chicago-centric 1906 World Series, Smith aimed higher when he organized his team's schedule in 1907. In June, the Smiths hosted the Cuban Stars of Havana. Jimmie Brown, the hometown pitcher, allowed two first-inning runs and received no offensive support. The barnstormers blanked the Smiths, 2–0.[23]

In late July, Seattle High School's team descended upon Dwight promoting the upcoming Alaska-Yukon-Pacific Exhibition. The Smiths "lacked the fast, snappy work that won so many games" earlier that year.[24] That afternoon, 16-year-old Charlie Schmutz—a future Brooklyn Robins pitcher[25]—stymied the local squad and the Seattleites won, 6–5.[26]

In mid-September of that year, Mabel Hite, eccentric ballplayer Mike Donlin's wife, revealed the secret of her husband's inexplicable disappearance. The actress and comedian shared that he was a patient at Dwight's Keeley Institute receiving the so-called "Keeley cure" under an assumed name.[27] Donlin opted for the vaudeville circuit with his wife following a preseason contract dispute with the New York Giants. He even played for Jimmy Callahan's Chicago semipros, the Logan Squares.[28] Ever the opportunist, Smith enlisted Donlin's services for a significant engagement.

Smith and Callahan coordinated to bring one of the two pennant-winning teams to West Side Park. They

Col. Frank Leslie Smith

arranged for the American League's pennant-winning Detroit Tigers to challenge the Smiths in Dwight on Tuesday, October 22.[29]

The Tigers arrived via train and were warmly greeted by a throng of local baseball fans.[30] Businesses were encouraged to close shop that afternoon and happily obliged.[31] More than 1,500 fans flooded the ballpark as the Tigers thumped the Smiths, 8–1.[32]

The game remained scoreless until the fourth inning, when Ty Cobb reached first safely on a Donlin error. Cobb stole second base, then scored on Claude Rossman's single. The Tigers padded their lead with single runs in the fifth and sixth.[33] Detroit sealed the Smiths' fate with a four-run eighth and an insurance run in the ninth, winning 8–1.

The umpires cut the Smiths some slack. During one at-bat, Donlin singled to right field. Cobb, aware that Donlin loafed toward first base, fielded and fired the ball to Rossman and beat the runner. When the umpire ruled Donlin safe, Cobb erupted into hysterics at the blatant hometown favoritism, unable to contain his laughter.[34]

Higgins, the 19-year-old local starting pitcher, limited the Tigers to nine hits, and perhaps with stronger defense, the result would have been closer. Dwight's defense committed five errors that afternoon. For good measure, Smith played shortstop and recorded four assists and one putout. He reached base on a ninth-inning fielder's choice, but the game ended when he interfered with Donlin's groundball toward first.[35]

Three-I League scouts were impressed and signed Higgins and George Cutshaw to the Bloomington (Illinois) Bloomers squad. Higgins joined the Cardinals in 1909 and played 18 total major-league games. Cutshaw enjoyed a 12-year major-league career with Brooklyn, Pittsburgh, and Detroit, playing second base for the

Brooklyn Robins in all five games of the 1916 World Series.

President Theodore Roosevelt appointed Smith as internal revenue collector in Illinois' Springfield district.[36] That role proved beneficial and strengthened his connection with William Howard Taft, Roosevelt's handpicked presidential successor.[37] As Smith's political ambitions strengthened, his passion for bringing baseball attractions to Dwight increased. On October 15, 1908, a hodgepodge of players identified as the American League's Washington Senators arrived in town. Initial promotions billed a pitching duel between Eddie Higgins, now a member of the Bloomers, and Walter Johnson.[38] Few actual major leaguers played with the remainder of the lineup selected from Chicago's amateur ranks at the last moment.[39] The Smiths jumped on Burt Keeley, a former Dwight R&S pitcher with no relationship to the Keeley Institute, but Washington managed to win, 4–3.[40]

As 1910 waned, Giants manager John McGraw received word that Arthur "Bugs" Raymond would curtail his drinking by entering Dwight's Keeley Institute.[41] The Times (Streator, Illinois) noted that Smith's players should gain some sage pitching insight from the National League hurler, but whether he tutored any Smiths is unknown.[42] The Keeley Institute expelled Raymond quickly due to excessive horseplay.[43]

Though a competitive squad with a winning record, the Smiths' talent waned for several seasons. In 1911, Col. Smith's team traveled north to Dellwood Park—a lavish park constructed by the Chicago and Joliet Electric Railway to encourage ridership—for a series of games against the Joliet Standards in July and August.[44] Typically known for top-notch quality of play, the Smiths' decline was memorialized by The Joliet News after their 11–10 win on July 30, calling it "a slow game crowded with many stupid, asinine plays, faulty work and rotten judgment."[45]

The Smiths' performance regressed and wrapped the 1912 season with a 14–12 record, but concluded play with a contest against the Chicago Cubs on October 24.[46] The Cubs trotted out their regulars, except for Johnny Evers who remained in Chicago.[47] That same day, Cubs owner Charlie Murphy selected Evers as the team's manager for 1913.[48] Despite Smith securing Polly Wolfe, who played one game for the Chicago White Sox that season, the Cubs pounded the Smiths, 9–3.[49] Cubs' third baseman Heinie Zimmerman electrified the crowd with his hard hitting.[50] After scoring five runs in the opening frame, the Cubs never relinquished the lead. Chicago plated another run in the second and three in the fifth. Spectators were buzzing after Zimmerman clubbed a home run and Jimmy Archer hammered a long foul ball that cleared a neighboring barn.[51]

Burt Keeley returned to Dwight on June 4, 1913, helming Chicago's upstart Federal League franchise.[52] Lacking a formal name, newspapers at the time frequently referred to his squad as the Keeleys, Browns, or playfully, the Keeley Cures.[53,54] The Smiths played well; outhitting the minor leaguers and extended a 5–4 lead into the bottom of the fifth. The Keeleys answered with five runs and defeated Dwight, 11–7.[55]

With business thriving, Smith focused upon the 1916 gubernatorial election in Illinois.[56] He flexed his political muscle and brought three high-profile contests

The Dwight, Illinois, train station, photographed between 1900 and 1905.

to Dwight during 1915. First, the Smiths faced Chicago's Sixth Ward Republican Club squad and lost a late-May contest, 8–2.[57] Smith also arranged for two Federal League games.

On June 7, 1915, the Pittsburgh Rebels sat atop the Federal League standings, and squared off against the Smiths at West Side Park in ankle-deep mud. Player-manager Rebel Oakes tapped Charles "Bunny" Hearn to face Eddie Higgins. With a biting wind and sub-optimal conditions, Oakes opted to rest his starters for the exhibition game.[58] The Smiths plated five early runs and carried a 6–3 advantage into the eighth. Pittsburgh ultimately forced extra innings and plated the two winning runs on a throwing error in the top of the 11th.[59]

The Smiths concluded the 1915 season before a large crowd on October 12, with a 9–0 throttling by Joe Tinker's Chicago Whales. Local rooters witnessed a game that *The Pantagraph* labeled "neither interesting nor spectacular."[60] Chicago's Mordecai "Three Fingered" Brown pitched in relief and puzzled the Smiths' batters that afternoon. After scoring three runs in the third, the Whales never looked back.

Determined to secure the Republican gubernatorial nomination in 1916, Smith's campaign managers insisted that sports fans would vote for him. Chick Evans, winner of the 1916 US Open golf championship, endorsed Smith.[61] To sway Cook County, the Friends of Col. Frank L. Smith booster club appealed to Chicago's split baseball allegiance. The club organized with Joe Tinker as president and Ray Schalk as secretary. Other members included Buck Weaver, Jimmy Callahan, Art Wilson, Burt Keeley, Art Zangerle, and Billy Niesen.[62] Despite the athletic horsepower, Smith finished third in the Republican primaries.[63]

After years of relentless campaigning, Smith served in the United States House of Representatives from 1919 to 1921.[64] For all his political bluster, nothing significant distinguished his service. Rather than run for reelection, he sought the Senate nomination and lost.[65] While serving, his connection with his baseball team is unclear as other Dwight-based teams emerged, namely the Midgets and Cubs, and the Smiths disbanded in July 1921.[66,67] A team branded as the Smiths played in 1922, but Col. Smith's connection is unknown.

Local coverage declared similar sentiments as in 1868 that "Dwight is not a baseball town," and noted that attendance barely surpassed 200 per game.[68] The Midgets were described as "remnants of the Frank L. Smiths and promising youngsters."

Governor Len Small appointed Smith as chairman of the Illinois Commerce Commission in April 1921, a regulatory body overseeing public utilities. He served in that role until September 1926.[69] During his tenure, he built powerful relations with Samuel Insull, a business magnate who controlled much of Chicago's public transportation.[70]

As quickly as Smith's team crumbled, so did his political career. In 1926 Smith ran against incumbent Illinois Senator William B. McKinley. During his campaign, rumors circulated about excessive primary expenditures. Despite these rumors, Smith defeated McKinley in a landslide and won the November election, but the Senate launched a campaign-spending investigation.[71] When McKinley died unexpectedly in December 1926, Governor Small appointed senator-elect Smith to fill the remainder of his term set to expire in March 1927.

On January 19, 1928, the United States Senate, by a 61–23 vote, determined that Smith was not qualified to fill Illinois' vacant seat due to fraud and corruption charges.[72,73] The investigation determined that Smith spent more than $400,000 ($6.8 million in 2023) during the campaign and received $125,000 ($2.1 million in 2023) from Insull.[74] Smith claimed, in an August 1931 open letter, that Chicago millionaire Julius Rosenwald offered him $555,000 ($9.4 million in 2023) worth of Sears Roebuck stock to withdraw his candidacy, but rejected said offer.[75]

Smith made a final unsuccessful run at political office in 1930. Following his defeat, he remained an active member of the Republican National Committee and continued his business pursuits in Dwight, but never organized another Dwight baseball team.[76]

Col. Frank L. Smith passed away at his home early in the morning on Wednesday, August 30, 1950, following a two-week illness. He was 82 years old. When he passed, Smith's estate was valued at $400,000 ($4.8 million in 2023[77]).[78] ∎

Notes

1. "'Big Bill' Uses Spicy Lingo in Talks at Election Rallies," *The Baltimore Sun*, April 8, 1928.
2. "He is a Candidate for Lieut. Governor," *Streator* (Illinois) *Daily Free Press*, November 30, 1903, 1.
3. "Frank L. Smith, 82, Dies; Long a GOP Leader," *Chicago Sun-Times*, August 31, 1950, 33.
4. "Brief Ball Notes," *Rockford* (Illinois) *Daily Register-Gazette*, April 9, 1892, 3.
5. "Base Ball," *Wilmington* (Illinois) *Independent*, June 3, 1868, 5.
6. "News Items," *The Star*, (Dwight, Illinois), July 23, 1868, 1.
7. *The Star*, (Dwight, Illinois), July 30, 1868, 3.
8. Dwight Centennial Committee. *Dwight Centennial, 1854–1954: A Great Past—A Greater Future* (1954), 18.
9. "'Maple Lane' Col. Frank L. Smith's Model Farm," (Bloomington, Illinois) *Pantagraph*, July 22, 1916.
10. "Flies," *Dwight* (Illinois) *Star & Herald*, September 9, 1899.
11. "Notes," *Dwight* (Illinois) *Star & Herald*, August 25, 1900.

12. Carroll H. Wooddy, *The Case of Frank L. Smith: A Study in Representative Government* (Chicago: University of Chicago Press, 1931), 71.

13. "Livingston County," (Bloomington, Illinois) *Pantagraph*, June 9, 1871, 2.

14. "Military Display at Dwight, Ill.," *Chicago Tribune*, August 15, 1874, 7.

15. "Telegraphic Brevities," (Chicago) *Inter Ocean*, August 15, 1874, 4.

16. Anonymous. *The Biographical Record of Livingston and Woodford Counties, Illinois* (Chicago: S.J. Clarke Publishing Company, 1900), 32.

17. "Took Dwight's Scalp," *Dwight* (Illinois) *Star & Herald*, August 31, 1901.

18. Nelville S. Hoff, D.D.S., *The Dental Register* (Cincinnati: Samuel A. Crocker & Co., 1903), 533.

19. "Took Dwight's Scalp," *Dwight* (Illinois) *Star & Herald*, August 31, 1901.

20. Carroll H. Wooddy, *The Case of Frank L. Smith: A Study in Representative Government* (Chicago: University of Chicago Press, 1931), 72–73.

21. Paul R. Steichen, "Dwight Baseball of Bygone Days Full of Interest," *Dwight* (Illinois) *Star & Herald*, August 11, 1938.

22. Carroll H. Wooddy, *The Case of Frank L. Smith: A Study in Representative Government* (Chicago: University of Chicago Press, 1931), 78–79.

23. "Base Ball Dope for the Fans," *Dwight* (Illinois) *Star & Herald*, June 8, 1907.

24. "Defeated by Seattle H.S. Boys," *Dwight* (Illinois) *Star & Herald*, July 27, 1907, 1.

25. "C.O. Schmutz, Former Major Leaguer, Dies," *Seattle Daily Times*, June 28, 1962, 49.

26. "High School Boys to Take Southern Trip," *Seattle Daily Times*, July 25, 1907, 15.

27. "On the Water Wagon," *Streator* (Illinois) *Free Press*, September 19, 1907, 6.

28. Rob Edelman and Michael Betzold. "Mike Donlin," SABR Baseball Biography Project, https://sabr.org/bioproj/person/mike-donlin, accessed February 20, 2023.

29. "Detroit Tigers Coming," *Dwight* (Illinois) *Star & Herald*, October 19, 1907.

30. Paul R. Steichen, "Dwight Baseball of Bygone Days Full of Interest," *Dwight* (Illinois) *Star & Herald*, August 19, 1938.

31. "Detroit Tigers Coming," *Dwight* (Illinois) *Star & Herald*, October 19, 1907.

32. "Tigers Whale Dwight," *Detroit Free Press*, October 23, 1907.

33. "Ee-Yah!," *Dwight* (Illinois) *Star & Herald*, October 26, 1907.

34. Paul R. Steichen, "Dwight Baseball of Bygone Days Full of Interest," *Dwight* (Illinois) *Star & Herald*, August 19, 1938.

35. Paul R. Steichen, "Dwight Baseball of Bygone Days Full of Interest," *Dwight* (Illinois) *Star & Herald*, August 19, 1938.

36. Genevieve Forbes Herrick. "Frank L. Smith is a Hero in His Own Home Town," *Chicago Tribune*, April 15, 1926.

37. Doris Kearns Goodwin, *The Bully Pulpit: Theodore Roosevelt, William Howard Taft and the Golden Age of Journalism* (New York: Simon & Schuster, 2013), 11.

38. "Local News," *The* (Fairbury, Illinois) *Blade*, October 9, 1908, 14.

39. *Washington* (DC) *Herald*, April 15, 1909.

40. "F.L. Smiths Play Against the Washington Senators of the American League," *Dwight* (Illinois) *Star & Herald*, October 17, 1908.

41. "'Bugs' Says He Will Behave," *Chicago Tribune*, December 31, 1910, 10.

42. "Trains at Dwight," *Streator* (Illinois) *Daily Free Press*, December 31, 1910, 5.

43. Don Jensen. "Bugs Raymond," SABR Baseball Biography Project, https://sabr.org/bioproj/person/bugs-raymond, accessed February 20, 2023.

44. http://lockporthistory.org/dellwoodpark/dellwoodpark.htm (accessed February 16, 2023).

45. "Dwight Takes Farcical Game," *The Joliet* (Illinois) *News*, July 31, 1911.

46. "A Resume for the Year of the F.L. Smith Club," *Dwight* (Illinois) *Star & Herald*, December 7, 1912.

47. "Big Leaguers Defeat F.L. Smiths," *Dwight* (Illinois) *Star & Herald*, October 26, 1912.

48. Jason Cannon, *Charlie Murphy: The Iconoclastic Showman Behind the Chicago Cubs* (Lincoln: University of Nebraska Press, 2022), 237.

49. Paul R. Steichen, "Dwight Baseball of Bygone Days Full of Interest," *Dwight* (Illinois) *Star & Herald*, September 2, 1938.

50. "Cubs Defeat Dwight," *The* (Bloomington, Illinois) *Pantagraph*, October 25, 1912.

51. "Big Leaguers Defeat F.L. Smiths," *Dwight* (Illinois) *Star & Herald*, October 26, 1912.

52. "South Wilmington," *The* (Joliet, Illinois) *Herald News*, June 5, 1913, 7.

53. "St. Louis Feds Even Up Series with Chicagos," *The* (Chicago) *Inter Ocean*, June 4, 1913, 13.

54. "Federals Home to Tackle Covingtons Thursday Matinee," *St. Louis Star and Times*, June 4, 1913, 8.

55. "Chicago 'Feds' Win at Dwight," *Chicago Tribune*, June 5, 1913.

56. "1916 Pot Boiling," *The* (Springfield, Illinois) *Forum*, March 13, 1915, 1.

57. "Home Team Wins Another Game," *Dwight* (Illinois) *Star & Herald*, May 29, 1915.

58. "Rebels Lose in Race by Idleness," *Pittsburgh Press*, June 8, 1915, 28.

59. "Win One and Lose One," *Dwight* (Illinois) *Star & Herald*, June 12, 1915.

60. "Whales Defeat Dwight," *The* (Bloomington, Illinois) *Pantagraph*, October 13, 1915, 5.

61. "Hull is Gaining Fast, Says Banker Friend," *Chicago Daily News*, August 18, 1916, 5.

62. "Merely Politics," *Chicago Day Book*, September 9, 1916, 29.

63. Carroll H. Wooddy, *The Case of Frank L. Smith: A Study in Representative Government* (Chicago: University of Chicago Press, 1931), 94-95.

64. "Smith, Frank Leslie," History, Art & Archives: United States House of Representatives.

65. Carroll H. Wooddy, *The Case of Frank L. Smith: A Study in Representative Government* (Chicago: University of Chicago Press, 1931), 96.

66. "Defeat Dwight Midgets," *Dwight* (Illinois) *Star & Herald*, June 25, 1921.

67. "A Tie Ball Game," *Dwight* (Illinois) *Star & Herald*, May 20, 1922, 1.

68. "F.L. Smith Team Quits," *The* (Streator, Illinois) *Times*, July 28, 1921, 4.

69. Carroll H. Wooddy, *The Case of Frank L. Smith: A Study in Representative Government* (Chicago: University of Chicago Press, 1931), 9.

70. "The (Other) Man Who Tried to Buy a Senate Seat," NBC 5 Chicago, June 3, 2011.

71. Sue Cummings, "Stormy Career Marked Dwight's 'Big Mover,'" *The* (Streator, Illinois) *Times-Press*, November 22, 1982.

72. "Senate Bars Smith by Vote of 61 to 23; Lorimer in Running," *Baltimore Sun*, January 20, 1928, 1.

73. "… article about Frank L. Smith isn't entirely accurate.," *The* (Dwight, Illinois) *Paper*, July 6, 2022, 7.

74. "The (Other) Man Who Tried to Buy a Senate Seat," NBC 5 Chicago, June 3, 2011.

75. "Smith Details Offer to Quit Senate Race," *Baltimore Sun*, August 17, 1931, 3.

76. "Smith, Frank Leslie," History, Art & Archives: United States House of Representatives.

77. https://smartasset.com/investing/inflation-calculator (accessed on February 19, 2023) "Frank L. Smith Estate Valued at $400,000," *The Times-Press* (Streator, Illinois), September 21, 1950, 4.

78. "Frank L. Smith Estate Valued at $400,000," *The* (Streator, Illinois) *Times-Press*, September 21, 1950, 4.

The 1906 World Series

The First World Series with Umpire Hand Signals

R.A.R. Edwards

While the World Series returns to us annually, some Series live in legend forever. One of those classics was surely the 1906 World Series, which pitted the Chicago Cubs against the Chicago White Sox.[1] The 1906 World Series was full of firsts. Being an all-Chicago affair, it was the first twentieth century "Subway Series"[2] and marked the first twentieth-century appearance in the World Series for both teams.[3] And while it would not be their last, their 1906 World Series appearance was the first for the Cubs' famous infield of Joe Tinker, Johnny Evers, and Frank Chance.[4] Sportswriter Franklin Pierce Adams would cement their legacy with these famous words, four years later: "These are the saddest of possible words: Tinker to Evers to Chance."

But all of those firsts would be of little consequence if it were not a series that rewarded fans with unexpected drama, ending in a huge upset. The heavily favored Cubs, with the best record in baseball (116–36), were defeated by the White Sox, the so-called "Hitless Wonders," who had the worst team batting average in the American League (.230) during the regular season. On their way to victory, the White Sox truly managed to outdo themselves in the Series, batting a mere .198 as a team.[5]

These are the important reasons that the 1906 World Series is memorable. Yet, arguably, its most lasting impact on baseball history lies elsewhere. This World Series was the first in which the umpires called the games with gestures behind home plate. In 1906, Jim Johnstone of the National League worked alongside American League umpire Francis "Silk" O'Loughlin. It was O'Loughlin's first World Series appearance. Already recognized as "one of the greatest umpires that ever stepped on the field," O'Loughlin made history in 1906.[6]

As the *Chicago Tribune* reported:

Fans who were fortunate enough to see the world's series in this city last fall will recall that the din of rooting was so great it was impossible to hear an umpire's decision. Umpire Johnstone, who worked behind the plate in the first game, had difficulty in making even the batteries understand his decisions. Next day, 'Silk' O'Loughlin supplemented his clarion voice with his characteristic gestures and his decisions were apparent to all. …(Before) the third game, both umpires were instructed to raise their right arms for strikes and their left arm for balls.[7]

There is a lot to unpack here. First, the impact of an intra-city Series leaps out. The noise was literally deafening. Second, what were these "characteristic gestures?" Third, how long had O'Loughlin been using them? Obviously, long enough that the *Tribune* thought of them as characteristic of the way that O'Loughlin called a game. Still, they were clearly not in use by most umpires. After all, it had not occurred to Jim Johnstone to use them, even as he struggled to make himself understood verbally. Fourth, where had these gestures come from?

The year 1906 holds all the answers. In April, just as the season was getting underway, the *Washington Post* reported that "O'Loughlin sprained his larynx Tuesday…and had no voice today. Instead of calling the decisions, he employed 'Dummy' Hoy's mute signal code, which certainly was a novelty for Silk."[8] Over the course of the season, the use of Hoy's signal code went from a "novelty" to a "characteristic" feature of O'Loughlin's work.[9]

The reporters in 1906 acknowledged that the credit for the system should not go to O'Loughlin but to Hoy. The *Post* stated directly that O'Loughlin "employed 'Dummy' Hoy's mute signal code." Though not the first deaf player in major league baseball, Hoy was without question the most impactful. A center fielder, his career began with the Washington Nationals in 1888 and ended with the Cincinnati Reds in 1902.[10]

His system went with him from team to team. The *Tribune* described it in this way: "When Dummy Hoy was playing in the big leagues, his only method of ascertaining decisions on pitched balls was by watching the coach at third base, who held up his right hand

William Hoy, shown in his 1888 Old Judge portrait for the Washington Statesmen.

when a strike was called on Hoy and his left hand for a ball."[11] The *Tribune* knew that fans had seen this system in baseball before and it was not original to hearing umpires.

Would O'Loughlin have seen Hoy's system in use? In 1902, O'Loughlin was a rookie umpire. Hoy had just finished playing in Chicago, and was moving on to Cincinnati, taking his signal system with him. But it had left an indelible impression by this point, on both major leagues. The *Washington Post* reporter instantly recognized the thrust right hand for strikes and the upraised left for balls when O'Loughlin tried it out in April 1906 as "Dummy Hoy's mute signal code."

Hoy stated back in 1900 that his system was "well understood by all the League players." He added that fans liked the system too, as "I have often been told by frequenters of the game that they take considerable delight in watching the coacher signal balls and strikes to me, as by these signals they can know to a certainty what the umpire with a not too overstrong voice is saying." He further explained that the "reason the right hand was originally selected by me to denote a strike and the left hand to denote a ball was because 'the pitcher was all right' when he got the ball over the plate and because 'he got left' when he sent the ball wide of the plate."[12]

The *Chicago Tribune* was confident that Hoy's signs were coming to baseball permanently. "The movement for a system of signals to indicate an umpire's decisions

during a baseball game...seems to be spreading," the paper declared in January 1907, predicting that baseball "will adopt some such system before another playing season arrives."[13] *Sporting Life* had reached a similar conclusion by February 1907, noting, "The umpire arm-signal plan, so well demonstrated during the world's championship series, is growing in favor, and, from appearances, will be in general use next season."[14]

But just as *Sporting Life* thought the matter settled, the *Tribune* broke a story in February 1907 revealing that "electrical score boards operated from near the home plates probably will be adopted by the American league clubs to indicate to spectators every decision made during a game instead of the signal system by umpires' gestures, which has been under consideration."[15] *Sporting Life* picked up the same report, with additional sourcing, explaining that "the scoreboard idea results from the protest of Hank O'Day and other knights of the indicator on the making of themselves human windmills trying to interpret balls and strikes to the fans in the bleachers."[16] The scoreboard would replace the gesture idea. Such boards were considered "simple," "practical," and "reliable."[17]

Unconvinced, the *Tribune* pointed out the obvious weakness to the scheme; namely, the scoreboard operator still needed to know what the call was in order to post it. Without implementing a gesture system for the umpires, the scoreboard operator would have to guess at the call. Besides, the paper went on, "the real fan does not like to take his eyes off the play long enough even to glance at a scoreboard except between innings....From the patron's standpoint, therefore, no scoreboard can replace an umpire's gestures."[18] In this way, the *Tribune* essentially argued that all baseball fans are deaf; they all rely on vision, not hearing, to understand the game unfolding on the field before them.[19]

Things came to a head in 1907. Umpires formally came out "against the proposed rule to have umpires wave their arms to designate balls and strikes."[20] But, at the turn of the century, their resistance was hardly surprising. Given that the system of gesturing originated with a deaf ballplayer, it would have been directly associated with deafness and with sign language, both of which were increasingly stigmatized as abnormal at the turn of the century.[21]

American Sign Language was under attack, as educators sought to eliminate it from schools. By 1907, teachers argued that "our first and foremost aim has been the development of the deaf child into as nearly a normal individual as possible."[22] Only by speaking, and never signing, could a deaf child become normal. A new ideal was emerging for deaf people, the ideal of "passing" as a hearing person.[23] Deaf students who failed to do so were mocked; as historian Susan Burch notes, they "found themselves labeled as 'oral failures' and ridiculed as 'born idiots.'"[24]

Deaf people were under attack in other ways. In 1907, the federal government updated the Immigration of Act of 1882 to bar entry to persons with "a physical defect being of a nature which may affect the ability of such an alien to earn a living." Deaf immigrants found themselves turned away at Ellis Island, as hearing immigration officials assumed that deafness would render them unemployable.[25]

The American deaf community had few defenders of either its members or its language in the early twentieth century. But they had William Hoy. Hoy became a prominent symbol of deaf success in a hearing world. He signed, and did not speak, and he valued his deafness, arguing that it offered him an advantage over hearing players. In 1902, Hoy explained how being deaf positively affected all parts of his game:

In batting there is really little handicap for a mute. I can see the ball as well as others....I think, perhaps, the fact that I have to depend so much on my eyes helps me in judging what the umpire will call a strike, and if the ball delivered is a little off I wait for four bad ones. In base running the signals of the hit and run game and other strategies are mostly silent, the same as for the other players. By a further system of signs my teammates keep me posted on how many are out and what is going on about me.... Because I can not hear the coaching I have acquired the habit of running with my neck twisted to watch the progress of the ball. I think most players depend too much on the coachers and often a man is coached along too far or not far enough, when, if he knew where the ball was himself, he would know what chances were best for him to take. In judging fly balls I depend on sight alone and must keep my eye constantly on the batsman to watch for a possible fly, since I can not hear the crack of the bat. This alertness, I think, helps me in other departments of the game. So it may be seen, the handicaps of a deaf ball player are minimized.[26]

Hoy challenged the expectations of hearing Americans; they saw hearing loss but Hoy saw deaf gain.[27]

At least in baseball, hearing reporters and fans came to recognize the benefits and contributions of deaf people. The deaf way to communicate, by gestures, was seen as superior to the hearing solution of screaming louder. In the face of the umpires' resistance, the *Tribune* changed tactics. It moved to attack them, complaining that there was "too much consideration for the umpires."[28] *Sporting Life* did likewise, arguing, "The umpire who cannot use the arm signal system without confusion or trouble is not fit even for amateur umpiring...The system was tried in the world's championship series and worked to a charm..."[29] The press hoped that umpires would voluntarily agree to experiment with it.

It seems that this is what happened. Though umpires, as an organized body, resisted the system, some of their number reluctantly tried their hand at it. Bill Deane notes that "umpires' hand signals were in mass usage by 1907, though standardization was lacking."[30] Unsurprisingly, O'Loughlin kept using gestures. *Sporting Life* noted his work, writing, "Silk O'Loughlin...is also in a class by himself. Silk yells 'Stri-i-ik' with particular emphasis on the 'I' and draws his right hand back over his shoulder and points his thumb at the grandstand. When he calls a ball, he makes no movement with his hands. Silk calls two 'TUH,' which never fails to raise a laugh."[31]

The signs of baseball did not have much longer to wait. In 1909, they were made mandatory in both leagues. A majority of umpires had apparently concluded that such a system would not be too difficult to use. Perhaps O'Loughlin's continued use of the system had helped to change minds. Or, perhaps, umpires had finally been persuaded that baseball was indeed a business. Catering to the needs of paying customers was a priority for baseball owners. As the *Sporting*

Umpire "Silk" O'Loughlin, photographed here at the 1915 World Series.

LIBRARY OF CONGRESS / BAIN COLLECTION

Life acidly commented in 1907, "It is a reflection on the intelligence of umpires that they should require command to uniformly employ so simple a method of pleasing the patrons of the sport."[32]

Fans at the World Series in Chicago in 1906 could scarcely have imagined what the future would hold. How could it be that Chicago would not see another Subway Series in the remainder of the century? How could the Cubs go from three consecutive World Series appearances, which yielded two championships, to a century-and-change long World Series drought? At least, Tinker to Evers to Chance would live forever.

Sadly, the contributions of Hoy and O'Loughlin would not. There remains resistance in baseball to the historical fact that Hoy brought the signs to baseball. A 2012 book flatly called it "a myth."[33] In truth, "Dummy Hoy's mute signal code" entered baseball, was popularized during the 1906 World Series, and those signals are with us still.[34] But the man himself has not been given the recognition that he deserves. Neither has O'Loughlin. He died in 1918, a victim of the flu pandemic. With his career cut short, his pathbreaking part in bringing Hoy's signs to baseball was soon forgotten. Today, if you visit the National Baseball Hall of Fame, neither Hoy nor O'Loughlin have plaques. Instead, visitors learn that the man who brought the signs to baseball was umpire Bill Klem. As his plaque reads, in part, "Umpire. National League 1905–1951. Umpired in 18 World Series. Credited with introducing arm signals indicating strikes and fair or foul balls."

This plaque provides an unexpected twist to the story, namely, a surprise ending. In 1906, O'Loughlin could hardly have imagined that the credit for his achievement would someday be given to a man whom he helped to break into major league baseball. O'Loughlin helped to arrange the professional introductions for

Bill Klem that allowed him to advance out of the minor leagues and into the National League in 1905.[35] Klem's first World Series appearance came in Chicago, too—but in 1908, when the Cubs faced the Tigers, two years after O'Loughlin brought Hoy's signs to the World Series, where they have been ever since. ∎

Notes

1. For more on this Series, see Bernard A. Weisberger, *When Chicago Ruled Baseball: the Cubs-White Sox World Series of 1906* (New York: Harper, 2006).

2. While the term "Subway Series" for an intra-city World Series was not widely popularized until after the World Series became a regular all–New York City affair, it may be applied in spirit to the city of Chicago, despite Chicago not having a subway until 1943.

3. The Cubs had been in the 1885 and 1886 "World's Series."

4. For more on the trio, see David Rapp, *Tinker to Evers to Chance: The Chicago Cubs and the Dawn of Modern America* (Chicago: The University of Chicago Press, 2018).

5. This might seem like the performance floor, but in a list of the thirteen worst team batting averages in the history of the World Series, my Boston Red Sox managed to come in both first (1918 appearance, with an average of .186) and last (2013 appearance, with an average of .211). Talk about winning the hard way. And no, a decade later, I am still not entirely sure that the 2013 win makes up for the 2011 collapse, thanks for asking. And thanks, ESPN, for providing an online list to torture ourselves with.

6. Timeline of his career in "Silk O'Loughlin King of Umps," *Sunday Vindicator*, April 29, 1906, 13.

7. "Gestures to Tell Umpire's Ruling," *Chicago Tribune*, January 6, 1907, A1.

8. "Nationals Lose Game," *Washington Post*, Thursday, April 19, 1906, 8.

9. "Silk O'Loughlin Unique Umpire," *Meriden Daily Journal*, October 16, 1906, 11.

10. For more on Hoy's career see R.A.R. Edwards, *Deaf Players in Major League Baseball: A History, 1883 to the Present* (Jefferson, NC: McFarland & Co., 2020).

11. "Gestures to Tell Umpire's Ruling," *Chicago Tribune*, January 6, 1907, A1.

12. "Calling Balls and Strikes," *The Sporting News*, January 27, 1900, 5.

13. "The Referee: Sporting Comment of the Week," *Chicago Tribune*, January 20, 190, A1.

14. "Easy To Execute," *Sporting Life*, February 23, 1907, 4.

15. "Electrical Score Boards for the American League," *Chicago Tribune*, February 13, 1907, 12

16. "Johnson's Idea," *Sporting Life*, February 23, 1907, 10. O'Day remains the only man to play, manage, and umpire in the history of the National League. He served as an umpire in the World Series in 1903, and would serve in 10 World Series over the course of his career. When O'Day died in Chicago on July 2, 1935, former NL president John Heydler called him one of the greatest umpires ever in terms of knowledge of the rules, fairness, and courage to make the right call. Umpire Bill Klem, however, referred to him as a "misanthropic Irishman," while Christy Mathewson said that arguing with O'Day was like "using a lit match to see how much gasoline was in a fuel tank" (David Anderson, "Hank O'Day," SABR Baseball Biography Project).

17. "Electrical Score Boards for the American League," *Chicago Tribune*, February 13, 1907, 12. The Yankees are usually credited for first using an electronic scoreboard in baseball, in the original Yankee Stadium, when it opened in 1923. See G. Edwards White, *Creating the National Pastime: Baseball Transforms Itself, 1903–1953* (Princeton: Princeton University Press, 1996), 41–42. These 1907 articles, however, repeatedly point to this forerunner apparently in use in St. Louis as the inspiration for Johnson's plan to adopt them throughout the American League. For more on the history of electronic scoreboards in baseball, see Rob Edelman, "Electric Scoreboards, Bulletin Boards, and Mimic Diamonds," *Base Ball 3*, 2, Fall 2009, 76–87.

18. "The Referee: Sports Comment of the Week: Signaling Balls and Strikes," *Chicago Tribune*, February 17, 1907, A1.

19. In theorizing fans as deaf, I follow the lead of Lennard Davis, who argues that the rise of reading in the eighteenth century similarly transformed hearing people. "Even if you are not Deaf," he writes, "you are deaf while you are reading. You are in a deafened modality or moment. All readers are deaf because they are defined by a process that does not require hearing or speaking (vocalizing)." See Davis, *Enforcing Normalcy: Disability, Deafness, and the Body* (New York: Verso, 1995), 4, 50–72.

20. "Echoes of the Diamond," *Washington Post*, March 1, 1907, 8.

21. See Douglas C. Baynton, *Forbidden Signs: American Culture and the Campaign Against Sign Language* (Chicago: University of Chicago Press, 1996).

22. Oralist teacher as quoted in Baynton, *Forbidden Signs*, 146.

23. For more on passing, see Baynton, *Forbidden Signs*, 146–48. See also Susan Burch, *Signs of Resistance: American Deaf Cultural History, 1900 to 1942* (New York: New York University Press, 2002), especially 146–49, and R.A.R. Edwards, *Words Made Flesh: Nineteenth-Century Deaf Education and Growth of Deaf Culture* (New York: New York University Press, 2012), especially 158–9, 200.

24. Burch 27.

25. See Douglas Baynton, "'The Undesirability of Admitting Deaf Mutes': U.S. Immigration Policy and Deaf Immigrants, 1882–1924," *Sign Language Studies* 6, 4, Summer 2006, 391–415. See also Douglas C. Baynton, *Defectives in the Land: Disability and Immigration in the Age of Eugenics* (Chicago: University of Chicago Press, 2016).

26. Dummy Hoy as quoted in "How A Mute Plays Ball," *Rochester Democrat and Chronicle*, January 5, 1902, 22.

27. For more on 'deaf gain,' see H-Dirksen L. Bauman and Joseph J. Murray, eds., *Deaf Gain: Raising the Stakes for Human Diversity* (University of Minnesota Press, 2014).

28. "The Referee: Sporting Comment of the Week: Too Much Consideration for the Umpire," *Chicago Tribune*, April 14, 1907, A1.

29. "Easy to Execute," *Sporting Life*, February 23, 1907, 4.

30. Bill Deane, *Baseball Myths: Debating, Debunking, and Disproving Tales from the Diamond* (Lanham, MD: Scarecrow Press, 2012), 20.

31. *Sporting Life*, October 19, 1907, 8.

32. "Timely Topics," *Sporting Life*, May 18, 1907, 7.

33. Bill Deane, *Baseball Myths: Debating, Debunking, and Disproving Tales from the Diamond* (Lanham, MD: Scarecrow Press, 2012), 17, 21.

34. In Peter Morris's book, *A Game of Inches* (2010, Ivan R. Dee Publishers), he attributes the earliest use of the umpire hand signals to Ed Dundon in 1886. Dundon had been a teammate of Hoy's at the Ohio School for the Deaf. See Brian McKenna, "Ed Dundon," SABR BioProject, https://sabr.org/bioproj/person/ed-dundon.

35. Klem discussed his professional relationship with O'Loughlin in William J. Klem and William J. Slocum, "I Never Missed One in my Heart," *Collier's*, March 31, 1951, 59. See also David Anderson, "Bill Klem," entry in The Baseball Biography Project, SABR.org.

The Chicago Green Sox

Steven M. Glassman

In 1912, Chicago was under consideration by two upstart baseball leagues. On February 12, John T. Powers's Columbian League awarded a franchise to Chicago (along with Cleveland, Detroit, Indianapolis, Kansas City, Louisville, Milwaukee, and St. Louis), but the venture failed to materialize due to a lack of money. On April 3, an official announcement was made that Columbian League would not operate in 1912, but might come back in 1913. The United States League was formed on December 21, 1911. Following a March 16 meeting, the league announced that Charles White and his New York franchise had until noon on March 18 to secure a field. A franchise for Chicago was sought by a representative for that city.[1] According to the *Chicago Tribune*, "the majority of the promoters, it is understood, believe Chicago would help to balance the western end of the circuit and that its admission would give the league more prestige. The western men are strong supporters of Chicago."[2] After White failed to meet the deadline, New York was out of the league, to be replaced by either Baltimore, Buffalo, or Chicago. League President William A. Whitman was appointed a committee of one to choose among these three cities.[3] He awarded the franchise to Chicago Gunthers owner William C. Niesen on March 23.

In addition to the Green Sox, Chicago newspapers referred to the new team by many names, including the Outlaws, Sams, US Leaguers, US Recruits (during the preseason), and Uncle Sams. The Green Sox played their home games at the 5,000-seat Gunther Park, owned by J.D. Cameron. Originally built in 1905, the park was located at the intersection of Clark Street and Leland Avenue, and served as home for the Chicago City League's Gunther Nine. The field had a wooden fence in the outfield and a covered grandstand.

On April 5, the Green Sox began their preseason with more than 30 players. Their April 6 debut against the Gunthers at Gunther Park was cancelled due to rain after two innings. On April 7, an intersquad was played between the "Raymonds" and "Keeleys" at Gunther Park. The "Raymonds," named for pitcher Bugs Raymond, defeated the "Keeleys," named for pitcher Burt Keeley, 7–5. The preseason schedule included games versus the Gunthers and Chicago American Giants. Keeley signed on as the Green Sox player-manager on April 11. He had previously pitched for the Washington Nationals (1908–09). This was his first manager's job.

The 126-game schedule was announced in the April 8 *Chicago Tribune*. Following a league meeting in Pittsburgh, a revised schedule was announced in the April 18 *Inter Ocean*, with the Green Sox opening the season on the road in Cincinnati on May 1. Their home opener was on May 8 versus Cleveland. The Green Sox were scheduled to finish their season on the road at Cleveland on September 22.

The 15 players announced on May 1 were as follows: Ed McDonough and Daly at catcher.[4] The pitchers were Charley Gardner, Tom McGuire, Walter Parker, Henry Paynter (or Painter), and Bugs Raymond. The infielders were Crowley (first), Al Schall (second), Bob Meinke (shortstop), and Herman Walters (third).[5] The outfielders were Jim Stanley (left), Lou Gertenrich (center), and "Bibbie" Lynch (right). Handy Andy wrote the following in the May 1 *Chicago Tribune*: "'Bugs' Raymond, who has signed a contract, may not pitch for some time, as he is still on the reserve list of the New York National league [sic] club. Owner Niesen expects to have him in the fold without causing a clash with the supreme body of baseball."[6] Gertenrich, Ernie Johnson, James McDonough, McGuire, and Meinke were Chicago natives. McDonough (Elgin) and Keeley (Wilmington) were Illinois natives. Stanley (Plymouth, Pennsylvania) was the only known player who was born outside of Illinois.

Only four players could boast of major-league experience. Ed McDonough played six games for the Philadelphia Phillies (1909–10). Meinke played two games for the Cincinnati Reds (1910). Gertenrich's baseball journey began in 1891 as a pitcher with the American Boys team.[7] After playing outfield in Milwaukee (1901) and Pittsburgh (1903), he played for the following Chicago City League squads (seasons unknown): Logan Square, Gunthers, Rogers Park, West

Ends, Riverviews, and Anson's Colts. Gertenrich also played for Springfield (Central) and Decatur (Three-I) in 1905.[8] In 1909, the Brooklyn Superbas offered Gertenrich an opportunity to play for them while he was playing in the Chicago City League. He was playing for the Gunthers before he was signed by the Green Sox at the age of 36. Raymond's professional career began in 1903 with Appleton (independent). He pitched in 136 games, including 95 starts, for the Tigers (1904), Cardinals (1907–08), and Giants (1909–11). He was kicked off the Giants due to alcoholism, and was pitching in semi-pro ball in Chicago before signing with the Green Sox.

With the season about to start, Niesen was optimistic about the league's future. "'We are on the shady side just now,' he said last night, 'but judging from reports from around the circuit, it will not be long before we cross into the sunshine. There is great interest in our league among the fans in the towns, and we hope to have good attendance from the start.'"[9] The season began on May 1 for Chicago, Cincinnati, Cleveland, New York, Pittsburgh, Reading, Richmond, and Washington. Pregame festivities in Cincinnati included music, a parade of automobiles, speeches, and Mayor Henry T. Hunt throwing the first pitch. The Green Sox won the season opener, 5–4, in front of 5,000 Cincinnatians. Meinke sent a ninth-inning single into left field, driving in McDonough for the go-ahead run. Raymond lost in his debut on May 2, 6–5. The Green

Sox next traveled to Cleveland, ending their two-city road trip 1–3–1 with one rainout.

Before the home opener on May 8, Chicago Mayor Carter H. Harrison II and Illinois Democratic gubernatorial candidate Edward F. Dunne led an auto parade including aldermen and local politicians down Clark Street from Hotel Sherman to Gunther Park. Despite scoring five runs in the bottom of the fourth and leading 8–4 in the eighth, the Green Sox fell 15–8 to Cleveland. Cold weather and rainouts hampered Chicago's early season schedule. Between May 5 and 16, five games were cancelled, including four out of a five-game stretch.

Around the league, poor weather and attendance led to a lack of money, which led to clubs dropping out. Washington disbanded first on May 23. Cleveland followed suit the very next day, as players were quitting because they were not getting paid. David Pietrusza wrote in his book, *Major Leagues*, "On May 27 New York forfeited a game on its own field to Chicago when just 50 fans showed up. Owner Tom Cronin, a Bronx politician, gave up the next day, and declared the franchise forfeit."[10] On June 1, Reading declared bankruptcy and Richmond dropped out of the league. Marshall Henderson replaced Whitman as league president. Cincinnati disbanded on June 3 and was sued the next day by 14 players who were owed salaries. Chicago resumed its schedule against the remaining teams, Cincinnati and Pittsburgh. The Green

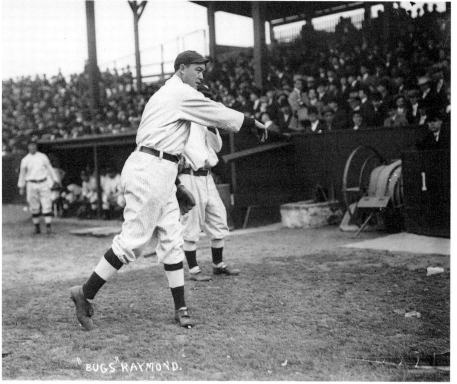

LIBRARY OF CONGRESS / BAIN COLLECTION

Pitcher "Bugs" Raymond, shown in 1911 with New York, was one of only four Green Sox with big-league experience.

Sox played nine more games. On June 23, they defeated the Pittsburgh Filipinos, 9–4, in their last league game. They finished by winning six of their last seven games and ended the season in third place.[11]

Table 1. Final Standings[12]

Team	W	L	T	Pct	GB
Pittsburgh	27	17	0	.614	—
Richmond	21	14	0	.600	1.5
Chicago	17	15	1	.531	4
Cincinnati	14	13	1	.519	4.5
Reading	12	12	2	.500	5
Washington	6	8	1	.429	6
Cleveland	8	13	0	.381	7.5
New York	2	15	1	.118	11.5[13]

Burt Keeley, shown here with the 1908 Washington squad, was signed by the Green Sox to pitch and serve as manager.

LIBRARY OF CONGRESS / BAIN COLLECTION

The Green Sox continued to play after the league officially disbanded on June 23. They played against local teams such as the All-Professionals, Cubans, Chicago Giants, Chicago American Giants, Chicago Typos, Fred Schmitt's (or Schmidt's) Joliets, Logan Squares, Professionals, Gunthers, Roselands, and West Ends. The July 9 *Chicago Tribune* and the *Inter Ocean* mentioned a possible four-team league with the Cubans, Giants, and Americans, but it would have needed approval from the Cubans' Nat Strong. The Green Sox also played against out-of-state teams including the Cheyenne Indians, Chinese Giants (from Hawaii), Cincinnati (formerly of the United States League), Crawfords, Gary (Indiana), and St. Louis Giants. They last played together on November 3 in a South Side semiprofessional championship series that featured the Green Sox and the All-Professionals at Gunther Park, and the Roseland Eclipses and Woodlawn Ramblers at Roseland.

Raymond, who last pitched for the Green Sox on May 6 against Cleveland, was a spectator at a semiprofessional game in Chicago on September 1. According to the *1913 Reach Official American League Guide*, "some one [sic] threw a piece of pottery which struck the pitcher on the face. Raymond picked up the missile and struck [Fred] Cigranz with it, and in the fight that followed, Raymond was knocked down and kicked in the head a number of times."[14] Six days later, Raymond was found dead at Hotel Veley in Chicago "from [a] cerebral hemorrhage due to a fracture of the skull."[15] Some of his Green Sox teammates served as pallbearers at his September 9 funeral. Fred Cigranz was arrested and confessed to murdering Raymond. It is not known how much prison time Cigranz (or Cingrang) served

The Green Sox did not return for the United States League's second attempt in 1913. New York, Reading, and Washington returned along with newcomers Baltimore, Brooklyn, Lynchburg, Newark (New Jersey), and Philadelphia. The 126-game schedule began on May 10 and was intended to end on September 27. However, the return was short-lived. The season ended on May 12, after just three days.

Chicago returned as part of the Federal League from 1913 to 1915. The team was known as either the Chifeds (*Encyclopedia of Minor League Baseball*, and also styled the ChiFeds or Chi-Feds), the Keeleys, or the Whales (Baseball-Reference.com). Some of the Green Sox players played for the 1913 team under Keeley: Gertenrich, Lynch, James McDonough, John McDonough, McGuire, Painter, Schall, and Stanley. Their 57–62 record was good for fourth, 17½ games behind the Indianapolis Hoosierfeds. McGuire and Stanley returned in 1914 under new manager Joe Tinker. James McDonough was on the 1914 Chifeds roster, but did not play.[16] The Chifeds finished second at 87–67, just 1½ games out of first place. None of the Green Sox were on the roster for the first place 1915 team.

McGuire made one appearance for the White Sox in 1919. Johnson had the longest Major League career after the Green Sox. He played 813 games for the White Sox (1912, 1921–23), St. Louis Terriers (1915), St. Louis Browns (1916–18), and the New York Yankees (1923–25).

Gunther Park was abandoned in 1913, shortly before the construction of Wrigley Field.[17] It was later turned into a park by the Lincoln Park Commission, and renamed Chase Park, after Treasury Secretary and United States Supreme Court Chief Justice Salmon P. Chase.[18] According to the Ravenswood-Lake View Historical Association: "In 1914 the Ravenswood Improvement Association and local residents petitioned the Lincoln

Park Commission to convert the former baseball stadium into a public park. The park commission acquired the land in 1920. Within two years tennis courts, a playground, an athletic field, a wading pool and a field house were constructed… The original field house was replaced with the current building in 1976." A few miles away in Lincoln Park, a fountain was dedicated to William C. Niesen in 1955. Funded by the Old Timers' Baseball Association, it still stands near the South Athletic field house and Niesen Field.[20] ■

Sources

In addition to the sources mentioned in the notes, the author referred to Baseball-Reference, Newspapers.com, and Retrosheet for box scores, play-by-plays, and other pertinent information.

Notes

1. "U.S. League Wants Chicago," *Chicago Tribune*, March 17, 1912, 24.
2. "U.S. League Wants Chicago," *Chicago Tribune*, March 17, 1912, 24.
3. "No U.S. League Club in Gotham," *Chicago Tribune*, March 19, 1912, 11.
4. I could not find a first name for Daly.
5. I could not find a first name for Crowley.
6. Handy Andy, "U.S. League to Start Today," *Chicago Tribune*, May 1, 1912, 13.
7. His early amateur, semiprofessional, and professional career also included stops with the Clyburn Juniors (1892), Brands (Chicago City League, 1894), Garden Cities (Chicago City, 1895); Maroons (season unknown), and Auburn Parks (seasons unknown)
8. According to website Baseball History Daily: "For the next four seasons, Gertenrich remained one of Chicago's best local athletes. At 33-years-old in 1908 he was still a good enough runner to win the City League Field Day title of fastest player; The *Daily News* said he rounded the bases in 14 and ⅕ seconds." https://baseballhistorydaily.com/2014/07/07/this-wealth-of-mr-gertenrich-has-cost-the-game-an-a-1-player.
9. "U.S. Leaguers To Open Up Tomorrow," *Chicago Inter Ocean*, April 30, 1912, 4.
10. David Pietrusza, *Major Leagues* Jefferson, NC: McFarland & Co., 1991), 205.
11. *The 1913 Reach Official American League Base Ball Guide* (Philadelphia: A.J. Reach Company, 1913), 113.
12. *The 1913 Reach Official American League Guide*'s standings differ. They do not include games that Chicago played against Cincinnati and Pittsburgh after June 3.
13. Pietrusza, 339.
14. *The 1913 Reach Official American League Base Ball Guide*, 113.
15. *The 1913 Reach Official American League Base Ball Guide*, 113.
16. "Chicago Feds Name Lineup," *Reading Times*, March 4, 1914, 8. McDonough was also purportedly rostered by the Cubs but did not play. See Bill Hickman, "Near Major Leaguers," SABR.org. https://sabr.org/research/article/near-major-leaguers.
17. Ravenswood-Lake View Historical Association, January 9, 2010, https://www.ravenswoodhistorical.com/tag/chicago-green-sox.
18. The Official Website of the Chicago Park District, https://www.chicagoparkdistrict.com/parks-facilities/chase-salmon-park.
19. Ravenswood-Lake View Historical Association.
20. The Official Website of the Chicago Park District, https://www.chicagoparkdistrict.com/parks-facilities/william-c-niesen-memorial-fountain.

For Whom the Ballgame Tolls

Ernest Hemingway Attends a White Sox Game Before Shipping Off to War

Sean Kolodziej

Baseball played a big part in Ernest Hemingway's life. The subject was featured in many of his novels and short stories, including *A Farewell to Arms* and *The Old Man and the Sea*. One game that he attended in 1918 was so meaningful to him that he kept the ticket stub with him throughout his service in WWI as a volunteer ambulance driver and for many years after.

Ernest Hemingway was born in 1899 in Oak Park, Illinois, located just west of Chicago. It was a great place to be a fan. From the age of four until he left to serve in WWI at the age of eighteen, he witnessed exceptional baseball. During that time, at least one Chicago baseball team finished no worse than third place in their respective leagues every year, and the Chicago White Sox and Chicago Cubs each won two World Series. The Chicago Whales of the Federal League also finished in first place in 1915.

Hemingway was such a fan of the Chicago baseball teams that he ordered "action pictures" of Cubs players Mordecai "Three Fingered" Brown, Jimmy Archer, and Frank "Wildfire" Schulte from an advertisement in *The Sporting News*.[1] He also ordered posters from *Baseball Magazine* of White Sox pitchers Big Ed Walsh and Ewell "Reb" Russell.[2] He went to games with his father and would study the upcoming schedules to pick out certain games to attend. In a letter to his father from early May 1912, Hemingway asked if they could go to the May 11 game between the Chicago Cubs and New York Giants.[3]

The 1917 World Series between the Chicago White Sox and the New York Giants made a big impression on Hemingway and he would later write about it in his short story "Crossing the Mississippi." The young man in the story, Nick Adams, would go on to appear in many Hemingway short stories and is partly inspired by Hemingway's own experiences. After witnessing Happy Felsch's game-winning home run at Game One in Chicago, in the story Nick travels to Kansas City to find work. Hemingway, in his real life, also went to Kansas City around this time to work for the *Kansas City Star*. While on the train, Nick (and one can assume

Hemingway himself) finds out that the White Sox have won the Series and is filled with a "comfortable glow."[4]

While at the *Kansas City Star*, Hemingway had the opportunity to interview members of the Chicago Cubs as they traveled to spring training in March 1918. He bought Coca-Colas for Claude Hendrix, Pete Kilduff, and Grover Cleveland Alexander, whom he referred to as "the worlds (sic) greatest pitcher."[5]

In early 1918, Hemingway joined the war effort when he volunteered to be an ambulance driver for the American Red Cross in Italy. He was sent to New York City on May 13, 1918, for training. On Wednesday, May 22, right before he was to ship out to Europe, Hemingway was able to attend a ballgame. Luckily for him, the Chicago White Sox were in town playing the New York Yankees at the Polo Grounds.

As the United States had entered WWI about a year prior to this game, the Yankees announced that 25% of the gross receipts from the game would be given to the Clark Griffith Bat and Ball Fund, which provided baseball equipment for soldiers who were stationed in Europe. The *New York Tribune* stated that "no less than nine companies of soldiers, many of them with their bands, will be on hand."[6] Prior to the game, the soldiers were paraded around the field. Because of the overcast weather, only 5,200 total fans attended the game that day, although the Polo Grounds could have held around 38,000 spectators.

The White Sox, winners of the prior year's World Series, had just lost their star outfielder, Shoeless Joe Jackson, less than two weeks earlier; he went to work at a Delaware shipyard to avoid the draft. To make matters worse, their starting pitcher for the game, Eddie Cicotte, was still winless with an 0–5 record.

The Yankees would be starting Herb Thormahlen, who was carrying a 19-inning scoreless streak into the game. Having appeared in only one game the previous season, the 21-year-old lefthander was unfamiliar to the Chicago sportswriters. His "name makes you think of some kind of tooth powder or disinfectant," wrote I.E. Sanborn of the *Chicago Daily Tribune*.[7]

The game went into extra innings as both pitchers were dominant throughout. In the 12th inning, Buck Weaver hit a drive to right field that looked like it might clear the fence, but Frank Gilhooley "leaped into the air and caught the ball as it was about to impinge on the stands, and then fell headlong in the mud."[8]

Both teams saved their most dramatic play for the 14th inning. In the top half of the inning, the White Sox loaded the bases with only one out. Unfortunately for the White Sox rooters, Buck Weaver could only manage to hit a grounder to third baseman Frank "Home Run" Baker, who threw home to easily force out Nemo Leibold. Chick Gandil then flew out to center field to end the inning.

With one out in the bottom of the 14th, the Yankees' Baker and Del Pratt hit back-to-back singles. Wally Pipp then hit a single to center that drove in Baker for the winning run.

It was a tough loss for the White Sox, especially for Cicotte. He gave up only four hits through thirteen innings before finally losing the game one inning later. The *Buffalo Enquirer* reported that "Eddie Cicotte's opinion of that fourteen-inning 1-to-0 defeat at the hands of the Yankees had been deleted by the censor."[9]

The game must have made an impression on Hemingway. On July 18, 1918, Hemingway was badly wounded in both legs while bringing chocolate and cigarettes to the soldiers on the front line in Italy. He spent six months at the Red Cross Hospital in Milan, and did not return to the United States until January 1919. Throughout all of this, the ticket stub remained with him. The stub from that New York game between the White Sox and Yankees can now be found in the Hemingway Archives in Special Collections at the Oak Park Library.

The following year, the Chicago White Sox lost the 1919 World Series to the Cincinnati Reds. Hemingway believed that the White Sox were playing on the level and bet on them to win. After Shoeless Joe Jackson, Eddie Cicotte, and Lefty Williams confessed to throwing the series, a friend made fun of Hemingway for betting on the White Sox. As he wrote to a friend, "I was informed by Deggie that it served me right to lose when I bet on the Sox last fall. Thinking the series was honest."[10]

Even after the scandal, Hemingway remained enough of a White Sox fan that he attended a White Sox-New York Giants exhibition game in France in November 1924.[11]

Later in life, Hemingway would reminisce about growing up watching baseball. He used a baseball metaphor to describe his own writing: "When I was a

The ticket stub that Ernest Hemingway kept with him throughout the war.

boy a pitcher named Ed Walsh, spit-ball pitcher for the Chicago White Sox, won 40 ball games one year for a team that rarely gave him more than a one run lead. Am working on this precept. Somebody said of him, Walsh, that he was the only man who could strut sitting down. I can strut when on my ass and will."[12] Based on Hemingway's reputation as one of the greatest writers of the twentieth century, winning the 1954 Nobel Prize in Literature, one can assume that he was right. ∎

Acknowledgments
The author would like to thank Kheir Fakhreldin, archivist in Special Collections at the Oak Park Library, who provided considerable research assistance in the writing of this article.

Notes
1. Ernest Hemingway letter to Charles C. Spink and Son, circa 1912 in *The Letters of Ernest Hemingway 1907–1922. Vol. 1*; eds. Sandra Spanier and Robert W. Trogdon (Cambridge: Cambridge University Press, 2011), 11.
2. Ernest Hemingway letter to *Base Ball Magazine*, April 10, 1915 or 1916, in *Letters, Vol. 1*, 18–19.
3. Ernest Hemingway letter to Clarence Hemingway, circa second week of May 1912, *in Letters, Vol. 1*, 12.
4. Ernest Hemingway, *The Nick Adams Stories* (Amereon Limited: New York, 1972,) 134.
5. Ernest Hemingway letter to Clarence Hemingway, March 14, 1918, in *Letters, Vol. 1*, 90.
6. "Soldiers to Get Baseball Goods at Polo Grounds" *New York Tribune*, May 22, 1918, 14.
7. I.E Sanborn, "Sox Lose 14 Round Battle to Yankee Slab Rookie, 1 to 0," *Chicago Daily Tribune*, May 23, 1918, 11.
8. "Thormahlen Pitches 34th Runless Inning," *New York Tribune*, May 23, 1918, 12.
9. Jack Veiock, "Score Board Reflections," *Buffalo Enquirer*, May 23, 1918, 14.
10. Ernest Hemingway letter to Grace Quinlan, September 30, 1920, in *Ernest Hemingway: Selected Letters, 1917–1961*. Ed. Carlos Baker (New York: Scribners, 1981), 41.
11. Ernest Hemingway letter to Howell Jenkins, February 2, 1925, in *Selected Letters*, 148.
12. Ernest Hemingway letter to Charles Scribner, August 25–26, 1949, in *Selected Letters*, 667.

The White Stockings' Fleet-Footed Preacher

Billy Sunday vs. the Alcohol Machine

Joseph L. Thompson

Mike "King" Kelly, Arlie Latham, Cap Anson, and Albert Spalding were among the most popular and respected players of nineteenth-century baseball. But despite the players' successes on the field, the public often viewed them as part of a working-class culture frequently associated with saloons and rowdy behavior. A minister in 1889 referred to ballplayers as "men without character" who "would engage in no legitimate occupation."[1] Newspapers of the late nineteenth century stereotyped ballplayers as thus: "A gentleman of leisure six months of the year, who arose at 10 AM during the season, had a 'snug' breakfast, read the papers, smoked a Reina Victoria, napped before his 2 o'clock dinner, strolled to the ball park at about 3, where he took a little exercise for a couple of hours, and then returned for supper, smoked, went with girls to the theatre, and of course drew his salary."[2] Players would hold this reputation until the public began to view them differently. Chicago White Stockings outfielder William "Billy" Ashley Sunday would be different.

Billy Sunday left the game of baseball behind after the 1890 season and became America's biggest temperance spokesman against the abuses of alcohol. His message helped propel him to become the country's most influential evangelist in the first half of the twentieth century. Using his celebrity status as a ballplayer, Sunday would attract large crowds almost everywhere he went. His campaign against alcohol helped fuel a movement that would eventually lead to the passage of the National Prohibition Act in 1919. His success in this campaign can not only be attributed to how he managed an effective organization, but also to how he used the newspaper medium.

William Ashley Sunday's battle against alcohol began when he was a child. Born in Ames, Iowa, in 1862, his father died during the Civil War. Sunday's mother soon remarried. Her second husband was a drunkard who provided little support for the family and soon left. Sunday went to live with his grandfather on his farm where his hatred for alcohol increased. "My poor dear old Grandfather used to drink oh so much and abuse me and when sober he would feel so sad about it."[3] Years later in his autobiography, Sunday described how the experiences of his youth helped foster within him a life-long confrontation with alcohol which he often described as his personal "enemy." Sunday even went so far to blame bootleggers for selling liquor to his Grandfather. "Grandfather used to have periodic spells of several months apart when he drank liquor, but never bought the liquor himself; he would get it from the bootleggers. You see, I began to hate booze in my youth, and as the years come and go my hatred for the cursed business and the bootlegger increases. It was the same back in those early days— the bootlegger was the scourge of society; and it takes two to make a bootlegger—the fellow who sells the stuff and the one who buys it."[4]

Sunday's professional baseball career started in 1883 when Adrian Constantine "Cap" Anson offered him a tryout with the Chicago White Stockings. Anson often

Sunday practiced temperance while he was a professional ballplayer. When his hard-drinking teammates would reach for beer or gin, he said he would have "lemonade or sarsaparilla."

spent his winters in Marshalltown, Iowa, where Sunday played baseball. Locals told Anson about a very fast young center fielder who always ran down fly balls. His aunt also tried to persuade Anson to give Sunday a tryout. The next spring, Anson telegrammed Sunday and invited him to a team tryout in Chicago. Anson met Sunday in the White Stockings locker room when he arrived, reportedly saying, "Billy, they tell me that you can run some. Fred Pfeffer is our crack runner. How about putting on a little race this morning?"[5] According to Sunday, he beat Pfeffer in the race by fifteen feet. "You can imagine how the boys razzed Fred for letting a raw country boy beat him," Billy wrote in his autobiography. "Winning that race opened the hearts of the players to me at once, and I'll always be thankful to Cap for giving me that chance to show off to the best advantage."[6] Sunday signed a contract to play with the Chicago White Stockings for the 1883 season. His biggest weakness as a ballplayer, he would say, was hitting. His speed and fielding were the tools where he really shone on the playing field. "I could run a hundred yards in ten seconds, and was the first to circle the baseball diamond in fourteen seconds from a standing start, touching all bases," Billy claimed.[7]

When Albert Spalding fined some of Sunday's White Sox teammates for their rowdy behavior and excessive drinking, Sunday was not among them. He turned away from the rambunctious lifestyle of ballplayers, and during the 1886 season he became an avid Christian. Soon after his conversion to Christianity, Sunday joined a local church, began teaching, and frequently spoke at his local YMCA. Sunday's conversion did not keep him from socializing with his teammates, as he explained: "I used to go to the saloons with the baseball players, and while they would drink highballs and gin fizzes and beer, I would take lemonade and sarsaparilla."[8]

Sunday officially retired from professional baseball in 1890 to become a Christian evangelist. In 1907, he held a revival function in the town of Fairfield, Iowa. Preaching to a half-empty hall, Sunday decided to use his status as a former major leaguer to drum up interest in his evangelical message. Sunday organized the local businesses into two baseball teams and scheduled a game between them. Sunday arrived wearing a uniform from his days as a ballplayer and played a couple of innings for both teams. Iowa newspapers spread the story of Sunday's antics.

In November of that same year in Muscatine, Iowa, large crowds gathered to hear Sunday's message. Sunday started a petition drive for a referendum on local-option Prohibition after the sermon, and Muscatine

Sunday preached to as many as 50,000 people a day in his revivals, giving him a larger platform than many politicians.

soon went "dry." The town of Ottumwa, Iowa, went "dry" after Sunday held a revival in the town a year later. Statewide Prohibition was not approved by Iowa until 1915, but Sunday's efforts to help spread the message of the "evils of alcohol" helped spur public interest that influenced legislative action.[9]

On April 8, 1917, in New York City, Billy Sunday addressed the largest crowd of his career. Sunday reminded the crowd of his former career. "I noticed you are the same warm-hearted, enthusiastic bunch you used to be when you sat in the grandstand and bleachers when I played at the old Polo Grounds. It didn't matter if a fellow was on the other side or not. If he made a good play he got the glad hand rather than the marble heart." Sunday's revival in New York City lasted until the end of June. During his time in New York, he made his first calls for National Prohibition, stating, "This whiskey business is a question for the government, not the states to battle, and you know it."[10]

After years of fighting for it, Sunday witnessed the Eighteenth Amendment become law on January 17, 1920, prohibiting the manufacture, transportation, and sale of alcohol. Although the law would eventually be repealed in 1933, Sunday's mission had been completed. According to Mark Lender, "While his precise impact is hard to judge, many [of his] contemporaries were convinced that the popular evangelist was of crucial importance in establishing public support for the passing of the Eighteenth Amendment."[11]

Sunday's biographer W.A. Firstenberger estimated that by 1915, Sunday had spoken to over forty million people on the dangers of alcohol. "For weeks at a time, as many as 50,000 people a day heard him preach on the evil of liquor. No one else commanded numbers like that—not entertainers, not even presidents."[12]

Sunday's ability to use his ball-playing fame to spur the press to drum up interest and to get his message across would not be lost on ballplayers who came after him.

Fast forward almost one hundred years and ballplayers are now using all kinds of media and technology to push their messages and defend themselves against those who might besmirch their reputations, in particular the phenomenon dubbed "social media" in which individuals can broadcast directly to a wide, public audience with no editorial curation or control. Social media platforms like Facebook and Twitter have revolutionized public access to athletes. Previously, the only way people could interact with their favorite players was at the stadium or through a special event that often cost considerable money. Social media changed the interaction between athletes and the public, as Jimmy Sanderson wrote in his 2011 book, *It's a Whole New Ballgame: How Social Media is Changing Sports,* "One of the more dynamic outcomes produced by social media is the increased ability for fans to access athletes. Social media acts [sic] as a conduit that connects these two groups, serving as a communicative bridge that facilitates interaction opportunities."[13]

Sanderson also argues that the way social media sites and apps have dramatically changed the way athletes, the public, and sports journalists interact with each other, has also empowered another "important shift in sports media reporting"—the rise of "tabloid" sites like "Deadspin," "drunkathlete.com," and "TMZsports.com." These sites often featured dirt on the private lives of players to draw readers.

Josh Hamilton became one of baseball's first players to have his alcohol and drug-related indiscretions broadcasted worldwide for all to see.[14] Hamilton's wife, Katie, suffered deeply from the embarrassing pictures posted online. She described receiving disturbing phone calls from people who could not imagine why she would stay with her husband after his embarrassing episode. She recalled people saying "I don't know how you can get out of bed in the morning" and another who asked, "How can you go grocery shopping or show your face?"[15]

Have these tabloid websites returned ballplayers to the reputation of rowdyism and drunkenness? Social media allow fans personal access to their favorite players as never before. One could only imagine the influence Billy Sunday might have had if he had been able to log in to his own social media accounts to spread his message of temperance. ■

Notes

1. Harold Seymour, *Baseball: The Early Years* (New York: Oxford University Press, 1960), 330, 331.
2. Seymour, *Baseball: The Early Years*, 330,331. John P. Rossi, *The National Game: Baseball and American Culture* (Chicago: Ivan R. Dee, 2000), 25–37. "The Baseball Season Near," *New York Tribune*, February 21, 1892.
3. W.A. Firstenberger, *In Rare Form: A Pictorial History of Baseball Evangelist Billy Sunday* (Iowa City, IA: University of Iowa Press, 2005), 72. Wendy Knickerbocker, "The Baseball Evangelist throws out John Barleycorn: Billy Sunday and Prohibition," in *The Politics of Baseball: Essays on the Pastime and Power at Home and Abroad*, edited by Ron Briley, Chapter 2 (Jefferson, NC: McFarland & Co., 2010).
4. Billy Sunday, *Sawdust Trail: Billy Sunday in His Own Words* (Iowa City, IA: University of Iowa Press, 2005), 67. *Papers of Billy and Helen Sunday, 1882–1974*, Collection 61, Archives of the Billy Graham Center, Wheaton College, Wheaton, Illinois.
5. Billy Sunday, *Sawdust Trail*, 67.
6. Billy Sunday, *Sawdust Trail*, 71.
7. Billy Sunday, *Sawdust Trail*, 73.
8. Billy Sunday, *Sawdust Trail*, 77.
9. Billy Sunday, *Sawdust Trail*, 1–20.
10. Knickerbocker, "The Baseball Evangelist Throws Out John Barleycorn."
11. Mark Edward Lender, *Dictionary of American Temperance Biography: From Temperance Reform to Alcohol Research, the 1600s to the 1980s* (Westport, CT: Greenwood Press, 1984), 476. Knickerbocker, "The Baseball Evangelist throws out John Barleycorn."
12. Firstenberger, *In Rare Form*, 72.
13. Jimmy Sanderson, *It's a Whole New Ballgame: How Social Media Is Changing Sports* (New York, NY: Hampton Press, 2011), 69.
14. Anderson, *It's a Whole New Ballgame*, 21.
15. Josh Hamilton and Tim Keown, *Beyond Belief: Finding the Strength to Come Back* (New York: Faith Words, 2010), 274.

Guilty as Charged

Buck Weaver and the 1919 World Series Fix

Bill Lamb

In mid-March 1921—amid delay in the criminal proceedings pending against those accused of corrupting the 1919 World Series—baseball commissioner Kenesaw Mountain Landis placed the eight indicted Chicago White Sox players on the game's ineligible list. "Baseball is not powerless to defend itself," an impatient Landis declared. "All these players must vindicate themselves before they can be readmitted to baseball."[1] Some four-plus months later, the Not Guilty verdicts returned by the Black Sox case jury put Landis's resolve to the test. In the defining moment of his tenure, the newly installed commissioner reacted to the trial outcome swiftly and forcefully, proclaiming:

> Regardless of the verdict of juries, no player that throws a ball game; no player that undertakes or promises to throw a ball game; no player that sits in conference with a bunch of crooked ballplayers and gamblers where the ways and means of throwing games are planned and discussed and does not promptly tell his club about it, will ever play professional baseball.[2]

And with that, Shoeless Joe Jackson, Eddie Cicotte, Buck Weaver, and the other acquitted Black Sox were permanently banished from Landis's domain of the American and National Leagues and their affiliated minor leagues, consigning them to playing out their careers in outlaw exhibitions.

Since its promulgation, the Landis edict has been construed as confining its condemnation of third baseman Weaver to his failure to act upon pre-Series knowledge that teammates and gamblers were intent on throwing the Fall Classic. According to his champions, Weaver himself was not a fix participant. Nor did he accept any kind of payoff from those who financed the Series fix. Rather, Weaver was an honest player punished for his refusal to inform on his corrupted teammates, his permanent banishment from the game designed to serve as a warning and deterrent to players disposed to look the other way on game-fixing in future.

The purpose of this piece is to assay the legitimacy and proportion of the Weaver banishment via forensic analysis of the historical record. Unhappily for some, this exercise does not sustain the thesis that Weaver was no more than a silent confidante of Series corruption. To the contrary, the record yields persuasive evidence that Buck Weaver took an active part in the fix from start to finish, and that Weaver was among the White Sox players who threw games during the 1920 season, as well. There is no basis, therefore, to second-guess the sanction visited upon Weaver a century ago, as expulsion was a mandatory punishment for game-fixing. The deterrence rationale also justified Weaver's banishment. To place these conclusions in context, we precede argument with a Weaver-centric review of the 1919 World Series and its aftermath.

A. BUCK WEAVER AND THE RUN-UP TO THE 1919 WORLD SERIES

By the time of the 1919 World Series, 29-year-old Buck Weaver had supplanted Home Run Baker as the American League's premier third baseman. A rangy switch-hitter, Weaver joined the White Sox as a lineup regular in 1912 but both his hitting (.224 batting average) and fielding at shortstop (71 errors) were marginal. Over time, both skills improved, particularly after Buck was switched to third base in 1917. That season, Weaver was a reliable role-player on an American League pennant-winning club (100–54, .649) that featured three future Hall of Famers—second baseman Eddie Collins, spitballer Red Faber, and catcher Ray Schalk—as well as Cooperstown-caliber outfielder Joe Jackson and 28-game winner Eddie Cicotte. Buck then chipped in a solid World Series performance as the Sox topped the NL champion New York Giants in six games.

Batting .300, Weaver came into his own in 1918 but the season was a trying one for the Chicago White Sox. The manpower demands of World War I eviscerated the club's roster, with Eddie Collins, Red Faber, and pitcher Jim Scott enlisting in the military, while other Sox players—including Joe Jackson, outfielder Happy Felsch, and pitcher Lefty Williams—left the club for shipbuilding work and other defense industry jobs.

Buck Weaver

Despite having piloted his charges to a championship the previous season, a sixth-place finish (57–67, .460) cost Sox manager Pants Rowland his job. At the same time, a staggering drop-off in home attendance (from 684,521 in 1917 to only 195,081 in 1918[3]) cost club owner Charles Comiskey dearly in the wallet.

Despite the financial setback, Comiskey rewarded Weaver for his stalwart performance, inking him to a handsome three-year contract in March 1919. His new pact yielded Buck $7,250 per annum and made him the second-highest paid third baseman (after Home Run Baker) in the big leagues. Meanwhile, the return of Eddie Collins, Red Faber, Joe Jackson, and the others who had left the 1918 club heralded likely restoration of the White Sox to championship form. But the clubhouse that they were returning to was not a healthy place. Long-simmering resentment of the highly paid ($15,000), college-educated, and socially superior Collins by more hardscrabble teammates like Chick Gandil and Buck Weaver, and Comiskey's public disdain of Joe Jackson, Happy Felsch, and other defense industry "slackers" who had avoided military service contributed to a fractious team atmosphere, with the club divided into two hostile cliques.[4] Aligned with team captain Collins were Faber, Schalk, and outfielders Eddie Murphy, Nemo Leibold, and Shano Collins (no relation). In the other corner were Gandil, Cicotte, Weaver, Felsch, shortstop Swede Risberg, and sub infielder Fred McMullin, while quiet road roommates Joe Jackson and Lefty Williams mostly kept to themselves. Placed in charge of this talented but torn squad was new manager Kid Gleason, a coach on the 1917 World Series champion club.

Despite personal antagonisms, the 1919 Chicago White Sox were a powerhouse ballclub, ranking first in team batting average and leading the league in runs per game.[5] Joe Jackson (.351/.422/.506), Eddie Collins (.319/.400/.405), and Nemo Leibold (.302/.404/.353)

paced the batters with Buck Weaver (.296/.315/.401), Chick Gandil (.290/.325/.383), and Happy Felsch (.275/.336/.448, with 86 RBIs) also making significant contributions. Meanwhile on the mound, Eddie Cicotte (29–7, 1.82 ERA) and Lefty Williams (23–11, 2.64 ERA) hurled a combined 600+ innings, and were capably supported by undersized lefty Dickey Kerr (13–7), filling in for the frequently sidelined Red Faber (11–9). Chicago led the AL pennant chase for most of the campaign and secured the crown with a 6–5 victory over the St. Louis Browns on September 24, Kerr notching the win in relief of ineffective starter Cicotte. Yet even before the pennant was clinched, the plot to dump the upcoming World Series against the Cincinnati Reds had been hatched.

B. THE PLAY OF BUCK WEAVER IN THE 1919 WORLD SERIES

In many respects, the fix of the 1919 World Series remains a murky affair to this day. Among the unsettled details are the number of Series fix conspiracies (as there were at least two and perhaps a third); the identity of the fix financiers; how many Series games the fix actually lasted; and the timing, dollar amount, and method of payment of the corrupted White Sox players—all topics beyond the scope of this essay. For now, suffice to say that Sox teammates Eddie Cicotte, Joe Jackson, Lefty Williams, and Chick Gandil, as well as fix insiders Bill Burns and Billy Maharg, all later identified Weaver by name as a fix conspirator. But as in the case of Joe Jackson, Weaver's Series stats—at least superficially—belie the charge. Playing in all eight Series contests, Weaver batted (11-for-34) .324, second only to Jackson's .375 Series average and, like Jackson, made no errors in 27 chances. On the minus side, Weaver registered zero RBIs, failing to drive in any of the 15 teammates on base when he came to the plate.

Going in, the White Sox were heavy Series favorites[6]—until a last-minute surge of money on Cincinnati installed the Reds as a slight betting favorite. Most sportswriters and other baseball cognoscenti, however, remained confident of a Chicago victory. But a few, including syndicated *Chicago Herald-Examiner* columnist Hugh Fullerton, were disquieted by rumors that the Series outcome had been rigged.

The Series began on a sour note for Weaver and the White Sox. In the top of the first, Buck came to bat with Eddie Collins on first. Recriminations ensued when Collins was caught trying to steal. Once back in the dugout, Collins accused Weaver of ignoring the hit-and-run sign that Collins had flashed him, with Buck replying that Collins just wanted an alibi after getting thrown out.[7] Three innings later, an abrupt meltdown by pitching ace Cicotte put the Sox on the road to a stunning, 9–1, loss.

In Game Two, a curious one-inning loss of control by Lefty Williams provided the baserunners needed by the Reds to prevail, 4–2. A three-hit, 3–0, shutout thrown by Dickey Kerr in Game Three got the Sox in the win column, but thereafter Chicago bats went silent. With heart-of-the-lineup batters Weaver, Jackson, and Felsch unproductive, baseball's highest-scoring club went an astonishing 26-consecutive innings without scoring a run, dropping Game Four (2–0, losing pitcher Cicotte) and Game Five (5–0, losing pitcher Williams) in the process.

With the White Sox trailing 4–1 in Game Six and on the brink of elimination, Reds left fielder Pat Duncan and shortstop Larry Kopf played Weaver's catchable sixth-inning pop fly into a double. And with that, slumbering Chicago bats suddenly came alive. A three-run Sox rally tied the score. Gritty pitching by Kerr then kept the Reds off the board until Weaver led off the tenth inning with a legitimate double. A bouncing ball single by Chick Gandil later brought him home with the run that gave the White Sox a Series-extending 5–4 triumph. The following day finally yielded the result that Series prognosticators had been expecting all along: an easy 4–1 Chicago win behind a sterling pitching performance by Eddie Cicotte.

In Game Eight, however, the World Series comeback hopes of White Sox fans were dashed early when starter Lefty Williams failed to make it out of the first inning. With the Sox in a quick four-run hole, Weaver came to bat in the bottom of the first with runners on second and third—and took a called third strike. By the eighth inning, the Reds lead had grown to an insurmountable 10–1. After a four-run Sox rally reduced the margin to 10–5, Weaver came to bat in the ninth with two runners on. But his lazy fly ball to right brought the Series to within an out of its close. Joe Jackson then grounded to second, making the Cincinnati Reds the World Series winner.

Although confounded by the outcome, most sportswriters accepted the Reds triumph magnanimously, heaping praise on the astute managing of Cincinnati skipper Pat Moran and extolling the standout work of the club's pitching staff. Meanwhile, complacency and overconfidence were generally cited as the basis for the Sox downfall. Few blamed the likes of Joe Jackson or Buck Weaver for the Chicago defeat. Rather, Lefty Williams (0–3, with a 6.61 ERA), shortstop Swede Risberg (2-for-25/.080 BA, plus four fielding errors), outfielder Nemo Leibold (1-for-18/.056 BA), and manager Kid Gleason provided more logical scapegoats.

C. THE REVELATION OF WEAVER'S ROLE IN THE SERIES FIX

Suspicion that the 1919 World Series had been fixed was the subject of several post-Series columns by Hugh Fullerton. But only a handful of fellow pressmen subscribed to fix rumors and over time, the subject faded from public consciousness. But in the Series aftermath, both White Sox club boss Charles Comiskey and American League president Ban Johnson launched discreet inquiries into the bona fides of Sox play during the Series. And neither liked what those investigations uncovered. For the time being, however, each man sat on findings that the Series had been corrupted. Meanwhile, the 1920 baseball season started, with the AL pennant race soon devolving into a tense, three-club battle between the White Sox, New York Yankees, and Cleveland Indians.

In early September, Judge Charles A. McDonald, the presiding judge of the Cook County (Chicago) criminal courts, invited a newly-impaneled grand jury to investigate the recent report that a meaningless late-August game between the Chicago Cubs and Philadelphia Phillies had been fixed by gamblers. The grand jury was also encouraged to probe Chicago's lucrative but illegal baseball pool-selling rackets. No mention, however, was made by Judge McDonald of the previous season's World Series. But by the time the panel undertook a substantive look at baseball later that month, its primary focus had changed. Instigated by a private meeting between avid baseball fan McDonald and AL president Johnson, the grand jury commenced inquiry into the integrity of the 1919 World Series. And in flagrant disregard of the legal command that grand jury proceedings remain secret, panel doings were reported daily in the press.[9]

On September 25, 1920, it was widely reported that Comiskey had withheld the World Series checks of eight White Sox players, including that of Buck Weaver.[10] Other press reports intimated that these eight players were now targeted by the grand jury for indictment on fraud-related charges.[11] Two days later, the scandal dike burst with publication of a Series fix exposé in the *Philadelphia North American*, courtesy of local club fighter and one-time Philadelphia Phillies gofer Billy Maharg.[12] Reportedly, White Sox players had thrown Games One, Two, and Eight of the 1919 World Series in return for a $100,000 payoff from gamblers.[13] Within hours, wire service dispatch made the Maharg allegations known across the country.

Summoned to the office of White Sox corporation counsel Alfred S. Austrian on the morning of September 28, an unnerved Eddie Cicotte quickly broke down under questioning. According to Cicotte, the plot to rig the Series outcome in return for a payoff from gamblers was unveiled by Chick Gandil at a like-minded players-only meeting held at the Ansonia Hotel in New York City. Under pressure from Gandil, Swede Risberg, and Fred McMullin, Eddie reluctantly joined the conspiracy. Cicotte's price was the $10,000 placed under his room pillow after a follow-up Warner Hotel meeting with fellow Sox conspirators and a pair of gamblers.[14] Whisked to the Cook County Courthouse, Cicotte repeated those assertions before the grand jury that afternoon.[15] Pertinent for our purposes, Cicotte identified Buck Weaver by name as one of the eight White Sox players taking part in the fix, and as attending the Warner Hotel meeting with fix gamblers.[16] Immediately following Cicotte's testimony, grand jury foreman Henry Brigham "sent for the newspaperman and in the jury's presence announced the voting of [true] bills and the names of the players [charged]."[17] Among the accused was Buck Weaver who, along with the other charged Sox players, was immediately suspended by club owner Comiskey.[18]

Later that day, the above exercise repeated itself with Joe Jackson. After being interrogated in the Austrian law office and thereafter confiding his culpability in the Series fix to Judge McDonald in chambers, Jackson testified before the grand jury.[19] Analysis of the conflicted, often self-contradictory Jackson testimony

Eddie Collins

LIBRARY OF CONGRESS / BAIN COLLECTION

can be found elsewhere.[20] For present purposes the germane point is Jackson's naming of Buck Weaver as a Series fix conspirator.[21]

Weaver strenuously denied the accusations against him, citing his solid Series batting average as "a good enough alibi."[22] But his protests were largely drowned out by deeply incriminating post-testimony statements made by Jackson to the Chicago press and by the next-day grand jury testimony of Lefty Williams.[23] Like Cicotte and Jackson before him, Williams had been summoned to the Austrian office that morning. Once there, he quickly admitted his Series fix complicity. And like Cicotte and Jackson, Williams identified Chick Gandil as the fix ringleader, revealing that Chick had first importuned him outside the Ansonia Hotel. Lefty also identified Buck Weaver as a fix participant, placing Weaver at the fix meeting conducted at the Warner Hotel and at an eve-of-Game One conspirator conclave held at the Hotel Sinton in Cincinnati.[24] The Hotel Sinton meeting related to a second fix proposition. This one was received from ex-major league pitcher-turned-gambler Bill Burns and former featherweight boxing champion Abe Attell, a sometimes bodyguard of New York City underworld financier Arnold Rothstein. But Williams never saw any of the $20,000 payoff that he expected from joining the Burns/Attell plot.[25]

Williams repeated his story before the grand jury that afternoon. But until the long-lost transcript of the Williams grand jury testimony resurfaced in 2007, it was not known to historians that Williams had expanded his account of the Warner Hotel fix meeting.[26] The historical record now includes the Williams revelation that after he and the others had entertained the pitch of gamblers Sullivan and Brown, Lefty, Buck Weaver, and Happy Felsch discussed ways that Series games might be thrown during the walk back to their respective apartments. "If it became necessary to strike errors [*sic*] or strike out in the pinch or anything, if a critical moment arrived, strike out, boot the ball, or anything" were ways "how we would do it," testified Williams.[27]

At the conclusion of the Williams testimony, the grand jury voted to indict the vaguely identified gamblers Sullivan and Brown. For purposes of clarity, readers should understand that Sullivan was Joseph "Sport" Sullivan, reputedly Boston's biggest bookmaker. The true identity of Brown remained a mystery throughout the proceedings but Black Sox researchers now believe him to have been Nat Evans, a capable Rothstein lieutenant and junior partner in several Rothstein casino operations. The two men likely served as emissaries of World Series fix bankroller Rothstein who funneled on the order of $80,000 through them to player ringleader Chick Gandil. Gandil then parceled out undersized portions of the payoff to corrupted Sox teammates while probably keeping the lion's share (perhaps $35,000) of the loot for himself. This fully consummated fix is separate from the $100,000 payoff that the Burns/Attell cartel subsequently reneged on.[28]

With their roster decimated by player suspensions, the White Sox gamely pressed on during the season's final week. But their outstanding final record of 96–58 (.623) was second-best to the 98–56 (.636) of the pennant-winning Cleveland Indians.[29] Meanwhile, outfielder Happy Felsch became the fourth White Sox player to confess his complicity in the 1919 World Series fix. In the privacy of his home, Felsch unburdened himself to *Chicago Evening American* reporter Harry Reutlinger. Happy declined to name the other player conspirators but averred that everything contained in the publicly reported grand jury confession of Eddie Cicotte was the truth.[30]

D. THE TRIAL, ACQUITTAL, AND BANISHMENT OF THE BLACK SOX

In mid-March 1921, recently-elected Cook County State's Attorney Robert E. Crowe administratively dismissed the original indictments returned in the Black Sox case for strategic reasons. The case would be brought to trial on superseding true bills that expanded both the criminal charges and the roster of gambler defendants.[31] Thereafter, Abe Attell and several other gambler defendants evaded an appearance in court by avoiding process, successfully resisting extradition, or pleading illness, while the charges against Sox infielder Fred McMullin had to be severed for trial at a later date when he did not arrive in Chicago in time for mid-June jury selection. That left Buck Weaver, six other White Sox players, and four gambler defendants in the dock when trial proceedings began.

While waiting for the Black Sox trial to commence, Commissioner Landis exercised the plenary powers granted to him by the major-league club owners when he assumed office in January. On March 24, 1921, he permanently expelled Phillies infielder Gene Paulette for suspected collusion with St. Louis gamblers in a game-fixing scheme.[32] The Paulette banishment was ordered pursuant to the unfettered discretion accorded Landis to take whatever action he deemed necessary to further "the best interest of the national game of baseball."[33]

After prolonged jury selection, the Black Sox criminal trial began in earnest on July 18, 1921. During those proceedings, the prosecution's star witness was gambler defendant-turned-State's evidence Bill Burns who

coolly recounted his part of the World Series fix over the course of three days on the witness stand. When it came to Buck Weaver, Burns identified him as one of the White Sox players in attendance at the pre-Game One fix meeting conducted at the Hotel Sinton.[34] Due $40,000 after the Black Sox dumped Game Two, conspirators Chick Gandil, Eddie Cicotte, Swede Risberg, Fred McMullin, and two other Sox players whom Burns did not then recall gathered in Room 708 of the Hotel Sinton to await their payoff. But when Burns only produced $10,000—procured from cash-flush but greedy fix partner Abe Attell—Gandil angrily accused Burns of a double-cross. Nevertheless, Chick assured him that the Black Sox would stick to the prearranged plan to lose Game Three, and Burns and Maharg bet accordingly. The hapless pair were then wiped out when Dickey Kerr pitched Chicago to an unscripted 3–0 victory.[35] Later in the proceedings, Billy Maharg corroborated the Burns testimony, including the identification of Weaver as a pre-Game One fix-meeting attendee at the Hotel Sinton. Affable and seemingly guileless, Maharg was deemed a credible and effective prosecution witness by most observers.[36]

After a mid-trial suppression motion had been denied by the court, the prosecution also introduced in evidence the grand jury confessions of Eddie Cicotte, Joe Jackson, and Lefty Williams.[37] Same were placed before the jurors via the reading of grand jury transcript colloquies by Special Prosecutor Edward Prindiville and grand jury stenographer Walter Smith. But here, constitutional protections and courtroom rules prohibiting the admission of hearsay evidence redounded to the benefit of Weaver and the other non-confessing accused.[38] Where the grand jurors had heard Buck Weaver, Chick Gandil, et alia, identified by name as Series fix participants, the trial jurors heard only the anonym *Mr. Blank* wherever the name Weaver, Gandil, or others appeared in the transcripts—a process that rendered parts of the confession evidence largely unintelligible.[39]

At the conclusion of the prosecution case, the court dismissed the charges against gambler defendants Ben and Lou Levi on grounds of evidential insufficiency. Trial judge Hugo Friend also expressed reservation about the force of the proofs against Weaver, Felsch, and gambler Carl Zork. But as a prima facie case had been presented against each, the court reluctantly allowed their prosecution to continue, but reserved the right to overturn any conviction that might be returned against them by the jury. The strength of the prosecution case against the remaining defendants, however, was manifest and not the subject of legal challenge.

Apart from gambler defendant David Zelcer, neither Buck Weaver nor any other of the accused took the stand when the defense turn came.[40] For the most part, defense counsel simply stood up and rested their cases. Following brief prosecution rebuttal, two days of attorney summations, and Judge Friend's instructions on the law, the case against the Black Sox was submitted to the jury.[41] A breathless two hours and 47 minutes later, Not Guilty verdicts were returned for all defendants on all charges.[42] This despite the fact that the prosecution had presented an overwhelming and unrefuted case against defendants Cicotte, Jackson, and Williams, and a strong, if more circumstantial one, against Gandil, Risberg, and Zelcer.[43]

A raucous defendant-juror celebration ensued in the courtroom.[44] After the taking of a group photo of smiling defendants, defense counsel, defense supporters, and trial jurors on the courthouse steps, the Black Sox and those who had acquitted them repaired to a nearby Italian restaurant.[45] There, jurors expressed both disdain of star prosecution witness Bill Burns and their affection for the erstwhile defendants.[46] Stretching into the early morning hours, the player-juror revelry reportedly concluded with a rousing chorus of "Hail, Hail, The Gang's All Here!"[47]

The celebration proved short-lived. Within hours of the rendering of the jury's verdict, Commissioner Landis promulgated his edict permanently banning the eight accused-but-acquitted White Sox players from all professional baseball affiliated with his major leagues.[48]

E. CIVIL LITIGATION REVELATIONS

In March 1921, Charles Comiskey officially severed all connection with the Black Sox, terminating their contracts with the club and unconditionally releasing all eight banished players. In time, four of these ballplayers instituted lawsuits against the White Sox corporation. The first was a breach-of-contract action filed by Buck Weaver which sought payment of his $7,250 salary for the 1921 season, his withheld 1919 World Series share, and other damages totaling $20,000.[49] More expansive lawsuits against the White Sox were thereafter filed in Milwaukee on behalf of Happy Felsch, Joe Jackson, and Swede Risberg.[50]

Although the lawsuits were lodged in different court venues, it was agreed that any evidence developed during the pretrial discovery period would be admissible in all proceedings. This produced developments little noted at the time but facially dispositive of the "Weaver as innocent fix bystander" claim if deemed credible: the civil trial depositions of Bill Burns and

Billy Maharg. Interrogated under oath in Chicago on October 5, 1922, Burns repeated his familiar account of fix-related events, but with one major addition—an expanded account of his delivery of the post-Game Two player payoff at the Hotel Sinton. This time when Burns related the events, he named Buck Weaver among the seven White Sox awaiting his arrival in Room 708.[51] And Weaver was named as present when the $10,000 (of the $40,000 then due) was counted out on the bed by Chick Gandil.[52]

When deposed in Philadelphia on December 16, 1922, Billy Maharg provided corroboration of Burns's account. Although Maharg had not accompanied Burns to Room 708 for the fix payoff, when Burns had returned to their hotel room, the two had spoken about the delivery of the $10,000 and the players' angry reaction to the shortchange. And Maharg averred that Burns had specifically mentioned Buck Weaver by name as being among those present when the payoff was delivered.[53]

F. THE CAMPAIGN TO REHABILITATE BUCK WEAVER

Of the civil lawsuits, the Joe Jackson suit was the only one litigated to a verdict. But the Black Sox scandal was old news by the time that the Jackson case came to trial in January 1924, and little, if any, press notice was taken of the deposition revelations of Bill Burns and Billy Maharg.[54] And those depositions did nothing to slow a simmering campaign to rehabilitate the image of Buck Weaver. Although pleas and petitions for reinstatement by Weaver himself to Commissioner Landis were repeatedly rejected, Buck gained some traction pleading his cause to the press. New-found Weaver advocates in the Fourth Estate included nationally syndicated sports columnist Westbrook Pegler who declared that "Buck Weaver was the victim of a singularly hypocritical deal in the reform that followed the [Black Sox] expose. ...Weaver was lynched because he just happened to be standing around the corner when the posse came yelling along with a rope."[55] Sportswriter John Lardner opined that "Joe Jackson and Buck Weaver were guilty of no more than thoughtlessness, under strong provocation."[56] Arguments for Weaver's pardon, however, were invariably premised on the notion that Weaver had only been culpable of having "guilty knowledge" of the fix. Buck had not participated in the throwing of Series games. Nor had he received any type of fix payoff presumed Weaver's press defenders.

Endorsement of that position came from a curious quarter: Black Sox gambler defendant Abe Attell. Attell had avoided removal to Chicago via extradition proceedings that bordered on courtroom farce.[57] He then escaped prosecution altogether when Cook County State's Attorney Crowe later administratively dismissed the indictments still pending against Attell and the other fugitive accused.[58] "I am not telling all I know, but an injustice was done Weaver when he was barred with the other players," Attell confided to a Minneapolis sportswriter in 1934. "I know positively that Buck refused to be a party to the deal and never accepted the money proffered to him. ...I always have felt sorry for Weaver," Attell continued. "I wrote a number of letters to Judge Landis in which I explained Weaver's innocence, but of course the judge wouldn't take my word for anything."[59]

Attell would continue sporadic efforts to clear Weaver over the next thirty years (while cashing in on diminishing interest in the Black Sox scandal for his own benefit). This included a factually dubious first-person scandal account published in the October 1961 issue of the cheesecake magazine *Cavalier*.[60] Here, Attell once again absolved Weaver of fix involvement. But publication of the Attell yarn had been preceded by an equally suspect first-person scandal exposé that kneecapped the Weaver cause: "This Is My Story of the Black Sox Series" by Arnold (Chick) Gandil as told to Mel Durslag.[61] Appearing in the high-circulation weekly *Sports Illustrated*, the Gandil account placed Buck Weaver among the White Sox players recruited by Eddie Cicotte and Chick for the original World Series fix proposed by Sport Sullivan. "Weaver suggested we get paid [the promised $10,000 per player] in advance. Then if things got too hot, we could double cross the gambler and also take the big end of the Series cut by beating the Reds. We all agreed this was a hell of a plan."[62] Weaver was also an enthusiastic backer of the second fix proposition offered by Bill Burns. "We might as well take his money, too," quipped Buck, "and go to hell with all of them."[63] But Gandil further maintained that the players had gotten cold feet before the Series started and never went through with the fix. Still, he accepted that in being permanently banished from baseball, the Black Sox "got what we had coming."[64]

However improbable and unnoticed, the Attell article in *Cavalier* netted the Weaver rehab campaign an unanticipated benefactor. The piece had been ghostwritten by novelist and television screenwriter Eliot Asinof. And in short order, Asinof became Buck Weaver's foremost champion. In his seminal 1963 scandal book *Eight Men Out: The Black Sox and the 1919 World Series*, Asinof portrayed Weaver as "a ferocious bulldog to the Cincinnati Reds" who had spurned overtures to join the Series conspiracy and came to be

Lefty Williams

regarded as "the enemy" by fix ringleader Gandil. But "Weaver didn't care: He was there to play ball."[65]

When *Eight Men Out* was converted into a movie 25 years later, co-screenwriter Asinof and film director John Sayles elevated Buck Weaver to the role of the wrongfully accused hero of the drama, equipping him with fictional street urchins to whom Weaver could express his bewilderment and anguish over the poor World Series play of teammates. Toward the end of the film Asinof and Sayles also inserted a make-believe courtroom soliloquy that allowed Weaver to proclaim his innocence regarding the Series fix.[66] And lest the audience somehow mistake the film's position on Buck, Asinof proclaimed to movie reviewers that "Weaver was a total innocent. The only thing he did wrong was not rat on his buddies. He never took a dime."[67]

Release of the *8MO* film in 1988 was probably the high-water mark of the Buck Weaver rehabilitation effort, its heroic portrayal shaping the lasting public perception of Weaver. Shortly thereafter came a friendly, if little-read, Weaver biography, and submission of a strenuously argued if factually selective petition for Weaver's posthumous reinstatement crafted by Chicago attorney Louis Hegeman.[68,69] Baseball commissioner Fay Vincent, however, declined to entertain the application, deeming "matters such as this are best left to historical analysis and debate."[70]

As a new century unfolded, Weaver's cause was adopted by some in the Black Sox scandal research community, including SABR Black Sox Committee founder Gene Carney. In Carney's view, Buck "gave his best effort in every [Series] game...and was banned nevertheless for having 'guilty knowledge' of the fix and failing to inform his club."[71]

G. THE OPPOSING VIEWPOINT RESURFACES

Those with an unsympathetic take on Buck Weaver mostly remained silent during the campaign to rehabilitate him. But the 2007 recovery of the Lefty Williams grand jury transcript and its incriminatory addenda to the Warner Hotel meeting provided new evidence of Weaver's culpability in the Series fix. But perhaps far more crippling to the Weaver cause was renewed examination of White Sox play during the 1920 season. At the time that the Black Sox scandal erupted in late-September 1920, contemporaneous concern about the integrity of Sox play that season had been expressed by various observers. During the close, three-way 1920 pennant race, Sox wins and losses seemed to coincide with how their principal rivals were faring on the scoreboard, and Yankees shortstop Roger Peckinpaugh later maintained that the accused players "were monkeying around so much that year you never could be sure" if they were playing on the level.[72]

White Sox captain Eddie Collins had no such doubts, attributing crucial Chicago losses to Buck Weaver and Eddie Cicotte. "The last series at Boston and New York was the rawest thing I ever saw," Collins complained in late October 1920. "If the gamblers didn't have Weaver and Cicotte in their pockets then I don't know anything about baseball."[73] Dickey Kerr evidently felt the same way. During an important late-season game against Boston, Weaver muffed a force-out throw from Kerr. When the inning was over, the pitcher walked over to Buck and shortstop Swede Risberg and told them "If you'd told me you wanted to lose this game, I could of done it a lot easier." Scuffles between antagonistic Sox player groups thereupon ensued.[74]

As the centenary of the 1919 World Series approached, scandal scholars returned attention to the White Sox 1920 season. In 2016, Bruce Allardice, the SABR Black Sox Committee's in-house expert on scandal gamblers, undertook a study of the Sox campaign. Surveying contemporary press reports, Allardice discovered that virtually every uncorrupted White Sox player had expressed misgivings or worse about the integrity of their accused teammates' play during 1920. In the end, Allardice's scrutiny of Black Sox player field performance led him to conclude that "the Sox threw games—at a minimum three, and perhaps as many as a dozen—in 1920."[75] More recently, a deep dive into the 1920 White Sox season was taken by baseball analyst Don Zminda.[76] He, too, uncovered much evidence of dishonest work by Black Sox players. His review of games involving suspect play, however, rarely focused on Weaver individually, and Zminda ultimately rendered an equivocal judgment on Buck: "Weaver's loyalty to his crooked teammates—and his performance in the games during the 1920 season that seem most likely to have been fixed—don't exactly put him beyond suspicion."[77]

ANALYSIS REVEALS BUCK WEAVER WAS ACTIVE IN THE FIX

Buck Weaver sympathizers have much in common with those who support the cause of Shoeless Joe Jackson. Both Weaver and Jackson were outstanding ballplayers and, by all accounts, nice men. The two also shared a deep love of baseball and were at or near their playing peaks when banished from the game. As for the 1919 World Series, Weaver and Jackson superficially appeared to hit well, both posting Series batting averages over .300. And from the time of their expulsion in 1921 until their deaths in the 1950s, Weaver and Jackson doggedly insisted that they were innocent of participation in the fix of the Series.

Buck Weaver and Joe Jackson have one more thing in common: a historical record containing near overwhelming evidence of their guilt in the Black Sox affair. That said, the cases against the two are not identical. (See the Spring 2019 issue of the *Baseball Research Journal* for this writer's brief for the prosecution in the Jackson case.[78])

Our point of departure on Weaver is, perhaps, an unlikely one: the content of the Landis banishment edict, particularly its condemnation of players who sit in conference with crooked ballplayers and gamblers intent on fixing baseball games and who do not report it to their clubs. It is universally agreed that Landis specifically directed this so-called "guilty knowledge" clause of his edict at Buck Weaver. What is mistaken is the long-prevailing notion that the grounds for Weaver's expulsion were necessarily confined to his guilty knowledge of the Series fix.

In law, judicial rulings—and Commissioner Landis remained a sitting federal district court judge at the time he issued his Black Sox banishment order—are often couched in the alternative. This *arguendo* or "even if" aspect of decisions affords the court a fallback basis for the outcome in the event that its primary grounds are found faulty or inadequate upon appellate review. In the Black Sox case, the belief that the expulsion of Buck Weaver was premised exclusively on his guilty knowledge of the Series fix is erroneous. As reflected in his denial of a 1927 Weaver reinstatement petition, Landis clearly deemed Weaver an active participant in Series corruption.[79] Among other things, Landis cited Weaver's incrimination in the grand jury testimony of Eddie Cicotte, Joe Jackson, and Lefty Williams, and Weaver's making "common cause [at trial] with these three players who had implicated you" in game-throwing.[80] Also cited by Landis was the trial testimony of "witness [Bill Burns] who acted as an agent between gamblers and the crooked players, arranging the fixing of the Series, and he also named you as one of the participants. Thus, there is on the record the sworn testimony of four admitted participants in the 'fixing' that you were implicated."[81] And finally, Landis disabused Weaver of the notion the jury's Not Guilty verdict "exonerated you and the other defendants of game fixing."[82] As far as Landis was concerned, it did not. Viewed in this light, the "guilty knowledge" clause of the banishment edict represents no more than Landis's fallback basis for the Weaver expulsion. First and foremost, Landis expelled Weaver as a World Series fixer.

As with Joe Jackson, Weaver supporters invariably cite his .324 Series batting average as proof-positive of his fix non-involvement. But again like Jackson, the stats argument is a malleable one, and just as easily susceptible to sinister construction.[83] As for clean-up batter Jackson, most of his gaudy .375 BA/team-high six RBI statistical line was compiled after Game Five, the outermost limit of the fix in the mind of many Black Sox aficionados. Prior to that, Joe was hitless with runners on base and failed to drive in any runs.

If Jackson's bat became dangerous toward the Series' close, Weaver's remained harmless throughout. Batting third in the lineup, Buck came to the plate 13 times with teammates on base—and produced zero RBIs. While he managed four singles in those at-bats (.308), the hits did little damage. As previously mentioned, Buck was next-to-useless with runners in scoring position. Here, Weaver's batting lowlights included a fly out with Shano Collins on second in the first inning of Game Seven and grounding into a double play with two more teammates on base in the third frame, his aforementioned called third strike in Game Eight, as well as the fly to right for the second-to-last out of the Series, snuffing a last-ditch rally.

As for affirmative proof of Weaver's active participation in the Series fix, the historical record reeks of it. Before the grand jury, Cicotte, Jackson, and Williams all specifically named Weaver as a fix conspirator. This is telling because, whatever their shortcomings, none of the three were malicious men or "had it in" for Weaver. To the contrary, all three were on friendly terms with Buck. More to the point, no evidence that Cicotte, Jackson, or Williams accused Weaver falsely has ever been uncovered—because none exists.

Weaver supporters concede Buck's presence at the pre-Series fix meetings conducted at the Ansonia (New York), Warner (Chicago), and Sinton (Cincinnati) hotels that Cicotte and Williams told the grand jury about. The question therefore arises: If Weaver was as resolutely uninterested in joining the fix plot as Asinof, Sayles, and other champions maintain, why did Weaver

attend a second fix meeting, this one with gamblers? Or a third, also with gamblers—and on the eve of Game One? Arguably, peer pressure, camaraderie, and/or curiosity may provide an excuse for Weaver's attendance at the initial fix gathering. But after that, no. The only plausible explanation for Buck's presence at follow-up meetings is that he was very much interested in getting a piece of the fix action.

The criminal trial produced more evidence of Weaver's complicity as gamblers Burns and Maharg testified that Weaver was in on it. At the risk of overkill, Weaver's participation in the fix can also be inferred from Felsch's admission that the widely publicized grand jury testimony of Cicotte was the truth, and by the stated belief of post-Game Three fix revival gamblers Harry Redmon and Joe Pesch that seven White Sox regulars and one substitute player were fix participants.[84] Doing the math here is just one more thing that puts Buck Weaver in the fix.

Decades after the fact, Chick Gandil's *Sports Illustrated* reminiscences raised the number of Series fix collaborators who implicated Buck Weaver to nine—six of whom cited Weaver by name (Cicotte, Jackson, Williams, Burns, Maharg, and Gandil), three by inference (Felsch, Redmon, and Pesch). And they all accused Buck of more than just having "guilty knowledge." These insiders portrayed Weaver as an active participant in the plot to throw the 1919 World Series.

Another Weaver talking point—the absence of evidence that he received payment for fix participation—is largely illusory, as proving a negative is always problematic.[85] More instructive here is evidence that Weaver was among the Sox players who threw games during the 1920 season, with Clean Sox Eddie Collins and Dickey Kerr making specific charges of game-throwing that season against Buck. The question then arises: Would Weaver have done gamblers' bidding in 1920 if he had not received payment for his efforts on their behalf in the previous year's World Series? The question seemingly answers itself.

Lastly, if deemed credible, the civil case depositions of Burns and Maharg drive the final nail into the Weaver coffin. According to Burns, after the Black Sox had dumped Game Two, the corrupted players (save Joe Jackson) gathered in Room 708 of the Hotel Sinton for an expected $40,000 payoff. But Burns only delivered $10,000, a shortchange that angered the players and caused their separation from the second (Burns-Attell) World Series fix. Burns's placement of Weaver in attendance at that payoff gathering was corroborated by sidekick Maharg. In his deposition, Maharg distinctly remembered Burns mentioning Weaver as one of the players in attendance. With the Black Sox criminal proceedings concluded and the two in no kind of legal jeopardy, there is no apparent reason why Burns, and especially Maharg, would have lied about the incident when deposed in 1922. Needless to say, if the Burns and Maharg depositions are believed, Buck Weaver has no defense—as there can be no innocent explanation for his presence in Room 708 at the time of the fix payoff.

PERMANENT EXPULSION WAS THE APPROPRIATE SANCTION

There was ample precedent for the lifetime banishment of ballplayers engaged in game-fixing,[86] and expulsion was the sanction compelled for game-fixing by the American League Constitution.[87] In the Weaver case, once Commissioner Landis determined that Buck had actively participated in the plot to rig the 1919 World Series, his permanent expulsion from the game was mandatory. The Weaver banishment was further warranted under the "best interests" command of the Commissioner's duties. As even Weaver supporters cannot dispute, the provision of the Landis edict that imposed banishment on ballplayers who "sit in conference" with those hatching game-fixing schemes had salutary deterrent effect. After the Weaver expulsion, game-fixing virtually disappeared from the American and National Leagues.[88]

In the final analysis, the historical evidence of Buck Weaver's participation in the fix of the 1919 Series is as strong as it is regrettable. And if corruption of the World Series, the game's ultimate event, would not warrant expulsion, then what would? So, to paraphrase Chick Gandil, with banishment, Buck got what he had coming. In the end, much like Joe Jackson, Weaver presents a sad figure, but hardly an innocent one. ■

Notes

1. As quoted in the *Boston Globe*, *Hartford Courant*, and elsewhere, March 13, 1921.

2. As reported in newspapers nationwide, August 3, 1921.

3. Robert L. Tiemann, "Major League Attendance," *Total Baseball* (Kingston, NY: Total Sports Publishing, 7th ed., 2001), 75.

4. Following the early 1918 season departure of Lefty Williams and back-up catcher Byrd Lynn for defense plant work, the vocally patriotic Chisox boss sneered, "I don't even consider them fit to play on my club." See "Comiskey Wipes 2 Shipbuilders Off Sox Roster," *Chicago Tribune*, June 12, 1918, 11. Later, Comiskey was reported as vowing to use "every ounce of my strength and the last cent I have" to keep defense plant jumpers Joe Jackson, Happy Felsch, and Williams "out of organized baseball forever." See "Shipyard Ballplayers Will Never Get Back, Says Comiskey," *Salt Lake Telegram*, September 17, 1918, 4.

5. See Fangraphs Leaderboards, 1919: https://www.fangraphs.com/leaders.aspx?pos=all&stats=bat&lg=all&qual=0&type=8&season=1919&month=0&season1=1919&ind=0&team=0%2Cts&rost=0&age=0&filter=&players=0&startdate=1919-01-01&enddate=1919-12-31&sort=20%2Cd.

6. Early Series odds ranged from 10–7 to 8–5 in White Sox favor, with comparably little money being bet on the Reds. For detailed analysis of the betting odds on the 1919 World Series, see Kevin P. Braig, "Don't Believe the Dope: Few Saw Fix Coming," *Black Sox Scandal Research Committee Newsletter*, Vol. 11, No. 1 (June 2019), 20–32.

7. As recounted by Rick Huhn in *Eddie Collins: A Baseball Biography* (Jefferson, NC: McFarland & Co., 2008), 152. The original source of the incident is an article by syndicated sportswriter Joe Williams published in the *New York Telegraph*, July 10, 1943.

8. Johnson and McDonald were longtime acquaintances, and Johnson had previously floated McDonald's name as a candidate for a vacant position on the National Commission, the three-man governing body prior to the anointment of US District Court Judge Kenesaw Mountain Landis as baseball commissioner in November 1920. A Landis biographer places the McDonald-Johnson meeting at Edgewater Golf Club on the outskirts of Chicago. See David Pietrusza, *Judge and Jury: The Life and Times of Judge Kenesaw Mountain Landis* (South Bend, IN: Diamond Communications, Inc., 1998), 164.

9. The only justification offered for this egregious breach of black letter law was the belated pronouncement that "officials of Chief Justice McDonald's court, desirous of giving the national game the benefit of publicity in its purging, lifted the curtain on the grand jury proceedings," per the Associated Press wire and published nationally. See e.g., "Two White Sox Players Confess; 8 Are Indicted; Comiskey Cleans Out Team," *Baltimore Sun*, September 29, 1920, 1, and "Officials Give Publicity to Purging of Game," *Grand Forks* (North Dakota) *Herald*, September 29, 1920, 1.

10. See e.g., "Jury Convinced Crooked Work Was Done by Players in League with Gamblers," *Philadelphia Inquirer*, September 25, 1920, 14; "More White Sox Players Involved in 1919 Scandal," *Salt Lake Tribune*, September 25, 1920, 10; "Scandal in Baseball Ranks," *Washington* (DC) *Post*, September 25, 1920, 10.

11. See e.g., "Name of Baseball 'Fixer' Is Known by Grand Jury," *Boston Globe*, September 25, 1920, 4.

12. Maharg is identified as an assistant trainer in a 1916 Philadelphia Phillies team photo and he played an inning in the Phils outfield in the final game that season. Earlier in 1912, the athletic Maharg had been a one-game replacement at third base during a brief Detroit Tigers players strike.

13. James C. Isaminger, "Philadelphia Gambler Tells of Deal with Chicago Players to Lose Series," *Philadelphia North American*, September 27, 1920, 1.

14. Per the transcript of the Cicotte statement given at the Austrian law office, September 28, 1920, and viewable online via the invaluable Black Betsy website. Readers should note, however, that the posted transcript is an abridged eight-paragraph version of the Austrian-Cicotte interview. A complete, unabridged account of the interview is not available.

15. In so doing, however, Cicotte endeavored to minimize his fix participation, presenting a significantly different picture of his own culpability as compared to the abject admissions that he had made earlier in the day at the Austrian office. For comparison and analysis of these differing Series fix confessions, see Bill Lamb, "Reluctant Go-Along or Fix Ringleader? Analysis of Eddie Cicotte's Role in the Corruption of the 1919 World Series," *Black Sox Scandal Research Committee Newsletter*, Vol. 12, No. 2 (December 2020), 3–9.

16. Like much of the Black Sox record, the transcript of Eddie Cicotte's grand jury testimony has been lost. A "Synopsis of Testimony of Edward V. Cicotte," however, is among the scandal artifacts contained in the Black Sox collection at the Chicago History Museum. In all probability, this 24-paragraph synopsis of the Cicotte testimony was created by Assistant State's Attorney Hartley Replogle or fellow Black Sox grand jury prosecutor Ota P. Lightfoot.

17. Per "Eight of White Sox Indicted," *Chicago Daily News*, September 28, 1920, 1. The public disclosure of charges prior to the completion of the probe was highly unorthodox and ran counter to lead grand jury prosecutor Replogle's previously stated preference that "all indictments…

be returned in a bunch" when the inquiry concluded. *Chicago Evening Post*, September 28, 1920.

18. As reported in "Jackson and Cicotte Admit Guilt; Cleveland Almost Sure of Pennant," *Cleveland Plain Dealer*, September 29, 1920, 1; "Comiskey Pulls Down Pennant Hopes to Steady Game's Foundations," *Tampa Morning Herald*, September 29, 1920, 7; and elsewhere.

19. The Jackson admissions in chambers were not memorialized, but testifying at the Jackson civil lawsuit against the White Sox in early 1924, Judge McDonald named Buck Weaver as one of the fix conspirators identified privately by Jackson to him. Transcript of Jackson civil trial, 552.

20. A detailed account of the Jackson grand jury testimony is provided by the writer in *Black Sox in the Courtroom: The Grand Jury, Criminal Trial and Civil Litigation* (Jefferson, NC: McFarland & Co., 2013), 52–54, and "An Ever-Changing Story: Exposition and Analysis of Shoeless Joe Jackson's Public Statements on the Black Sox Scandal," *Baseball Research Journal*, Vol. 48, No. 1 (Spring 2019), 38–40.

21. Transcript of Jackson grand jury testimony at 20–3 to 7.

22. As quoted in the *Boston Globe* and *The New York Times*, September 29, 1920. Weaver mistakenly gave his Series batting average as .333. He actually batted .324.

23. Among other things, Jackson complained about receiving only $5,000 of the $20,000 promised him for joining the Series fix and declared that "the eight of us did our best" to lose Game Three but were thwarted by the shutout pitching of "little Dick Kerr. ...Because he won it, the gamblers double crossed us because we double crossed them," first reported in the *Chicago Daily Journal* and *Chicago Tribune*, September 29, 1920.

24. Statement of Claude "Lefty" Williams, September 29, 1920, viewable on-line at www.famoustrials.com/blacksox, and elsewhere.

25. During his grand jury testimony, Williams stated that he received $10,000 from Chick Gandil the night before Game Five and that he gave half the money to Joe Jackson back at their hotel. Transcript of grand jury testimony of Claude Williams at 27–10 to 16. This money presumably emanated from the original Series fix arranged with Rothstein agents Sullivan and Brown.

26. The Williams grand jury transcript was among the scandal artifacts obtained at auction by the Chicago History Museum in December 2007. Although not publicly disclosed, the document's source is presumed to be the successor of the law firm of White Sox corporation counsel Alfred S. Austrian.

27. Williams grand jury transcript at 29–26 to 30–7. Prior to the recovery of the Williams grand jury transcript, many scandal researchers simply supposed that the content of the Williams testimony was identical to the long-available statement that he had given in the Austrian law office.

28. The Burns/Attell group included Burns's friend Billy Maharg and Des Moines gambler David Zelcer, with recently cashiered NY Giants first baseman Hal Chase facilitating matters. A nebulous post-Game Three fix revival effort orchestrated by St. Louis gamblers Carl Zork and Ben Franklin is yet another entry in World Series fix scenarios.

29. The excellent 95–59 (.617) record of the New York Yankees was good for no better than third place in the tight AL pennant chase of 1920. But the record-shattering 54 home runs swatted by Yanks pitcher-turned-everyday outfielder Babe Ruth that season would revolutionize the way that the game was played.

30. "I Got Mine, $5,000—Felsch," *Chicago Evening American*, September 30, 1929, 1.

31. In addition to reindicting all the previously named defendants, the March 1921, superseding indictments made Midwestern tinhorns David Zelcer, Carl Zork, Benjamin Franklin, and Ben and Lou Levi answerable to the charges.

32. As reported in the *Chicago Tribune*, *The New York Times*, and newspapers nationwide, March 25, 1921.

33. See Pietrusza, *Judge and Jury*, 173–74.

34. As is the case with the grand jury minutes, only fragments of the Black Sox criminal trial record survive. But extensive verbatim excerpts of the Burns testimony were published in the press. See e.g., "Burns Reveals Further Facts in Series Plot," (Indianapolis) *Indiana Times*,

July 20, 1921, 8; "World's Series Made to Order," *Philadelphia Inquirer*, July 20, 1921, 14.

35. As reported nationwide. See e.g., "Story of How Chicago Players Double-Crossed Gamblers When They Failed to Receive Bribe Money Is Revealed by Bill Burns on the Witness Stand," *Casper* (Wyoming) *Daily Tribune*, July 21, 1921, 4; "Burns Admits on Stand to Being Stakeholder in Baseball Conspiracy," *San Francisco Chronicle*, July 20, 1921, 14.

36. According to Eliot Asinof, Maharg was "an articulate witness [who] added a strong layer of testimony to the State's already strong case." *Eight Men Out: The Black Sox and the 1919 World Series* (New York: Henry Holt, 1963), 202.

37. No claim that the grand jury transcripts were inaccurate or unreliable was asserted by the defense. Rather, suppression was sought on the ground that the Cicotte, Jackson, and Williams grand jury testimony had been induced by broken, off-the-record promises of immunity. With questioning strictly limited to events occurring in and around the grand jury room, defendants Cicotte, Jackson, and Williams testified in support of the application out of the jury's presence. In response, former ASA Replogle and Judge McDonald countered that no such inducement had been offered. In denying the motion, trial judge Hugo Friend necessarily decided this swearing contest in favor of the prosecution witnesses.

38. Although it would be decades before the protections of the Sixth Amendment's Confrontation Clause would be applicable in state court prosecutions, the analogous provision in the Illinois State Constitution of 1870 shielded the non-confessing Black Sox defendants from the Cicotte/Jackson/Williams confessions.

39. As reported in newspapers across the country. See e.g., "Technicalities Galore Raised," *Grand Island* (Nebraska) *Daily Independent*, July 26, 1921, 3; "Baseball Trial Goes by Spasms, *Ogden* (Utah) *Standard-Examiner*, July 26, 1921, 6. This editing process is known as redaction and was required by Judge Friend before the prosecution could utilize the Cicotte, Jackson, and Williams grand jury testimony before the trial jury.

40. The defenses of Chick Gandil and Carl Zork presented proof but neither Zork nor Gandil testified.

41. A prosecution attempt to belatedly introduce the Felsch newspaper confession as rebuttal evidence was rejected by Judge Friend—the court ruling that this damning proof should have been offered during the prosecution's case-in-chief.

42. The Associated Press reported that jurors spent more time on mechanical chores like affixing their 12 signatures to multiple separate verdict sheets than they did deliberating on the proofs. See e.g., "'Black Sox' Doomed," *Bellingham* (Washington) *Herald*, August 3, 1921, 7.

43. In previous works this writer has postulated that certain of the acquittals were the product of a rare but dread courthouse phenomenon known as jury nullification. See e.g., "Jury Nullification and the Not Guilty Verdicts in the Black Sox Case," *Baseball Research Journal*, Vol. 44, No. 2 (Fall 2015), 47–56.

44. Jurors paraded around the courtroom with several of the player defendants on their shoulders, as reported in the *Atlanta Constitution*, *The New York Times*, and elsewhere, August 3, 1921.

45. Well known to Black Sox researchers, the group photo on the courthouse steps was originally published in the *Chicago Tribune*, August 3, 1921.

46. As reported in the *Des Moines Evening Times* and *Los Angeles Times*, August 3, 1921.

47. Per the *Des Moines Evening Times* and *Los Angeles Herald Examiner*, August 3, 1921.

48. Although occupied by his duties as a Chicago federal district court judge during the Black Sox trial, Landis had kept close watch over the proceedings via the trial transcript delivered daily to his chambers, as reported by the *Chicago Evening Post*, August 3, 1921. In banishing the Black Sox, Landis applied the precedent recently established by Pacific Coast League expulsion of ballplayers who had had game-fixing criminal charges dismissed by a Los Angeles court on statutory construction grounds.

49. The Weaver lawsuit was filed in the Chicago Municipal Court by attorneys Charles A. Williams and Julian C. Ryerson on October 18, 1921. Days

later, the action was transferred to federal district court on diversity of citizenship grounds, the defendant White Sox having been incorporated in Wisconsin.

50. The Felsch lawsuit was instituted on February 9, 1922, while the Jackson and Risberg cases were filed on May 12, 1922. Representing all three plaintiffs was young firebrand Milwaukee attorney Raymond J. Cannon, a one-time semipro teammate of Happy Felsch.

51. Of the Black Sox, only Joe Jackson was absent from the room.

52. Deposition of Bill Burns as admitted in evidence at the early 1924 trial of the Jackson civil lawsuit. See Jackson trial transcript at 695–98.

53. Deposition of Billy Maharg. See Jackson trial transcript at 730–34.

54. A $16,000+ civil jury award in Jackson's favor was promptly vacated by the trial judge who ruled that the judgment was based on perjured testimony. The suit was later quietly settled out of court for a pittance. A similar outcome attended the other actions. For more on the Black Sox civil litigation, see again William F. Lamb, *Black Sox in the Courtroom*, 149–98.

55. Westbrook Pegler, "Nobody's Business: Great Chance Reporters Muffed," *Omaha World-Herald*, November 13, 1932, 25.

56. John Lardner, "Hall of Fame Contenders Include Baseball Outlaws," *Springfield* (Massachusetts) *Republican*, January 22, 1938, 10.

57. Among other things, Attell defense counsel William J. Fallon shamelessly argued that there were actually two Abe Attells and that prosecutors were trying to extradite the wrong one. Perhaps more effectively, Fallon also bribed the prosecution's principal extradition witness (Chisox groupie Sam Pass) into testifying that the Abe Attell in court was not the gambler with whom he had placed high-stakes World Series wagers.

58. The outstanding indictments against defendants Attell, Fred McMullin, Sport Sullivan, Hal Chase, and Rachael Brown were dismissed by SA Crowe only days after the Not Guilty verdicts had been returned in court.

59. George A. Barton, "Sportsgraphs: Abe Attell Absolves Buck Weaver," *Minneapolis Tribune*, April 27, 1934, 30.

60. Abe Attell, "The Truth Behind the World Series Fix," *Cavalier*, October 1961, 9–13, 89–90.

61. *Sports Illustrated*, September 17, 1956.

62. Gandil, *Sports Illustrated*, above.

63. Gandil, *Sports Illustrated*, above.

64. Gandil, *Sports Illustrated*, above.

65. Asinof, *Eight Men Out*, 63.

66. In previous writings, this writer has dissected *8MO*'s historically unreliable treatment of the Black Sox saga, with particular scorn reserved for the fabrications of the movie version. See e.g., "Based on a True Story: Eliot Asinof, John Sayles, and the Fictionalization of the Black Sox Scandal," *The Inside Game*, Vol. XIX, No. 3 (June 2019), 35–43, and the *8MO* historical errata catalogue appended to the Black Sox Scandal Research Committee's online *Eight Myths Out* project. See also, Bill Lamb, "1919: A Loss of Innocence and a Few Key Facts," *Black Sox Scandal Research Committee Newsletter*, Vol. 13, No. 2 (December 2021), 11–16.

67. As quoted in Ed Sherman, "Chicago Strikes Out," *Chicago Tribune*, August 21, 1988, 288.

68. Irving M. Stein, *The Ginger Kid: The Buck Weaver Story* (Dubuque, IA: Brown & Benchmark, 1993).

69. Commentary on the Hegeman petition is provided in "Amnesty for Black Sox Third Baseman?" *Wall Street Journal*, January 17, 1992.

70. Same as above, quoting a December 12, 1991, letter from the commissioner's office to Hegeman.

71. Gene Carney, *Burying the Black Sox: How Baseball's Cover-Up of the 1919 World Series Fix Almost Succeeded* (Washington, DC: Potomac Books, 2006), 209.

72. As quoted by Donald Honig in *The Man in the Dugout: Fifteen Big League Managers Speak Their Minds* (Lincoln: University of Nebraska Press, 1977), 216.

73. Frank O. Klein, "Collins Charges 1920 Games 'Fixed,'" *Collyer's Eye*, October 30, 1920, 5.

74. As related in Kuhn, *Eddie Collins*, 172. The incident was originally revealed in a 1924 article published in *Baseball Magazine*.

75. Bruce S. Allardice, "'Playing Rotten, It Ain't That Hard to Do': How the Black Sox Threw the 1920 Pennant," *Baseball Research Journal*, Vol. 45, No. 1 (Spring 2016). The article title quotes Happy Felsch.

76. Don Zminda, *Double Plays and Double Crosses: The Black Sox and Baseball in 1920* (Lanham, Maryland: Rowman & Littlefield, 2021).

77. Zminda, *Double Plays and Double Crosses*, 270.

78. See again, Lamb, "An Ever-Changing Story."

79. The Landis ruling is re-produced verbatim by Daniel E. Ginsburg in *The Fix Is In: A History of Baseball Gambling and Game Fixing Scandals* (Jefferson, NC: McFarland & Co., 1995), 148.

80. Ginsburg, *The Fix Is In*, 148.

81. Ginsburg, *The Fix Is In*, 148. Billy Maharg, a fifth witness directly implicating Weaver in the Series fix, went unmentioned by Landis.

82. Ginsburg, *The Fix Is In*, 148.

83. Analysis of Joe Jackson's World Series stats appears in Lamb, "An Ever-Changing Story," 45.

84. According to the grand jury testimony of Redmon and St. Louis Browns second baseman Joe Gedeon (a personal friend of Swede Risberg) the fix-revival meeting was conducted at the Sherman Hotel in Chicago and chaired by subsequently indicted St. Louis gamblers Carl Zork and Ben Franklin. The meeting's intelligence that seven White Sox regulars and one substitute player were in on the fix was provided by the Levi brothers, also among those indicted.

85. This writer entirely discounts the putative, double-hearsay grand jury testimony attributed to Dr. Raymond Prettyman, the Weaver family dentist. Same concerned a package of cash supposedly delivered to the Weaver home by Fred McMullin. Both Weaver and McMullin denied the allegation, and it is unclear if Prettyman ever made it in the first place.

86. Expulsion of players engaged in game-fixing dated back to 1865. See John Thorn, *Baseball in the Garden of Eden: The Secret History of the Early Game* (New York: Simon & Schuster, 2011), 127–29. See also, Thorn, "Our Game: Baseball's Bans and Blacklist," February 8, 2016.

87. Adopted on February 16, 1910, the American League Constitution mandated the expulsion of any franchise that failed to terminate a player who had conspired to throw a league game.

88. Landis's swift expulsions of Phil Douglas (1922), Jimmy O'Connell and Cozy Dolan (1924) provided the coda on game-fixing in the majors.

The Endurance of Black Sox Mythology
Narrative Conventions and Poetic Form

Bill Savage and S.P. Donohue[1]

Historians and scholars of the Big Fix and the Black Sox Scandal often bemoan the endurance of myths about the 1919 World Series and its aftermath. Thanks to a complicated interplay between evolving literary representations of the events of 1919–20 and popular films like *Eight Men Out* and *Field of Dreams*, mention of "the Black Sox" calls forth a host of myths, chief among them that Charles Comiskey was a cheapskate owner who underpaid his team despite their greatness, and that the ballplayers were naïve dupes enticed by slick gamblers like Sport Sullivan and Arnold Rothstein. The reality that Comiskey was no cheaper than any other owner and that players Chick Gandil and Eddie Cicotte approached the gamblers just hasn't gained cultural traction beyond SABR circles, despite corrective journalism and other media representations of the historical reality.

Of course, "myth" has more than one definition: According to Merriam-Webster, one is "an unfounded or false notion," something contrary to the facts. Another, however, matters more: "a usually traditional story of ostensibly historical events that serves to unfold part of the world view of a people or explain a practice, belief, or natural phenomenon."[2] Despite their thorough debunking by SABR researchers, the myths synch with widespread American worldviews; their endurance results from aspects of how the Black Sox narrative plays into certain tropes of American literature, and the poetic power of the one key phrase instantly recognized even beyond the world of baseball fans: "Say it ain't so, Joe."[3]

Though today people militate to reinstate Shoeless Joe Jackson and place him in the Hall of Fame while Comiskey is derided, originally the dynamic of blame was the other way around. As Daniel Nathan has explored in *Saying It's So: A Cultural History of the Black Sox Scandal*, Comiskey was not the villain. He and countless fans were the victim of ballplayers and gamblers who betrayed ideals of sport and manhood that were thought to be the very basis of a uniquely American identity expressed through the national game.[4]

Many fans—a very few of whom became writers representing these cultural events—had refused to believe history even when it was happening right in front of them. James T. Farrell, in the essay "I Remember the Black Sox," writes the following account of a supposed incident late in the 1920 season, after a Sox home game:

> I went with the crowd and trailed about five feet behind Jackson and Felsch. They walked somewhat slowly. A fan called out:

> "It ain't true, Joe!"

> The two suspected players did not turn back. They walked on, slowly. The crowd took up this cry and more than once, men and boys called out and repeated:

> "It ain't true, Joe!"[5]

No one has corroborated Farrell's memory of this incident, and the American popular imagination embraced the mythic "Say it ain't so, Joe" instead.

But Farrell is not the key literary figure in the path to reverse the myths: his fellow Chicagoan and White Sox fan Nelson Algren is. About a generation after the events of the 1919 World Series—and Commissioner Judge Kenesaw Mountain Landis's banishment of the eight Black Sox "regardless of the verdict of juries"[6]—Algren began to turn that narrative around, first in his 1942 poem "The Swede Was a Hard Guy."[7] He continued in a 1951 representation of the scandal in "The Silver-Colored Yesterday."[8] His reversal culminates in the 1973 mixed-genre prose poem "Ballet for Opening Day: The Swede Was a Hard Guy."[9] In each of these works, Algren depicts the players as victims of Comiskey's miserliness and the gamblers' guiles, especially Shoeless Joe Jackson. Beyond any readers who might have been swayed directly by Algren, these mythic representations clearly influenced later writers and filmmakers.

To teach these mythic texts, and to challenge students to accept the reality, can be frustrating, but only if we fail to grapple with why the myths endure. Rebecca Kell, a student in "Baseball in American Narratives"—a class in the Big Fix's centennial year of 2019—helped me understand one key reason why the myths endure. After reading Algren and screening *Eight Men Out*, when presented with the historical reality in "Eight Myths Out," she replied: *OK, then, if I cannot blame Comiskey, I'll blame Rothstein.*[10] She argued that even if Gandil and Risberg and Cicotte initiated the Fix, the gamblers nonetheless were taking advantage of players who were all outsiders and underdogs, and who therefore deserved the sympathy of readers rather than condemnation. Most of them didn't even get paid! Sure, they were wrong to throw the Series, but they had justifications that suffice. While a philosophical purist might argue with the situational morality here (the gamblers, Jewish Arnold Rothstein and Irish-American Sport Sullivan, were also outsiders in their own ways) her argument resonates with a powerful tradition in American narrative literature of rooting for the outsider and the underdog against the dominant culture. From Hester Prynne to Huck Finn to Jay Gatsby to Tom Joad to John Yossarian to Randall Patrick McMurphy—just to name a few canonical literary figures—American authors, and by extension American audiences, tend to side with the marginalized.[11]

In "Ballet for Opening Day," Algren describes the White Sox ballplayers as all coming from regional or class subject positions outside of the dominant in American culture. Gandil had "been riding the Western rails since boyhood." Weaver had "come west from soft-coal country" in Pennsylvania. Risberg was "a rangy San Franciscan," and a "grammar-school dropout." Felsch also was a dropout, a factory worker and bartender from Milwaukee. Cicotte was "a French-Canadian family man." Williams was a "Missourian who kept his grievances to himself." Most importantly for the coming filmic mythology, "Joseph Jefferson [sic] Jackson was an illiterate son of an illiterate share-cropper…[whose]…flaw was fear. He saw himself as an ignorant rube among erudite city-wise Northerners."[12] Jackson's greatness, a putative inability to play bad baseball, is central to "The Silver-Colored Yesterday." In that story, young Algren, surrounded by Cubs fans, is challenged for his embrace of Swede Risberg as his "fayvrut player." After the Scandal breaks, Algren laments:

> Out of the welter of accusations, half denials and sudden silences a single fact drifted down: that Shoeless Joe Jackson couldn't play bad baseball

even if he were trying to. He hit .375 that series and played errorless ball, doing everything a major-leaguer could do to win. Nearing sixty today, he could probably still outhit anything now wearing a National League uniform.[13]

It seems highly unlikely that an elderly Joe Jackson would outhit anyone at that point, but such exaggeration comes naturally to the process of mythologizing the larger-than-life heroes of the past.

Algren's depictions are central to the groundbreaking journalistic representation of the Big Fix, Eliot Asinof's *Eight Men Out*. Together, Algren and Asinof create a skein of interwoven myths using each other's work as sources. Asinof quotes Algren four times, and even ends his book with the conclusion of Algren's 1942 poem, depicting Shoeless Joe as a tragic figure whose ghost haunts the game:

> Who made an X for his name and couldn't
>   argue with Comiskey's sleepers.
> But who could pick a line drive out of the air
>   ten feet outside the foul line
> And rifle anything home from anywhere in
>   the park.
>
> For Shoeless Joe is gone, long gone,
> A long yellow grass-blade between his teeth
> And the bleacher shadows behind him…[14]

Later, Algren quotes a paragraph from Asinof's depiction of Cicotte as an epigraph to the 1973 "Ballet for Opening Day." That paragraph reinforces the "Comiskey was a cheapskate" myth, and sets up the entire thrust of Algren's last version of the Black Sox story:

> [Cicotte] had grown up believing it was talent that made a man big. If you were good enough, and dedicated yourself, you could get to the top. […] In the few years he had been up, they had always praised him and made him feel like a hero to the people of America. But all the time they paid him peanuts. […] Meanwhile, Comiskey made a half million dollars a year on Cicotte's right arm.[15]

The evocation of the classic American Dream narrative, the idea that talent and hard work would be rewarded resonates with the characters' arcs common in "the Great American Novel," and creates the narrative framework that entices readers to accept the myth of Comiskey as an exploiter of his athletes.

Like an intergenerational Tinker-to-Evers-to-Chance, it's Algren to Asinof and back to Algren for a 3–6–3 mythic double play. Other writers join in a pepper game of spread-the-myths, including Tony Fitzpatrick and, most importantly, W.P. Kinsella. In his epic Chicago poem *BumTown*, Fitzpatrick defines Comiskey Park as a "shrine/The Old Roman built/On the backs of underpaid/Ballplayers. So cheap was Comiskey/That he'd only launder uniforms/Once a week."[16] Kinsella, in his novel Shoeless Joe, from which *Field of Dreams* was adapted, writes:

> '[Jackson] hit .375 against the Reds in the 1919 World Series and played errorless ball,' my father would say. 'Twelve hits in an eight-game series. And they suspended him,' Father would cry. Shoeless Joe became a symbol of the tyranny of the powerful over the powerless. The name Kenesaw Mountain Landis became synonymous with the Devil.[17]

The odd locution "played errorless ball" is directly from Algren, and shows the influence all of these writers had on each other. These writers, all clearly having read and been influenced by each other, weave the myths out of strands of reality. Jackson did indeed bat .375, and owners sure enough made more money than players. The dynamic of dominance and marginality here is the paraffin that makes the shine ball of mythology so hard to hit: along with their other ethnic or regional outsider identities, the players occupied subject positions at the bottom of the hierarchy of class.

But for every baseball fan who has read Algren, Farrell, Fitzpatrick, or Kinsella, maybe ten thousand have watched *Eight Men Out* and a million have seen *Field of Dreams*. John Sayles' 1988 adaptation of *Eight Men Out* explicitly extends the mythologies created by Algren and Asinof. The film depicts the players as an exploited working class, profited off of by greedy capitalist owners and slick gamblers. Vivid performances by the film's ensemble, especially D. B. Sweeney as Jackson, David Strathairn as Cicotte, and John Cusack as Weaver, evoke sympathy for the players which overwhelms the reality.[18] In the movie's coda, Jackson plays in a run-down minor league stadium under an assumed name. A fan thinks it's Joe Jackson after he has hit two homers and a double, and then makes a spectacular catch. But Buck Weaver, sitting forlornly nearby, says it isn't him. After he strokes a triple, some fans now are sure they know who he is despite his alias, "Brown." A child asks "Who's Joe Jackson?" and is told he is "one of them guys that

Joe Jackson in a 1920 photo.

threw the Series back in '19. One of them bums from Chicago, kid. One of the Black Sox."[19] Ironically, this scene shows the original embrace by fans of the reality that the players were guilty. This taste of truth, however, is overwhelmed by the film's primary depiction of the players as exploited outsiders only driven to throw the Series because of Comiskey's cheapness. Of course, the film centers on the scene on the courthouse steps where the urban urchin who worshipped Jackson cries out, "Say it ain't so, Joe!"

Field of Dreams extends the mythology even further. That film's depiction of Shoeless Joe Jackson as someone who just wanted to play ball, who would play for free, for the pure pleasure of the game, is a mirror image of the condemnation the players originally received for being greedy.[20] The ghost of Jackson is restored to the status of the pure hero, where belief in him can redeem you and restore broken connections between fathers and sons.[21]

But more than narrative convention perpetuates the mythology. Poetry also matters. The phrase "Say it ain't so, Joe!" has a certain magic to it.[22]

Like all the best slogans, ditties, chants, and nursery rhymes, this plaint is made memorable through internal rhyme, alliteration, and rhythmic mirroring.

The sentence is thick with rhyming vowel sounds: "S**ay**" rhymes with "**ai**(n't)"; "s**o**" rhymes with "J**oe**". And because "it" alliterates with "(ain')t", our ear is tempted to hear "ain't" as an almost-rhyme for "say't".

So there's a near-rhyme pair in the first half of the sentence and a full rhyme pair in the second, effectively dividing the sentence into two hemistichs (half-lines): "say it ain't" and "so, Joe," a structure further supported by two strong beats in each half:

```
   x    x   x    x
SAY it AIN'T SO JOE
 a        a    b  b
```

where the x's stand for vocal stress and the a's and b's mark the rhyme pairs. The twin sibilance of "say" and "so" (both words at the start of their hemistich) knit the two halves together.

As for rhythm: the line starts with a strong, stressed syllable on the imperative verb "Say"—a real command. Followed by an unstressed syllable, the phrase establishes a trochee, a falling rhythm. This initial trochee encourages us to stress "ain't" a little more than we otherwise might; we naturally want to alternate strong stress and weak stress, an on-off or off-on motion like a heartbeat or wave. Repeating this motion is what creates rhythm. Therefore, after the stress of "ain't," our ear expects another weak syllable, but instead we have to stress "so," a small word that carries a great deal of the sentence's castigation and regret in its sibilant hiss (and doesn't "so" conjure "no"?). The comma then pauses us, making our leap onto the final single syllable even stronger than it naturally is—proper nouns are always stressed. This means we

Chick Gandil

have three stresses in a row at the end of the sentence: *ain't so, Joe!* Wherever stresses cluster and crowd, they create great force and weight, further underscoring the lament.

Thinking of this as a chant, we're basically going to shout four stressed words, almost eliding over the "it"—SAY (it) AIN'T SO JOE. We can clap that out, it's a regular 1–2–3–4 musical phrase, with the "it" touching ever so lightly on the downbeat.

And surely the slangy "ain't" has something to do with the pleasure of the sentence.

In his 1942 poem, Algren misquotes the original as "Say it isn't so, Joe." Some form of lyric natural selection led the more poetic version to endlessly reproduce and thrive. This line, recycled by a legion of sports-page headline writers and quoted out of context in countless situations unrelated to baseball, is the poetic reason why myths of the Black Sox endure.[23]

In short, poetry and narrative defeat history every time.

Myths that coincide with readers' or viewers' ingrained predispositions regarding fictional characters (even those based on real-life people) influence how they interpret narratives. The power of poetic form can drill a mythic sentence into the public consciousness so deeply that it cannot be overcome by prosaic facts. Yogi Berra or Casey Stengel may or may not have said that "Good pitching beats good hitting, and vice-versa,"[24] but the endurance of the myths surrounding the Big Fix and the Black Sox Scandal suggest that good storytelling and poetry beat good history rather than the other way around. ∎

Notes

1. Professor Savage teaches the course "Baseball in American Narratives"; Professor Donohue teaches courses on creative writing, including technical matters of poetic form. Their distinct contributions to this essay should be clear.
2. Merriam-Webster, online edition. "Myth," https://www.merriam-webster.com/dictionary/myth?utm_campaign=sd&utm_medium=serp&utm_source=jsonld. Accessed March 6, 2023.
3. See *Scandal on the South Side*, ed. Jacob Pomeranke (Phoenix: SABR Publications, 2005). Also *Eight Myths Out*, https://sabr.org/eight-myths-out Accessed March 6, 2023.
4. Daniel Nathan, *Saying It's So: A Cultural History of the Black Sox Scandal* (Urbana and Chicago: University of Illinois Press, 2003), 11–57.
5. James T. Farrell, *My Baseball Diary* (Carbonsdale and Evansville: Southern Illinois University Press, 1998), 106.
6. Quoted in Eliot Asinof, *Eight Men Out: The Black Sox and the 1919 World Series* (New York: Henry Holt, 1963), 273.
7. Nelson Algren, "The Swede Was a Hard Guy." *Southern Review*, Spring 1942, 873–79.
8. Nelson Algren, *Chicago: City on the Make. 60th Anniversary Annotated Edition*, David Schmittgens and Bill Savage (Chicago: University of Chicago Press, 2011).
9. Nelson Algren. "Ballet for Opening Day: The Swede Was a Hard Guy." *The Last Carousel* (New York: G. P. Putnam's Sons, 1973) 268–98.

10. This paraphrase has been cleared with Ms. Kell. She also made a most cogent critique of *Bull Durham*, describing it as a sex-positive film about non-toxic masculinity. To paraphrase Nuke Laloosh: That's deep. Think about it.

11. I note the masculinist bias of this roster of "Great American Characters." I would add that rooting for the outsider is a powerful factor in representations of women's baseball, from Penny Marshall's *A League of Their Own* to the recent television series of the same title.

12. Algren, *Last Carousel*, 270–75.

13. Algren, *Chicago: City on the Make*, 38.

14. Asinof truncated Algren's poem; this truncated version appears in *Eight Men Out*, 293. The original was in *Southern Review*, 878–79.

15. This appears in Asinof, 257. In Algren, *The Last Carousel*, 268.

16. Tony Fitzpatrick. *BumTown* (Chicago: Tia Cucha Press, 2001), 13.

17. W. P. Kinsella. *Shoeless Joe* (New York: Houghton Mifflin, 1982), 7.

18. *Eight Men Out*, director: John Sayles (MGM, 1988).

19. This scene can be found on YouTube. MovieClips, "*Eight Men Out* (12/12) Movie CLIP—It's Him (1988) HD," https://www.youtube.com/watch?v=cMxPAkZgoy0. Accessed March 6 2023.

20. Phil Alden Robinson. *Field of Dreams* (Universal Pictures, 1989).

21. *Field of Dreams* exemplifies another aspect of baseball narratives my class engages with; the feedback loop between real and fictional baseball; we all expect everyday life to appear in fiction, but in baseball narratives, fiction creeps back into real world. Even before Major League Baseball games were played in 2021 and 2022 at the newly built professional ballpark at the movie site in Dyersville, Iowa, countless fans had travelled to the place as a shrine to a game of catch, and so helped perpetuate the myth of Shoeless Joe as innocent victim and redemptive hero.

22. Professor Donohue steps up to the plate here.

23. Among the many examples of the phrase escaping baseball and entering the pop-cultural landscape include the use of "say it ain't so, Joe" as a bridge-refrain in the 1981 song "Up All Night" by Irish rock band the Boomtown Rats, and the predictable headline in the *Atlanta Journal Constitution* when Joe Biden chose Chicago over Atlanta to host the Democratic National Convention.

24. Neither did, or at least neither originated the phrase, which is not attributed to either until the 1970s. One blogger and researcher into American vernacular English, Barry Popik, identifies the source of the quotation as Pittsburgh Pirates pitcher Bob Veale, and the original version, in 1966, as "Good pitching always stops good hitting and vice-versa." https://www.barrypopik.com/index.php/new_york_city/entry/good_pitching_will_always_stop_good_hitting. Accessed March 6, 2023.

Which Manager Knew First That the 1919 World Series Was Fixed?

Tim Newman

Several players on the 1919 Chicago White Sox agreed to lose that year's World Series, earning the nickname "Black Sox." Their manager William ("Kid") Gleason said publicly after the Series that "something was wrong. I didn't like the betting odds. I wish no one had ever bet a dollar on the team."[1] Gleason had good reason to know that his team had been fixed. White Sox owner Charles Comiskey passed along a tip to that effect on the morning before the second game. The tip came from well known gambler Monte Tennes, whom Comiskey apparently deemed credible.[2]

Gleason probably knew more, earlier, and from a source that he trusted.

BILL BURNS WAS CLOSE FRIENDS WITH BILLY MAHARG

The players first discussed the fix during a train ride one month before the Series.[3] At their hotel in New York City in mid-September, Black Sox Eddie Cicotte and Arnold Gandil sought money from a former major leaguer and outwardly prosperous acquaintance selling oil leases named Bill Burns. Unbeknownst to the players, Burns could not meet their financial demand, so he summoned his friend Billy Maharg from Philadelphia.[4]

Maharg was born in Philadelphia, and had left school when he was ten to work on a farm. At age thirty-eight in 1919, Maharg worked for the Baldwin Locomotive Company as a driller.[5,6] He enjoyed some local celebrity as a former boxer.[7]

In 1920, Maharg famously told the story of his involvement in the fix to legendary Philadelphia sportswriter James Isaminger. Maharg related how Burns wired him to come to New York City, and when he got there Burns was planning a hunting trip with White Sox pitcher Bill James.[8] Maharg had spent time hunting with Burns in Texas several years earlier.[9]

Burns had a long history of hunting big game with big leaguers. In 1910, he gathered a hunting party that included future Hall of Famer Tris Speaker.[10] During the 1911 season several players, including Phillie Tub Spencer, said that they would spend the winter on Burns' ranch in San Saba, Texas.[11] That October, Phils

rookie sensation and future Hall of Famer Grover Cleveland Alexander said that he would also go to Burns' ranch to spend a part of the winter.[12]

In 1916 Burns and his pack of bloodhounds met James in New Mexico to hunt bears and mountain lions.[13] Bill Rodgers, who spent most of 1916 in the Pacific Coast league and accompanied Burns and James on the 1916–17 trip, said that "Burns is a bug on dogs.[14] Some of his seven pups were good bear dogs." Maharg raised hunting dogs.[15] During a drive from Santa Rita, New Mexico, where the Chicago Cubs had lost to Burns' team of copper miners in a 1918 spring training game, Alexander and Burns shot crows and quail from their car.[16]

Just before his trip to New York City in 1919, Burns had visited Philadelphia, where he had some success selling oil leases. Around September 9 he sold an oil lease to Harry C. Giroux.[17] While neither Burns nor Maharg ever mentioned meeting the other in Philadelphia, Maharg's connection is beyond coincidental. Maharg was an accomplished dancer who found time to teach at the renowned Wagner Ballroom in Philadelphia.[18] Giroux worked at the Wagner Ballroom from 1918 until retiring as the manager in 1962.[19]

Burns saw Cicotte and other Chicago players while he was in Philadelphia.[20] Third-string White Sox catcher Joe Jenkins said later that blue laws in Philadelphia prohibited baseball on Sundays, so he played in a high-stakes craps game with Burns at the hotel.[21] The date was probably September 14, 1919, when the White Sox had a Sunday off.

After the World Series, Maharg bought two oil leases from Burns. On both, Maharg was part of a group that included Giroux and Charles Gey.[22] Gey led the Jazzy Jazz orchestra that played the Wagner.[23,24]

MAHARG WAS CLOSE FRIENDS WITH GROVER CLEVELAND ALEXANDER, BILL KILLEFER, AND PAT MORAN

Maharg might have been the only person whom Burns both trusted and thought might have the connections necessary to raise the money. Maharg met Burns in 1908 or 1909 when the latter broke in to the major leagues with Washington.[25] They probably came to know each other better when Burns was acquired by the Phillies in May 1911, where Burns joined a pitching staff headed by Alexander. Alexander lived with Maharg when he was a member of the Phils, and they remained lifelong friends.[26,27]

Three months after Burns joined Philadelphia, the Phillies purchased the contract of catcher Bill Killefer. Killefer and Alexander immediately meshed and were best friends off the field.[28] According to Isaminger, "From attending ball games at the Phillies' park [Maharg] became very friendly with Alexander and Killefer…Alexander had an automobile and Maharg drove it for him. The pitcher and catcher and Maharg were inseparable, and while Maharg's duty was to drive the car he was always 'one of the party.'"[29] It probably helped that Maharg was or had been an auto mechanic.[30]

By 1915 Burns was out of the major leagues, but Pat Moran—the backup catcher from that 1911 Phillies team—had been hired to manage the Phillies. During spring training Moran introduced the concept of catchers using combination signs to signal the pitcher, thus thwarting opposing baserunners from tipping the upcoming pitch to the batter.[31] Alexander won thirty-one games in 1915, and Killefer was the regular catcher.

Maharg was still around too—helping Moran steal the signals of teams visiting the Baker Bowl:

[I]n the spring of [1915] the Phillies suddenly changed their players' bench to the first base side of the field, the visiting teams occupying the bench at the third base side, which had always been used by the home team.

When they changed players' benches they had a small door at the back of their old bench which was now to be used by the visiting team closed up so that it was impossible to get from the players' bench under the stand without going around by way of the bleacher entrance.

Behind this wall, under the grandstand, a hole was dug in the soft ground, and Maharg was used as a spy to hide in this hole with his ear to the cracks of the nailed-up door so he could hear the conversation of the visiting players and catch their signals and plays. He would then report this information to Manager Moran by returning under the grandstand to the Phillies' bench, the door to which had not been closed, with the

Pat Moran   **Kid Gleason**

result that the Phillies usually knew every play their opponents were about to pull in advance.[32]

The Phillies won the National League pennant in 1915, a substantial improvement over their sixth place finish of the previous year. But they refused an offer to stage the coming World Series games at the more spacious Shibe Park several blocks away.[33] The Phils won the first World Series game at home, but then lost the next four and the Series.

Moran insisted that Maharg travel with the Phillies on occasion, and Maharg was identified in 1916 as the Phillies assistant trainer in their team photo.[34,35] Moran put him into that year's final regular season game. A Pennsylvania paper reported, "Butterball Maharg, the king of the chauffeurs, went to right in the ninth."[36] *The New York Times* called it "a travesty on the national game."[37]

KILLEFER WAS TIGHT WITH OTTO KNABE, WHO WARNED HIS LONGTIME FRIEND AND BUSINESS PARTNER KID GLEASON

After the 1917 season, the Phillies traded Alexander and Killefer to the Chicago Cubs. The move shocked the baseball world.[38] The trade did reunite Killefer with Cubs' coach Otto Knabe, who had been the Phillies' second baseman from the time it was ceded to him by his mentor Kid Gleason in 1907, until 1913.

The Phillies let Moran go as their manager when his contract expired following the 1918 season. That did not stop Moran from betting $500 on that year's World Series.[39] It is not known whether he bet for or against Killefer and the Cubs (who lost to the Boston Red Sox). For the 1919 season Moran was hired to manage the Cincinnati Reds, and Gleason was hired to manage the White Sox.

The train that pulled out of Chicago at 5 PM on August 11, 1919, carried Burns, Alexander, Killefer and Knabe.[40] It may have been during this trip that Burns

Pitcher Eddie Collins speaks with his skipper, Kid Gleason, in this photo dated 1921.

convinced Cubs Fred Merkle and Speed Martin, and manager Fred Mitchell, to buy an oil lease that Killefer held in trust.[41] Knabe left the Cubs for the year when the train got to Syracuse, to attend the famous horse races in Saratoga.[42] There is no telling whether Knabe saw alleged fix financier Arnold Rothstein win $200,000.[43]

After Saratoga at the end of August, Knabe headed back to Philadelphia to look after the business that he owned with Gleason. Knabe let it be known that he would share with Gleason any insights he had on Chicago's World Series opponent, Moran's Reds. Knabe also intended to bet on the Series.[44]

The business that Knabe and Gleason owned was variously described as a billiard hall and/or a bowling alley.[45,46] Knabe was indicted in 1938 for running a gambling house and "pool selling" in Philadelphia. The *Philadelphia Inquirer* said that Knabe had operated the place for many years.[47] At trial, the police described the operation as a sumptuous casino with former light-heavyweight boxing champion "Battling" Levinsky at the peephole.[48]

Whether or not they were the same business, sportswriter Effie Welsh said that the former one also made book. Welsh also said that Knabe had a pool of money he was prepared to bet on the White Sox to win the 1919 World Series when a ballplayer friend told him that the Sox had been fixed. Knabe corroborated the tip, and then informed Gleason. They quarrelled and the longtime partners split up.[49]

This scenario is perfectly plausible. White Sox executive Harry Grabiner identified the player who warned Knabe as none other than Bill Killefer.[50] The Cubs ended the 1919 season in Cincinnati, and Killefer stayed in town for game one of the Series. Knabe was at game one, so there was ample opportunity for him to have talked to Killefer.[51] Gleason arrived in Cincinnati with the White Sox on the day before the first game, so there was ample opportunity for him to have heard about the fix from his long-time friend Knabe before the Series started.

BUT IF KILLEFER TOLD KNABE, THEN HE PROBABLY TOLD MORAN, TOO

Would Killefer have told Knabe that the fix was in, but not Moran?

Killefer joined the parade after the Reds' clinched the National League pennant, and Moran asked Alexander and him to share their wisdom with the Reds' players before the Series started.[52,53] Presumably Alexander and Killefer were still around while their wives spent Game One in a box with Moran's wife.[54] Alexander and Killefer are also known to have visited the Reds' clubhouse after the fifth game in Chicago.[55]

Thus it seems likely that if Killefer told Knabe about the fix, then he probably told his old friend Moran as well.

But Moran never said when he learned of the fix, and Gleason never acknowledged getting any tips earlier than the morning of Game Two. The closest he came was in a column he wrote on the day that the Series ended. "I wasn't in the betting, but I know that a host of my friends in Philadelphia were backing my team…There never were so many rumors of crookedness floating around, as have been in the air since Labor day. One story had it that seven players on my ball club were on the Cincinnati end of it and had gobbled up some enticing odds in the series wagering."[56] Gleason told the grand jury investigating the fix that he had no definitive proof, only suspicions about his team's play, particularly in 1920.[57]

Moreover, Maharg was probably not the source of Killefer's information. They were clearly close friends, but at all relevant times Maharg was in Philadelphia while Killefer was with the Cubs in the West. Maharg also claimed to have kept quiet until he publicly exposed the scandal in 1920: "My closest friend is Grover Cleveland Alexander, and when he was here [in Philadelphia] with the Cubs this year [1920] I never said a word to him about it."[58] Alexander immediately acknowledged that "Maharg always impressed me as being truthful and honest."[59]

Maharg could have wired or phoned Killefer. But it is more probable that Burns told someone, maybe his old hunting buddy Bill James. In addition to the multiple instances already mentioned, Burns and James repeated their hunting trip in the winter of 1918–19.[60] On that day in September 1919 at the Ansonia Hotel when Cicotte and Gandil first broached the idea of the fix, Burns and James were planning another trip for that winter. But Burns said that the trip was postponed and then canceled, and that James never knew anything about the fix.

Finally, Knabe was a constant caller at Gleason's bedside while he was dying in 1933.[61] He also served as an honorary pall bearer (with Killefer) at his funeral.[62] Were Knabe's actions those of an estranged protege, or was there never any need to do that?

So who knew about the fix first, Gleason or Moran? You decide. ∎

Notes

1. *Chicago Tribune*, October 10, 1919, 19.
2. Deposition of Charles Comiskey taken March 24, 1923, pertaining to civil lawsuits filed by Oscar Felsch, Joe Jackson, and Swede Risberg against the White Sox. These records are in private possession, but are abstracted in Gene Carney, "New Light on an Old Scandal," *Baseball Research Journal* (Cleveland: Society for American Baseball Research, 2006) Volume 35, 74. Some details are missing from Carney's summary. The various reports of what Kid did with his information are ably summarized in Gene Carney, *Burying the Black Sox: How Baseball's Cover-Up of the 1919 World Series Fix Almost Succeeded* (Washington, DC: Potomac Books, 2006) 46–47.
3. William F., Lamb, *Black Sox in the Courtroom: The Grand Jury, Criminal Trial and Civil Litigation* (Jefferson, NC: McFarland & Co., 2013) 50; and sources cited therein.
4. Timothy Newman, "Why the Black Sox Almost Got Away With It," *The Inside Game*, 2023.
5. Maharg's testimony in the criminal trial of the Black Sox recounted in the *New York Herald*, July 28, 1921, 9.
6. Maharg's World War I draft registration card, dated September 1918.
7. See Bill Lamb's outstanding biography of Maharg at SABR BioProject: https://sabr.org/bioproj/person/billy-maharg.
8. James Isaminger, "My Part in '19 Fix–Maharg," *Philadelphia North American*, September 28, 1920 (reprinted in *Baseball Digest*, October–November 1959, 9).
9. Burns' testimony from the criminal trial appears, for example, in the *Philadelphia Inquirer*, July 20, 1921, 1.
10. *Arizona Republican*, September 2, 1910, 7; *Ft. Worth Star-Telegram*, November 11, 1910.
11. *Sporting Life*, August 26, 1911, 7; Gandil played semipro ball with Spencer in 1920. *Los Angeles Times*, February 12, 1920.
12. *Harrisburg (PA) Patriot*, October 17, 1911, 8. Maharg may have joined this trip. Maharg testified they did not see each other for several years after Burns left the major leagues in 1912. Deposition of William Maharg, taken December 16, 1922 (note 2).
13. *Western Liberal* (Lordsburg, NM), November 3, 1916, 1; *Oregonian*, February 22, 1917 (this report has Burns' dogs as Airedales). James at that time was playing for Detroit. James also collected a controversial payment from Gandil and White Sox shortstop Swede Risberg in 1917. James' biography is at https://sabr.org/bioproj/person/bill-james-2.
14. *Oregonian*, February 22, 1917.
15. At least later in life. Jerry Jonas, "He helped 'fix' the 1919 World Series," *Daily Intelligencer* (Doylestown, PA), October 11, 2009, 34.
16. Oscar C. Reichow, "Alex Expected to be a Sniper," *Chicago Daily News*, February 13, 1919, 2.
17. Assignments dated September 9, 1919, recorded in San Saba County, Texas.
18. Jonas (note 15).
19. Giroux's obituary is in the *Philadelphia Inquirer*, November 10, 1969, 10.
20. Deposition of William Burns taken October 5, 1922 (See note 2).
21. "Hanford's Jenkins, Black Sox Innocent, Talks of One Big Smirch on Baseball," *Fresno (CA) Bee*, May 13, 1962, 26. Jenkins also said that Abe Attell was there, which is harder to believe, but Burns was known to play poker and shoot craps. First tip of the cap to the late Gene Carney for his Notes, #388 discussing the deposition of Chicago sportswriter Hugh Fullerton.
22. Assignment dated October 20, 1919, recorded in San Saba County, Texas.
23. *Reading (PA) Times*, July 9, 1918, 5.
24. https://www.city-data.com/forum/philadelphia/1924588-whatever-happened-wagners-ballroom-3.html (accessed December 15, 2022). Another lease, to Hall of Famer Max Carey and several of his Pittsburgh Pirates teammates, was recorded on the same day. This suggests that the dates that the Assignments were recorded are not necessarily the dates that they were signed.
25. Deposition of William Maharg (note 12).
26. "My Part in '19 Fix–Maharg" (note 8) 13. It is unclear how much Maharg lived at the Hay Market Hotel. He may actually have lived at 1819 N. Park, at least in 1918 (the address he listed on his draft registration card) and 1919 (per the address on the telegram shown in this article).
27. Alexander's wife said in 1951 that her husband's "friend" Maharg had called her in 1929 about Alex's health. *Sporting News*, May 2, 1951, 14.
28. Killefer caught Alex on October 3, the first of 250 times they would be the starting battery in big league games. The SABR biography of Bill Killefer by Charlie Weatherby is at https://sabr.org/bioproj/person/bill-killefer.
29. *Pittsburgh Press*, July 24, 1921, 20; The author was unable to find this article in any other newspaper.
30. At the Hay Market Hotel (note 26). Maharg deposition (note 12).
31. Peter Morris, *A Game of Inches: The Story Behind the Innovations that Shaped Baseball* (Chicago: Ivan R. Dee, 2010) 236.
32. Jim Nasium, "Maharg Was Used by Moran as a Spy," *Philadelphia Inquirer*, September 29, 1920. Jim Nasium was the pen name of Edgar Forrest Wolfe.
33. The 1915 Philadelphia Phillies: National League Champions, https://www.philadelphiaathletics.org/history/the-1915-philadelphia-phillies-national-league-champions (accessed December 16, 2022).
34. *Philadelphia Inquirer*, September 29, 1920, 18 (note 32); *Pittsburgh Press*, July 24, 1921, 20 (note 29).
35. *Deadball Stars of the National League* (SABR, 2004) 185. Maharg is seen in the photo that was apparently taken very late in the 1916 season, standing on the far left, distinctive in suit and tie; Lamb's biography of Maharg says that the photo can also be found in Paul G. Zinn and John G. Zinn, *The Major League Pennant Races of 1916* (Jefferson, NC: McFarland & Co., 2009).
36. *Lancaster (PA) Daily New Era*, October 6, 1916, 8.
37. Lamb's biography of Maharg, note 17, citing *The New York Times*, October 6, 1916.
38. White Sox executive Harry Grabiner suggested that Alex and Killefer were traded by former NYC police commissioner William Baker "after they were crooked." William Veeck with Ed Linn, *The Hustler's Handbook* (Baseball America Classic Books, 1996) 226.
39. Sean Deveney, *The Original Curse* (McGraw Hill, 2010) 57; Gleason also bet on baseball at least once on a Labor Day 1917 game with the Tigers that Gandil and Swede Risberg alleged was fixed. Rick Huhn, *Eddie Collins: A Baseball Biography* (Jefferson, NC: McFarland & Co., 2008) 188, citing Collins' letter to Commissioner Landis dated February 24, 1921, in the Black Sox Scandal files at the National Baseball Hall of Fame Library in Cooperstown NY.
40. *Chicago News*, August 11, 1919.

41. Assignment dated August 30, 1919, recorded in San Saba County Texas.

42. *Pittsburgh Press*, August 16, 1919; *Chicago Tribune*, August 13, 1919, 15, has Knabe proceeding to NYC with Alexander, Killefer, Claude Hendrix, and Jim Vaughn.

43. *Collyers Eye*, August 16, 1919, 4; Cubs owner Charles Weeghman claimed this is where Tennes tipped him that the upcoming World Series was fixed.

44. *Philadelphia Inquirer*, August 31, 1919. Before the 1919 season, Gleason and Knabe attended a boxing match together. *Philadelphia Evening Public Ledger*, March 11, 1919.

45. *The Sporting News*, January 16, 1919, 8, discussing Gleason's appointment as manager of the White Sox. Gleason left his team at least once during the 1919 season to go to Philadelphia. "Sox to Battle Senators Today in Hot Capital," *Chicago Tribune*, September 9, 1919, 17.

46. See for example *Binghamton* (NY) *Press and Sun-Bulletin*, August 28, 1919, 14.

47. May 8, 1938, 2.

48. *Philadelphia Inquirer*, November 9, 1939, 19.

49. Statement of Effie Welsh, sportswriter for the *Wilkes-Barre* (PA) *Times Leader*, dated September 28, 1920, printed in the *Boston Globe* the next day (another shoutout to Gene) and in the *New York Sun and Herald*, 13. Welsh may have known Buck Weaver growing up. Weaver barnstormed with Babe Ruth to California, where they golfed with Bill James, Kerry Keene, Raymond Sinibaldi, David Hickey, *The Babe in Red Stockings: An In Depth Chronicle of Babe Ruth with the Boston Red Sox 1914–1918* (Sagamore, 1997) 282.

50. Veeck (note 38) 225; From the context of Veeck's discussion, the information may have come from detectives hired to investigate the fix rumors.

51. *Evening Public Ledger* (Philadelphia), October 1, 1919, 15.

52. As noted by Cubs' beat writer Charles Dryden's column dated September 27 in the *Richmond* (VA) *Times-Dispatch* September 28, 1919, 21.

53. Before they all left to attend the horse races across the river at Latonia. *San Francisco Examiner*, September 30, 1919 18.

54. Susan Dellinger, *Red Legs and Black Sox* (Emmis Books, 2006) 207, note 9, citing the *Cincinnati Enquirer*, September [*sic*: October?] 2, 1919. To be fair, Christy Mathewson wrote that Knabe served on Moran's "strategy board." *Detroit Free Press*, October 6, 1919, 12.

55. *Cincinnati Post*, October 1x, 1919. For good measure Alexander also visited the headquarters of the White Sox boosters, known as the Woodland Bards, after game two. *Cincinnati Post* October 1x, 1919.

56. See for example *Pittsburgh Press* October 10, 1919, 40. Taken with the quote from note 1, Gleason seemed to have more sympathy for the people who lost money than anger at the fixers or his guilty players.

57. Lamb (not 57 e 3) 70-71, note 38 and sources cited therein.

58. *Philadelphia North American*, September 28, 1920 (note 8).

59. See for example *Brooklyn Daily Times*, September 28, 1920, 1.

60. *Los Angeles Herald*, September 2, 1919, 15.

61. *Philadelphia Inquirer*, January 4, 1933, 14.

62. *Philadelphia Inquirer*, January 8, 1933, 37.

Major League Baseball in Iowa

Iowa's History of Hosting Negro League Contests

John Shorey and Kevin Warneke

The *Washington Post* described the so-called significance of the August 12, 2021, matchup between the New York Yankees and the Chicago White Sox played in Dyersville, Iowa—where the movie *Field of Dreams* was filmed—this way: "Thursday night, 30 years and a pandemic after the release of that movie, the state will host its first MLB game at a specially made field plowed into the cornfields outside Dyersville, not far from the diamond where the movie was filmed."[1]

Other news outlets carried similar messages. A *USA Today Sports* story predicted that "About 8,000 fans will be on hand to watch the New York Yankees and Chicago White Sox in the first MLB game ever played in the state of Iowa."[2] *Des Moines Register* writer Tommy Birch, days prior to the matchup, chronicled how the game had sparked renewed interest in the movie site. Birch shared how visitors to Iowa were making pilgrimages to Dyersville. "On Aug. 12, the New York Yankees and the Chicago White Sox, two historic franchises featured in the film, will play in the first official MLB game in Iowa history on a specially built field right next to the diamond featured in the movie."[3]

Not so fast, tweeted John Thorn, official historian of Major League Baseball. "Iowa did host some Negro Leagues games of 1920–1948 (the era included by MLB). Negro American League games were played in Davenport, Des Moines and Council Bluffs (neutral sites)—complicating the story of 'Iowa's first MLB game.'…"[4]

In between MLB's initial announcement of the game to be played in Dyersville and the game's first pitch, the commissioner of Major League Baseball, Robert Manfred Jr., had announced (in December 2020) that Major League Baseball was correcting "a longtime oversight" in the game's history by officially recognizing that the Negro Leagues were deserving of the designation "major," joining the Federal League, American Association, and a few other defunct leagues that share that status. The announcement stated that MLB was proud to showcase the contributions of those who played in seven distinct leagues from 1920 through 1948. "With this action, MLB seeks to ensure that future generations will remember the approximately 3,400 players of the Negro Leagues during this time period as Major League-caliber ballplayers. Accordingly, the statistics and records of these players will become a part of Major League Baseball's history."[5]

It turns out that Iowa has a robust history of hosting Negro League games. The authors, primarily using newspaper accounts, discovered at least 30 games between Negro League teams played in Iowa from 1937 to 1948. These games were played in the three Iowa cities mentioned by John Thorn in his tweet, along with others played in Sioux City and Charles City.

Documenting what counts and what doesn't count as an official Negro League game is challenging and an ongoing process. Retrosheet president Tom Thress explained that games played in communities other than the teams' home bases and during the regular season that were reflected in league standings typically count as official.[6] Those played in the offseason or those that involved only one Negro League team (typically played against a local team or another barnstorming team) are considered exhibition games.[7]

No teams that were members of one of the seven Negro Leagues now recognized as major league by MLB had franchises in Iowa. However, barnstorming was a major component of Negro League operations, and the Kansas City Monarchs and the Chicago American Giants were frequent visitors to Iowa. Sometimes they played local clubs, sometimes other barnstorming teams, and sometimes each other.[8]

As early as 1926, a brief article in the *Des Moines Tribune* advertised two coming games in June as the headline proclaimed, "Negro Teams to Play Exhibition in June."[9] However, the first game apparently played in Iowa now recognized as official by MLB pitted the Cincinnati Tigers and the Birmingham Black Barons on May 27, 1937—after the weather stymied three earlier attempts that year.

A preview story in the *Des Moines Register* that ran on May 16 proclaimed, "Two teams from the Negro major league will play at League park Wednesday and

Thursday nights of this week. The Chicago American Giants, who were seen here last season in games against Des Moines and the House of David, will play the Cincinnati Tigers of the same circuit."[10] Two days later, the *Register*'s sports editor, Sec Taylor, began his "Sittin' In" column with "Negro Stars Play Here. Games Count in the League."[11] Along with establishing the official nature of the game, he hyped the contest with the observation, "It was claimed before the Giants appeared here a year ago that at least six or seven of their players would be in the National or American leagues if they were white, and after the Negroes defeated the Des Moines Western leaguers and the House of David, there were few who would dispute those claims."[12]

Mother Nature failed to cooperate and both games were rained out. A week later, two newly scheduled contests were announced. "Teams from the Negro National league are going to try to play in Des Moines again… The Cincinnati Tigers, rained out of two scheduled games here last week with the Chicago American Giants, will return here Wednesday and Thursday nights but this time their opponents will be the Birmingham Black Barons, champions of the south, this year members of the league."[13] A subsequent article established that the game would count in the season's standings, and also added this incentive, "If attendance here warrants it, other league contests will be played here this season when the local Western league club is out of the city."[14]

The first of the two announced games between the Tigers and the Black Barons was also rained out. Finally, after three washouts, an official league game was played on Thursday, May 27, 1937. Cincinnati led 2–1 until a five-run outburst by the Black Barons in the top of the fifth. "Birmingham bunched five hits and took advantage of a pair of Tiger errors to push across their five tallies," read the *Register*'s game recap. "Herman (Red) Howard, husky Baron twirler, stopped the Cincinnati batters with his southpaw slants and scattered nine hits. The Tigers pushed across two runs in the eighth stanza to narrow the gap, but Birmingham came back with two runs to put the game on ice in the ninth frame." Final score: 8–4.[15]

Des Moines would have to wait until the next season for another turn at hosting a Negro League contest. In July 1938, the *Des Moines Tribune* announced that "The Chicago American Giants and the Kansas City Monarchs, crack teams from the Negro American league, will meet at League park, Des Moines, on Thursday night, July 28."[16] Sec Taylor, in his column, once again promoted the caliber of Negro League

baseball. "Thursday night the Kansas City Monarchs, pacesetters in the Negro American league, will meet the Chicago American Giants in a regularly scheduled game in the Negro American league. There is no need to point out the brand of baseball that is played in that league. Several of its teams have appeared here in former years and have proved conclusively that they measure up to double A, almost to major league standards, and have several players who if they were white, would now be playing under the big top."[17]

The Chicago American Giants pounded out 14 hits on their way to an 11–4 triumph over the Monarchs. Slugging third baseman Alec Radcliffe led the attack with two triples and a double. "A crowd of 1,500 persons saw some hard hitting, some thrilling plays, including great fielding," reported the *Des Moines Register*. "The spectators were so enthusiastic that [promoter] E. Lee Keyser decided to book another Negro American league game as soon as possible."[18]

The Kansas City Monarchs were frequent visitors to Iowa for official Negro American League games in 1939. The Monarchs roster that season featured five future National Baseball Hall of Famers. Pitcher Hilton Smith was the ace of the staff but didn't pitch in any of the three official games in Iowa. However, Iowa spectators did see the other four future Hall of Famers in player-manager Andy Cooper, Willard Brown, Norman "Turkey" Stearnes, and John "Buck" O'Neil. "Baseball hungry Des Moines scoffed at threatening skies Friday night and turned out 600 strong to watch the Kansas City Monarchs trounce the Indianapolis A.B.C.'s 11 to 2, behind the spectacular hitting of Willard (Willie) Brown, Negro baseball's Rogers Hornsby," described the game summary. "Brown, Monarch outfielder who led the American Negro league in home runs last year, whaled the tar out of Dad Mitchell's pitching with a pair of triples and a brace of doubles in five trips to the plate. All of his blows, which brought in three runs, rattled off the centerfield fence."[19]

In early July, the heavy-hitting Monarchs clashed with the St. Louis Stars, a team noted for their defensive prowess. "Great fielding plus a dozen hits let the St. Louis Stars wallop the Kansas City Monarchs, first half champions of the Negro American league, 9 to 5, before 1,000 fans at League park here Friday night."[20]

The Monarchs were slated to face their rival Chicago American Giants in late July. Besides pitting the top two teams from the Negro American League, the game preview featured an unusual promotion. "As an added attraction Pepper Bassett, catcher for the Giants, will work one inning while seated in a rocking chair. Bassett once caught an entire game in this manner, as

LIBRARY OF CONGRESS

Satchel Paige warms up before pitching for the Kansas City Monarchs.

the outgrowth of a wager, and will try it for one inning this evening."[21] The game story failed to report whether Bassett worked an inning from a rocking chair. Perhaps his antics were overshadowed by the Monarchs' onslaught as they combined 20 hits with eight errors by the Giants to whip them, 20–7. Turkey Stearnes helped lead the charge with two singles and a home run.[22]

The Monarchs and Giants squared off again in Des Moines in an official league game in 1940. This time O'Neil belted a home run to lead the Monarchs to a 7–3 triumph.[23]

After the 1940 contest, no official Negro League games were held in Des Moines for seven years. By 1947, the Negro League landscape had dramatically changed. On April 15, 1947, Jackie Robinson made national headlines when he broke the long-standing color barrier in the National League. "A Robinson To Play Here" proclaimed the headline of the *Des Moines Tribune* pregame story between the Kansas City Monarchs and the Chicago American Giants. "There will be a new Robinson at shortstop for the Kansas City Monarchs...He is Curt Robinson, 18-year-old flash from Berkeley, Cal...Of the four Negroes now playing in the majors, the Monarchs contributed three—Jackie Robinson and Henry Thompson, and Outfielder Willard Brown."[24]

Due to the top talent being increasingly siphoned off into the American and National Leagues, 1948 is the final season that MLB recognizes the Negro Leagues as major league caliber. Des Moines hosted its final major league game on June 24 of that year. "Kansas City Monarchs rallied for six runs on a lone

hit in the eighth inning to edge the Memphis Red Sox, 7–4." It was player-manager Buck O'Neil's three-run pinch-hit single, which followed five walks and an error, that provided the margin of victory. Future Hall of Famer Willie Wells went 2-for-4 for Memphis and had a stolen base in the losing effort. Willie Wells Jr. also played for Memphis, forming a rare father-son combination in the same game. The game was also notable in that Willard Brown and Henry Thompson were back with the Monarchs after their brief stints with the St. Louis Browns the previous season.[25]

Des Moines was the first city to host a major league baseball game in Iowa, but Davenport has hosted the most—at least 14 official Negro American League games were played in the Iowa community 1941–48. The Kansas City Monarchs were scheduled to take on the Birmingham Black Barons in the first major league game in Davenport, but due to a conflict in schedule, the Monarchs were unable to appear, so the Jacksonville Red Caps filled in, and the game was moved up one day to July 14, 1941.[26] "The hard swatting Birmingham Barons overpowered the Jacksonville Red Caps by an 8 to 3 count," began the game recap. "The Barons also looked great in the field, completing four lightning-like double plays and made many beautiful stops in the infield."[27]

The Kansas City Monarchs were able to keep a scheduled date later that summer and battled the St. Louis Stars. "Since the race for the second half title in the league is so close that neither the Monarchs nor the Blues [*sic*[28]] dare lose lest they might not get in the playoff, the game here should be a lulu since all the exhibition strings will be cut from the game. The boys will settle down to some real baseball."[29] Future Hall of Famer Hilton Smith was the starting pitcher for the Monarchs. He pitched through the sixth inning and left the game with a 3–2 lead. With Smith out of the game, St. Louis rallied for five runs in the top of the seventh to secure a 7–3 victory.[30]

After a one-year hiatus, Davenport baseball fans again attended official Negro American League games, only with a new wrinkle. In 1943 the famous barnstorming Ethiopian Clowns, who had been frequent visitors to Iowa over previous seasons, became the Cincinnati Clowns and an official member of the Negro American League. "They not only play a spectacular brand of baseball, but they also have the ability to put on clown acts which have the customers shouting for more," proclaimed an article previewing the game between the Clowns and the Memphis Red Sox.[31] Notable players for the Clowns included Reece "Goose" Tatum of Harlem Globetrotters fame and

In 1948, Willie Wells played for the Memphis Red Sox in the final major league game held in Des Moines.

Lloyd "Pepper" Bassett, the Rocking Chair catcher.[32] The Clowns performed their famous phantom infield practice for the entertainment of the fans during an intermission in the sixth inning, but it was the Red Sox who won the game, 6–1.[33]

A game between the Clowns and the Birmingham Black Barons a couple weeks later featured pregame contests: "Four of the fastest runners in the Negro American league will participate in a speed test…The managers of the two teams have selected their top men to compete in the base-running stunt, and the runner circling the bases in the best time gets first money…. In addition there will be a complete list of stunts… There will be long-distance hitting and throwing for accuracy."[34] The Clowns not only won the game, 5–3, but their players also swept the pregame contests. Clowns right fielder John Britton won the two speed contests as he circled the bases in 14.9 seconds and won the 100-yard dash in 9.6 seconds.[35]

World War II strained the country's resources and the Negro major leagues were no exception. "The Monarchs…are going to carry through for the duration despite the fact that the draft has hit them hard—if not harder—than any of the white clubs…with their 'murderer's row' of heavy hitters in the army and with three pitchers among those for whom the service stars wave, (they) still have an 'ace' to send out on the mound—Satchel Paige."[36] The Kansas City Monarchs were participants in two of the four official league games held in Davenport in 1944, with the Cincinnati Clowns featured in the other two games. Along with the games, a new promotion was added during the season. "The sideline features will be a jitterbug contest on a platform in front of the home plate and a bathing beauty contest for Negro participants. This program is expected to pack the park."[37] A crowd of 2,300 watched the Monarchs defeat the Chicago American Giants, 9–0, but also cheered for the participants in the jitterbug contest as the game summary described the dance contest in some detail.[38]

The anticipated highlight for the one official game played in 1945 in Davenport was Jackie Robinson. "The Monarchs have Jackie Robinson, a former UCLA grid great, at shortstop and the young man has been playing sensationally ever since he joined the Monarchs early this spring after receiving his medical discharge from the army…Robinson has been hailed as the greatest rookie in the Negro baseball circles this season. He is batting at a .349 clip and has a powerful throwing arm."[39] The Chicago American Giants defeated the Monarchs, 8–7. "But there was something more important happening. 'Many of the fans,' one sports writer wrote, 'were disappointed by the absence of Jackie Robinson, much publicized shortstop for the Monarchs.' Robinson was in Brooklyn [meeting] with Branch Rickey and the Brooklyn Dodgers."[40]

Three Negro American League games were played in Davenport in the final season designated as major league contests. All three games featured the Kansas City Monarchs and their new shortstop Gene Baker, a graduate of Davenport High School.[41] Baker would later play for the Chicago Cubs and team with fellow Monarch Ernie Banks to form the first black keystone combination in one of the formerly segregated major leagues.[42] Led by Baker's six hits over the three games, the Monarchs won two of three.[43]

On the Western side of the state, Council Bluffs looked to cash in on the crowds generated by traveling Negro League teams. However, the community's Legion Park lacked adequate lights for the preferred night games. The Rainbow American Legion Post voted in November 1945 to install "the best lighting system…at a cost of between $8,000 and $9,000…With installation of lights assured, Rainbow post plans to bring some outstanding baseball attractions here in 1946," proclaimed the *Nonpareil*. "It is probable that clubs in both the American and National Negro leagues will play some of their official league games here during the summer."[44]

Their effort to bring in fans after installing the new lighting system was rewarded in July 1946. "Indianapolis Clowns defeated Kansas City Monarchs 9 to 6 in a Negro American league ball game at American Legion park here Tuesday night before a crowd of 4,000, by far the largest of the season," crowed the game recap in the *Nonpareil*. The Monarch's lineup was still stocked with many future Hall of Famers, including pitcher Hilton Smith. However, on this particular day Smith played right field. He went 2-for-5, and barely missed hitting a game-tying three-run homer in the bottom of the ninth.[45]

The Monarchs returned to Council Bluffs in the spring of 1947 and were shut out on three hits by the Chicago American Giants despite a roster that included Willard Brown and Henry Thompson—who would be signed by the St. Louis Browns later that season.[46] The Indianapolis Clowns brought their legendary antics back to the Bluffs in August and an overflow crowd of 4,079 saw them fall to the Monarchs, 9–5.[47]

In their final season as a major league-caliber team, the Kansas City Monarchs split the two official Negro American League games they played in Council Bluffs.[48] But a national story involving their legendary pitcher, Satchel Paige, dominated the headlines. Although nominally a Kansas City Monarch from 1935–36 and 1939–48, in his final years affiliated with the Monarchs, Paige mainly barnstormed on his own, primarily with his Satchel Paige All-Stars. While his old team was losing to their archrivals, the Chicago American Giants, in Council Bluffs on July 7, 1948, "Leroy (Satchel) Paige, 39-year-old [sic] top-flight negro pitcher of 20 years standing, today was signed by the Cleveland Indians, President Bill Veeck announced. Terms of the deal in which the venerable hurler moves up from the Kansas City Monarchs of the Negro National league were not disclosed. But Paige admits he will make more money with the Indians."[49,50]

Sioux City hosted at least two official games. After playing against each other in Des Moines on July 7, 1939, the Kansas City Monarchs and the St. Louis Stars faced off again three days later at Stock Yard Ball Park in Sioux City. An ad for the game incorrectly identified the Stars as the Giants and that both teams were members of the Colored National League.[51] The Monarchs scored a single tally in the bottom of the eighth on a pair of doubles to win the game, 1–0.[52]

Eight years later, the Monarchs and the Indianapolis Clowns met in Sioux City the day before they took the 90-mile trip down to Council Bluffs for a game. The *Sioux City Journal* helped sell the attraction by emphasizing the "brilliant record" of the Monarchs

along with the endorsement that "The Clowns claim to have two of the funniest men in baseball—King Tut and Goose Tatum. Tut is the No. 1 cutter-upper and Clown fans declare that laughter could be heard for blocks around Blues stadium (Kansas City) when the Clowns and Monarchs played."[53] The next day's newspaper reported, "Kansas City's Monarchs defeated the Indianapolis Clowns, 4 to 1, Monday night in a Negro American league game played at Soos park before a crowd of about 4,000 fans."[54]

Charles City, a community with a population of approximately 8,000, hosted what is now an official major league game in 1939. "Negro Aces to Play in Tuesday Night Game on Lion Field" read the headline of the preview article. "The strong Crawfords took a doubleheader from the Kansas City Monarchs Sunday, and will feature the slugging of Oscar Charleston, husky outfield ace."[55]

"The fans assembled last night, one of the largest crowds of the season, enjoyed their money's worth." extolled the *Charles City Press*. The Crawfords were trailing 3–1 going into the bottom of the ninth. A double, an error and a single, sandwiched around two outs set the stage for a walk-off home run and a 5–3 win.[56]

The historic game in Dyersville, Iowa, in 2021 between the Chicago White Sox and the New York Yankees was significant not because it was the first major league game played in Iowa, but because it signified the return of major league baseball to Iowa. By 2022, with a game between the Chicago Cubs and the Cincinnati Reds, the message had changed. "Major League Baseball on Thursday returned to Dyersville, Iowa, the site of the classic movie *Field of Dreams*, for the *Field of Dreams* Game," FoxSports reported. "Last year's matchup between the New York Yankees and Chicago White Sox featured a host of magical moments. Thursday night's game was no different, as the Chicago Cubs and Cincinnati Reds met in a closely fought contest."[57] ■

Notes

1. *Washington Post*, www.washingtonpost.com/sports/2021/08/12/mlb-iowa-field-dreams-game, accessed December 21, 2022.
2. *USA Today*, https://sports.yahoo.com/mlb-field-dreams-game-2021-102502920.html?src=rss, accessed December 21, 2022.
3. *Des Moines Register*, www.desmoinesregister.com/story/sports/baseball/2021/08/08/field-of-dreams-game-mlb-movie-site-dyersville-chicago-white-sox-new-york-yankees-tickets/5467520001, accessed December 21, 2022.
4. John Thorn, tweet of August 21, 2021, https://twitter.com/thorn_john/status/1425441694481330179.
5. MLB. Press release, December 16, 2020. "MLB Officially Designates the Negros Leagues as Major League." MLB.Com, www.mlb.com/press-release/press-release-mlb-officially-designates-the-negro-leagues-as-major-league, accessed December 21, 2022.

6. Retrosheet was founded in 1989 for the purpose of computerizing play-by-play accounts of as many pre-1984 major league games as possible. In January 2021, after the announcement by Major League Baseball elevating seven Negro Leagues to MLB status, Retrosheet is working on documenting official Negro League games starting in 1948 and working back towards the inaugural 1920 season.

7. Tom Thress, telephone interview, January 25, 2023.

8. The last of the seven Negro Leagues recognized by MLB as major league caliber was created in 1937. That league, the Negro American League, included two of the Negro League teams from the original 1920 Negro National League: the Chicago American Giants and the Kansas City Monarchs.

9. "Negro Teams to Play Exhibition in June," *Des Moines Tribune*, May 25, 1926, 21.

10. "Negro Teams to Play Here," *Des Moines Register*, May 16, 1937, 24. Note that throughout the article, the capitalization usage is retained from the original newspaper articles.

11. In his column Sec Taylor incorrectly identified the teams as being members of the Negro National League. A preview story of the game a week later also incorrectly identified the league as the Negro National League. The summary story of the first game played in Iowa finally correctly identified the teams as members of the Negro American League.

12. Sec Taylor, "Negro Stars Play Here," *Des Moines Register*, May 18, 1937, 7.

13. "Negroes Play Contests Here," *Des Moines Register*, May 25, 1937, 8.

14. "Negroes Play Here Tonight," *Des Moines Register*, May 26, 1937, 9.

15. "Barons Defeat Tigers, 8 to 4," *Des Moines Register*, May 28, 1937, 17.

16. "Monarchs to Play Giants," *Des Moines Tribune*, July 21, 1938, 19.

17. Sec Taylor, "Good Baseball Booked," *Des Moines Register*, July 25, 1938, 5.

18. Sec Taylor, "Giants Beat Monarchs, 11–4," *Des Moines Register*, July 29, 1938, 9.

19. "Brown's Bat Lets Monarch Club Win, 11–2," *Des Moines Register*, May 27, 1939, 7.

20. "Stars' Fielding Wins 9–5 Game," *Des Moines Register*, July 8, 1939, 7.

21. "Crack Negro Nines Clash Here Tonight," *Des Moines Register*, July 28, 1939, 9.

22. "Kansas City's Negro Team Beats Chicago," *Des Moines Register*, July 29, 1939, 9.

23. Brad Wilson, "Monarchs Beat Giants, 7–3," *Des Moines Register*, June 11, 1940, 14.

24. "A Robinson To Play Here," *Des Moines Tribune*, July 29, 1947, 12.

25. Bob Thompson, "Monarch Rally Clips Memphis," *Des Moines Register*, June 25, 1948, 18.

26. "Birmingham Black Barons Will Meet Jacksonville Red Caps Here Monday," *Daily Times* (Davenport, Iowa), July 10, 1941, 18.

27. "Birmingham Trips Loop Rivals, 8–3," *Quad-City Times* (Davenport, Iowa), July 15, 1941, 8.

28. Newspaper stories leading up to the game misidentified the team from St. Louis as the St. Louis Blues instead of its correct name, which was the St. Louis Stars.

29. "Monarchs-Blues Game Here to Be League Contest," *Daily Times*, August 7, 1941, 20.

30. Jerry Jurgens, "Stars Rally in Seventh to Nip Monarchs, 7–3," *Daily Times*, August 13, 1941, 28.

31. "Clowns to Meet Memphis Team Here," *Daily Times*, July 15, 1943, 15.

32. "Famed Rocking Chair Catcher of Clowns To Be Here July 20," *Daily Times*, July 16, 1943, 22.

33. Francis M'Wane, "Red Sox Score 4 Runs in Opening Inning; Win 6–1," *Daily Times*, July 21, 1943, 16.

34. "Speed Events on Wednesday Show At Muny Stadium," *Daily Times*, July 31, 1943, 9.

35. Francis McWane, "Clowns Score Three Runs in Seventh to Defeat Black Barons," *Daily Times*, August 5, 1943, 16. (The byline name was spelled differently from the one listed in the July 21, 1943 story, and back to the different spelling in the June 2, 1944 story.)

36. Sam Smith, "Despite Draft, Monarchs Carry On," *Des Moines Tribune*, January 6, 1944, 19.

37. "Another Game," *Quad-City Times*, May 26, 1944, 16.

38. Francis M'Wane, "Monarchs Trim Chicago Negro Team by 9 to 0," *Daily Times*, June 2, 1944, 26.

39. "Negro Stars Here Tuesday For Ball Game," *Daily Times*, August 24, 1945, 24.

40. Joe Posnanski, *The Baseball 100* (New York, NY: Avid Reader Press, 2021), 423. The original quote says Robinson was in Brooklyn signing his contract with the Dodgers, but nothing was signed until October, when he signed his contract with the Montreal Royals, a Dodgers farm club.

41. "Gene Baker Rated as Best Shortstop On Monarchs Since Jackie Robinson; Plays Against Clowns Here May 30th," *Daily Times*, May 18, 1948, 16.

42. James A. Riley, *The Biographical Encyclopedia of The Negro Baseball Leagues* (New York, NY: Carroll & Graf Publishers, Inc., 1994), 46.

43. Retrosheet.org, https://www.retrosheet.org/NegroLeagues/boxe-setc/1948/Bbakeg1011948.htm, accessed December 23, 2022.

44. "Rainbow Post to Arclight Legion Park," *Council Bluffs Nonpareil*, November 15, 1945, 1.

45. "Clowns Beat Monarchs in Long Battle," *Council Bluffs Nonpareil*, July 24, 1946, 10.

46. "Monarchs Held to Three Hits," *Council Bluffs Nonpareil*, May 24, 1947, 7.

47. "Monarchs Defeat Clowns; Overflow Crowd Watches," *Council Bluffs Nonpareil*, August 20, 1947, 9.

48. Retrosheet.org, https://www.retrosheet.org/NegroLeagues/boxesetc/1948/1948GL.htm, accessed December 23, 2022.

49. The Kansas City Monarchs were members of the Negro American League in 1948.

50. "'Ole' Satch Signs With Cleveland As Relief Hurler," *Oelwein Daily Register*, July 7, 1948, 4.

51. "Baseball," *Sioux City Journal*, July 10, 1939, 7.

52. "Monarchs Win Over St. Louis Stars Here, 1–0," *Sioux City Journal*, July 11, 1939, 12.

53. "Negro Teams to Combine Humor and Fast Baseball," *Sioux City Journal*, August 16, 1947, 6.

54. "Clowns Fall To Monarchs," *Sioux City Journal*, August 19, 1947, 10.

55. "Negro Aces to Play in Tuesday Night Game on Lion Field," *Globe-Gazette* (Mason City, Iowa), August 14, 1939, 10.

56. "Large Crowd Watches Fast Negro Teams," *Charles City Press and Evening Intelligencer*, August 16, 1939, 2.

57. FoxSports, www.foxsports.com/stories/mlb/field-of-dreams-game-2022-top-moments-from-cubs-reds, accessed December 21, 2022.

Chicago, Latina Culture, and the Community of Women's Baseball

Emalee Nelson

While baseball's origin story began on the East Coast, the Midwest has been a vital part of the growth of America's pastime. Although a disastrous fire in 1871 temporarily stunted the city's growth, Chicago at the end of the nineteenth century was a growing hub for commerce and culture. As the United States expanded westward, Chicago turned from being a "city out west" to a midway point between the populated Eastern seaboard and the Western frontier. As a result, baseball quickly followed to the Windy City.

Following the Mexican Revolution in the early twentieth century, an influx of immigrants would find refuge in the Midwest, including Chicago and the surrounding area. Eager to build their new lives, Mexican Americans found solace in their Catholic faith and baseball. While many community teams sprang up for young men, a handful of women's teams were created during the 1930s and 1940s. In the years before World War II, local parishes created women's teams as opportunities for young women to gather in a safe environment and play baseball. Following the war, the Great Lakes region—notably Chicago and surrounding areas—would also attract Latina baseball players through the All-American Girls Professional Baseball League. This article will briefly discuss the intersections of women's sport and Latina culture in Chicago-area baseball. In doing so, this article also hopes to continue filling an understudied gap in the historical tapestry of women's baseball.

¡HOLA, CHICAGO!

To understand the importance of women playing baseball in Chicago and surrounding areas, it is crucial to begin with the city's baseball origins. The first club for men was organized in 1856. As with the early teams which formed in New York City, camaraderie and socializing were key aspects of these clubs. Following the Civil War, many Chicagoans looked to the sport as a premier avenue for physical recreation and fellowship. Tournaments held in the city attracted teams from nearby areas such as Detroit, Bloomington, Rockford, Milwaukee, and Freeport.

Unfortunately, these games didn't include all of the area's best players, because these teams, such as the Excelsior Club and the Chicago Base Ball Club, largely consisted of only White men. Even in a northern region which collectively mourned the assassination of their homegrown president—the man who delivered the Emancipation Proclamation—racially exclusionary practices were the norm in Chicago. This was evident in 1870 when a Black ball club known as the Blue Stockings was excluded from an amateur city tournament. Although the Blue Stockings would go on to become quite successful in the "colored" circuit of competition—even traveling to a handful of East Coast cities—a prominent theme was evident in Chicago baseball. In short, race mattered.

However, race was not a binary issue of Black or White during a time of increased Latino immigration. The Mexican Revolution was a violent conflict that was drawn out for nearly a decade between 1910 and 1920. Many Mexicans fled the fighting for the prospect of a more peaceful life. The Midwest was an enticing destination for them, and Mexican presence served as a sort of buffer in the middle of the racial divide. Segregation was becoming fully entrenched in the early twentieth century, even in northern cities, with baseball itself became increasingly segregated from the late nineteenth into the early twentieth century. Although professional teams affiliated with the American and National Leagues held to the "gentlemen's agreement" which excluded Black players from joining, certain Latino players were able to cross this color line.

Segregation throughout league-affiliated baseball in the United States did not discourage non-White athletes from picking up bats and gloves. Many of Chicago's first baseball fields were built around rail lines. Given that the railroad industry was a popular source of employment for many Mexican immigrants, America's pastime soon spread to these communities of new citizens. Given the popularity of the sport and the relative ease with which one could find a field and makeshift equipment, baseball helped these young immigrants prove their American-ness, while imitating a familiar memory of playing on teams in the barrios of their homeland.

FATHER, SON, AND HOLY SWING

Though it was a recreational pastime, baseball was crucial in fostering a strong sense of ethnic identity and pride within migrant communities. So was church-going, and places of worship were another space where Mexican immigrant families could congregate to create a sense of community and belonging in their new country. Catholic churches played a pivotal role in the formation of Mexican community sports teams, especially for youth. Young players were encouraged to participate for their physical health, but also their parents sought the positive impact teamwork and camaraderie could have on their children.

These teams were not just available for young boys in Chicago; teams for girls and women were formed, as well. One such was Las Gallinas, which emerged as a team affiliated with Our Lady of Guadalupe, a Catholic church in East Chicago, Indiana. Such women's teams were usually managed by all-male staff. The women's teams would often play on a field nearby where the men's teams were playing at the same time. Sometimes, the women would play in the morning and the men in the afternoon. The men's and women's teams would often travel together. This was evident with Las Gallinas (The Hens), the lady counterpart to Los Gallos (The Roosters). The church provided the equipment, the uniforms, and even a (male) coach for Las Gallinas. Frederick Maravila was the team manager of Las Gallinas during the 1937 season, but also played on the men's baseball team. Almost all the girls had some sort of affiliation with the church, according to Gloria Guerrero Fraire, a former player for Las Gallinas. Amidst the competitive spirit, religious tones of modesty were evident. Fraire recalls, "You could tell from the uniforms that the sisters wanted them to dress modestly. No shorts, and limbs were covered." This sentiment furthered the notion of religious influence and importance within the larger Mexican immigrant culture.

Fraire continues, "We used to play and then the Gallos used to play. It was a big festival day. Everybody would go out there and watch us play baseball... So with two games, it was a long day. Lots of people would take their sandwiches and tacos." Her teammate, Carol Garcia Martinez, also remembers, "Some young women were active in all types of sports in school. We formed community teams because we enjoyed sports. Most of our parents were supportive as long as our older brothers and male friends were watching over

us. We played nine innings and basically played by the same rules as the men. Our games were extremely competitive." These women were pioneers in their time during the 1930s and 1940s, often becoming some of the first girls to compete in varsity sports at their local high school, years before Title IX. The women were talented, deserving athletes, sometimes drawing crowds of a few hundred to their games.

Both men's and women's teams often had the responsibility to promote themselves and to find teams to barnstorm against. They would feature themselves in local newspapers to try to find a worthy competitor. Las Gallinas would play against teams in South Chicago, Whiting, Gary, and Hessville, indicating they would travel, but mostly within the state. Word of mouth remained the best method to find an opponent.

Surprisingly, most of the women playing were in their teenage years, not yet adults. This made them first generation Mexican Americans, rather than immigrants from Mexico like their parents. These parents made sure the girls were on time for all games and practice, implying that they were supportive of these young women playing baseball. This was quite opposite of the usual stigma associated with women participating in sport, especially a physically demanding sport like baseball. Furthermore, parents were supportive of their children joining sport teams because it gave them useful skills to be utilized in the political arena and fight for social justice.

A CUBAN CATCH

Although many of these smaller, church-affiliated teams folded during the wartime years, Latina presence would return to Chicago ballfields following World War II. During the war years, the All-American Girls Professional Baseball League (AAGPBL) was the creation of Chicago-based business magnates Philip Wrigley and Arthur Meyerhoff. The first teams called cities in the Great Lakes region their homes. After a handful of successful years, the AAGPBL expanded their efforts by creating a barnstorming tour outside of the Midwest to expand their fanbase, while also attracting the more talent. Before the 1947 season, the league held spring training in Havana, Cuba.

The AAGPBL teams played a series of exhibition games against each other while in Cuba, but also played a team of the best Cuban women baseball players. This proved to be top notch entertainment on the Caribbean island, since the women's games out-drew the crowds of the men's teams also training in Cuba, notably the Brooklyn Dodgers and their up-and-coming phenom Jackie Robinson. Wrigley and Meyerhoff used

LAS GALLINAS IN 1938
Back Row (L to R)
Manuel Vega (Coach), Unknown man,
Esther Ramirez, Juanita Cruz,
Loreto Torres, Ramon Ramirez (Coach)
and Fred Maravilla (Manager)

Middle Row (L to R)
Helen Aguirre, Carole Garcia,
Petra Gonzales, Petra Godoy and
Nena Bonilla

Front Row (L to R)
Frances Vela, Sally Gonzalez,
Bertha Munoz and Gloria Guerrero

these exhibitions to scout additional talent to join the league. As a result, a handful of Cuban women signed contracts and packed their bags for the United States.

While this was an unprecedented opportunity to play professional baseball, these women understood the significance of departing a country on the verge of turmoil. Similar to those only a few decades prior escaping the turbulent Mexican Revolution, the Midwest provided a haven of opportunity. Isabel Alvarez, who played for the Fort Wayne Daisies and other teams, recalls, "I left home tired and tense from all the endless preparations and from all the warnings about my safety in Communist country." Yet, Alvarez and her Cuban league-mates found a community of solidarity in sport.

Migdalia "Mickey" Perez bounced around between Chicago, Springfield, and Battle Creek before landing with the Rockford Peaches from 1952 through 1954. She was known for being a savvy, skillful utility player and pitcher, who "used a hole in a back fence as her pitching target and was never satisfied until she could hurl ten balls in a row without missing." While growing up in Cuba, she studied English and became the "official translator and foster mother of the other Cuban girls." During her time in Rockford, she met James Jinright, the groundskeeper for the Peaches. The pair tied the knot in July 1952, eventually residing in Florida until she passed away in October 2019.

However, when Mickey was not present, the language barrier did materialize. Ysora Castillo Kinney left Cuba when she was still a teenager to play for the Chicago Colleens in 1947. During the 1950 season, she

played for the Kalamazoo Lassies, and was kicked out of a game for talking back to an umpire in Spanish. She hardly remembers the incident. Instead, she recalls in an interview with *Huffington Post Miami*, "I said something I wasn't supposed to say. I don't remember. I was real happy all the time, and I was yelling all the time." The *Daily Oklahoman* referred to Castillo-Kinney as "the pretty Cuban third-baseman…[who] does not speak English, but she is a Spanish pepperpot once the game gets underway." With this spirited persona, she would serenade audiences in her native language, notably a Spanish rendition of "Yours (Quiéreme Mucho)" prior to a July 1949 scrimmage between the Springfield Sallies and Chicago Colleens in Austin, Texas.

In 1950, Isabel Alvarez was traded after the season from the Colleens to the Fort Wayne Daisies. Professionally for Alvarez, this was an upgrade, as the Daisies were a full-fledged league team, as opposed to the rookie-level touring Colleens. Unfortunately for Alvarez, none of her Cuban teammates were traded with her. She recalls her transition: "I was alone in Fort Wayne. Sometimes when you can't communicate, you feel maybe [others] don't want you around. Everyone has a clique, they run around in groups." In addition to feeling socially isolated, Alvarez believed the language barrier also inhibited her ability as a baseball player given her immense difficulty communicating with her new teammates.

These feelings of loneliness and isolation were not unique to this small group of Cuban women. "Indeed, the cultural chasm between U.S. and Latin societies, which included historical, religious, ethnic, and language differences was formidable and sometimes impassible." Even the most successful of players, male or female, were subject to discouragement, even questioning their purpose for playing baseball in the United States. For Alvarez, the homesickness was evident, and she returned to Cuba following the season. By then she had been in the league for two years but was just seventeen years old. At home, she told her mother of her difficulties communicating with her new teammates. She was sad and discouraged. Her mother, who had urged Alvarez to join the league two years prior, reminded her "[she] had to do her job and forget about Cuba." To her mother's happiness, she did return to Fort Wayne for the 1951 campaign.

Awaiting Alvarez in Fort Wayne for the 1951 season was sixteen-year-old Catherine "Katie" Horstman, the newest member of the Daisies. In an interview many years later, Katie laughingly recalled a particular encounter with her new teammate. "When I first started with Fort Wayne in 1951, I pitched a lot of batting practice. The very first girl I met spoke Spanish. It was Isabel Alvarez, who was Cuban. I thought, 'They've got Cubans on their team. I live sixty-five miles from Fort Wayne, and I never even heard of women's pro baseball!'"

CONCLUSION

While Chicago's baseball historical tapestry is typically represented by the ivy-covered walls of Wrigley and the 1919 Black Sox scandal, it is important to acknowledge that the city and surrounding area is home to many lively sporting histories on smaller sandlots. Immigration and the Manifest Destiny narrative are essential pieces of America's nineteenth century—and so is baseball. The promises of freedom and opportunity attracted migrants from all corners of the world eager to vie for a chance at the American dream. If any sport could embody this desire, baseball proved to be the perfect vehicle to celebrate new opportunity and build community pride. ■

Notes

1. Peter Morris, *Baseball Pioneers: 1850–1870*, "Excelsiors of Chicago, Prewar" (Jefferson, North Carolina, and London: McFarland & Company Inc., 2012).
2. Brian McKenna, "Sputtering Towards Respectability: Chicago's Journey to the Big Leagues," in *The National Pastime: Baseball in Chicago*, Society for American Baseball Research, 2015, https://sabr.org/journal/article/sputtering-towards-respectability-chicagos-journey-to-the-big-leagues. Accessed June 11, 2023.
3. McKenna, "Sputtering Towards Respectability: Chicago's Journey to the Big Leagues;" see also *Chicago Tribune*, September 17, 1870.
4. Adrian Burgos, *Playing America's Game: Baseball, Latinos, and the Color Line* (Berkeley: University of California Press, 2007).
5. McKenna, "Sputtering Towards Respectability: Chicago's Journey to the Big Leagues."
6. Richard Santillán, Gene T. Chávez, Rod Martínez, et. al., *Mexican American Baseball in Kansas City* (Charleston, South Carolina: Arcadia Publishing, 2018), 25.
7. East Chicago is aptly named, located so near to Chicago, Illinois, today it takes less than half an hour to drive from the site of the old Comiskey Park to Our Lady of Guadalupe. See Google Maps https://www.google.com/maps/dir/Our+Lady+of+Guadalupe+Church,+Deodar+Street,+East+Chicago,+Indiana/Guaranteed+Rate+Field,+333+W+35th+St,+Chicago,+IL+60616.
8. John Fraire. "Mexicans Playing Baseball in Indiana Harbor, 1925–1942." *Indiana Magazine of History* 110, no. 2 (2014): 120–45. https://doi.org/10.5378/indimagahist.110.2.0120.
9. Santillán, et al, 66.
10. Santillán, et al, 66.
11. Fraire, 136.
12. John Fraire. "Mexicans Playing Baseball."
13. John Fraire. "Mexicans Playing Baseball."
14. John Fraire. "Mexicans Playing Baseball."
15. Santillán, et al, 150.
16. John Fraire. "Mexicans Playing Baseball."
17. Meaghann Campbell, #Shortstops: Spring Training in Cuba, National Baseball Hall of Fame, Accessed June 4, 2023, https://baseballhall.org/discover/shortstops/spring-training%20in%20Cuba.
18. Terry Doran, "In Cuba, people are important," *Fort Wayne Journal Gazette*, April 28, 1996.
19. For a comprehensive summary of Isabel Alvarez's life, see Kat Williams's *Isabel "Lefty" Álvarez: The Improbable Life of a Cuban American Baseball Star* (Lincoln: University of Nebraska Press, 2020).
20. All-American Girls Professional Baseball League, "Migdalia Perez" Press Release, 1950.
21. "Migdalia Perez" Press Release, 1950.
22. W.C. Madden, *The Women of the AAGPBL: A Biographical Dictionary* (Jefferson, NC: McFarland & Co., 1997), 192.
23. Christiana Lilly, "Ysora Kinney, 79-Year-Old Hospital Volunteer, Talks Pioneering Past in Women's Baseball," *Huffington Post Miami*, May 9, 2012, accessed March 18, 2016, http://www.huffingtonpost.com/2012/04/04/ysora-kinney-womens-baseball_n_1403283.html. Accessed June 11, 2023.
24. Wally Wallis, "These Gals Expert at Running Bases," *Daily Oklahoman*, 1949.
25. "Colleens and Sallies Steam Up For Final Thriller Here Tonight," *Austin American*, July 8, 1949.
26. Marilyn Cohen, *No Women in the Clubhouse* (Jefferson, North Carolina: McFarland & Company, 2009), 67.
27. Samuel Regalado, *Viva Baseball: Latin Major Leaguers and Their Special Hunger* (Urbana: University of Illinois Press, 1998) 93.
28. Regalado, *Viva Baseball*.
29. Jim Sargent, *We Were the All-American Girls; Interviews with Players of the AAGPBL, 1943–1954* (Jefferson, NC: McFarland & Company, Inc., 2013) 15.

Hack Wilson: Pugilist

John Racanelli

"During his career in Chicago, Hack [Wilson] has indulged in four fistic encounters. All of the battles have tended to increase his popularity. Most ballplayers would be called rowdies or hoodlums for such outbreaks, but there is something about Hack's gladiatorial foray that makes the folks cheer instead of condemn. That is, folks who have not been targets for the pudgy one's onslaught."

—Edward Burns[1]

Unthinkably, just a year removed from hitting 56 home runs and knocking in 191 runs, Cubs outfielder Hack Wilson was persona non grata in Chicago. Thanks to a mediocre 1931 campaign and a season-ending suspension in September, he and pitcher Bud Teachout were traded to the Cardinals for 38-year-old spitballer Burleigh Grimes in December.[2] Wilson, however, was insulted by St. Louis's salary offer and refused to sign.[3] The Cardinals shipped him to Brooklyn in January, where he settled for $16,500 (approximately $360,000 today)—precisely half of his 1931 salary with the Cubs.[4] Determined to show he was still a valuable Major League slugger, Wilson found himself fighting for his career. But Hack Wilson was no stranger to a fight.

A MILKMAN GETS CREAMED

Near the end of an afternoon doubleheader at Wrigley Field on June 21, 1928, Hack Wilson grounded out to second base. Edward Young heckled Wilson from the grandstand, "When'll you bench yourself, you fat so and so!?"[5] Wilson did not appreciate the unsolicited advice and leapt into the stands where he reportedly "thump[ed] Mr. Young soundly before other players pulled him off."[6] Young claimed two other Cubs, Gabby Hartnett and Joe Kelly, also took some jabs at him during the melee despite having "ostensibly entered the box as peacemakers."[7]

Young, a milk wagon driver, was arrested for having incited a riot and pled guilty to a charge of disorderly conduct.[8] Wilson did not face criminal charges but was fined $100 by National League president John Heydler for "conduct unbecoming a ballplayer."[9]

On July 25, Young filed a personal injury lawsuit against the Cubs and Wilson, alleging, somewhat ironically, that the Cubs owed a duty to protect him against "disorderly persons" so he might "peacefully enjoy the game."[10] He sought damages of $50,000 (approximately $855,000 today) but would have to be patient for his day in court.[11]

FIREWORKS ON INDEPENDENCE DAY

The Cubs hosted the Reds for a doubleheader on July 4, 1929. In the fifth inning of the second game, Hack Wilson rapped a seemingly ordinary single off Pete Donohue. As Wilson stood at first base, Reds pitcher Ray Kolp ridiculed him with taunts of "bastard" and dared him to come into the dugout.[12,13] Wilson obliged—fists flying. He landed a blow on Kolp's jaw that even the Reds' hometown paper called a "neat piece of work."[14]

Once order was restored, Wilson and Kolp were ejected. Donohue, tagged for four earned runs in four innings, got the hook—but it would not be the last time he was roughed up that day. The Cubs and Reds gathered at Chicago's Union Station to catch the (same) train that would take the Cubs east to Boston and Reds to Pittsburgh, and the teams mingled near the gate. Still fuming, Wilson warned he was going to "make Kolp apologize."[15] Kolp, however, had arrived early and had "retired immediately to the privacy of his Pullman."[16]

As Wilson was talking peacefully with Reds pitcher Jakie May, Donohue butted in, "You're quite a scrapper, aren't you? If you want any more, come into our car."[17,18] Wilson saw no reason to wait, and popped Donohue where he stood, knocking him to ground. Members of both teams jumped in to pull the men apart and railroad officials diplomatically separated the teams into different sections of the train.

Wilson was unapologetic afterwards, "I'm no Dempsey, but when anyone says I'm yellow I am going to try to show 'em they're wrong. Kolp thought I wouldn't take his dare to come into the dugout after him Thursday. He didn't want to fight. He just wanted to make a little noise."[19] Wilson was fined $100 and suspended for three days by the National League. However, club president William Veeck took no disciplinary action against Wilson, whom he considered a "gentleman and conscientious baseball player."[20] Veeck added, "Boys will be boys, you know."[21]

THE MILKMAN RETURNS FOR ROUND TWO

When Edward Young's lawsuit was dismissed in October 1929 on procedural grounds, the Cubs and Hack Wilson likely felt some sense of relief. However, Young's attorney acted quickly to reinstate the matter. An amended complaint was filed in November in

Hack Wilson (left) pictured with Babe Herman.

which Young's claims against the Cubs were dropped. The revised pleading named Hack Wilson as the sole defendant and reduced the ad damnum to $20,000 (approximately $350,000 today).[22]

Wilson's response to the amended complaint included a plea of *son assault demesne*, in which Wilson claimed that if Young had been injured in the altercation, Wilson had acted in self-defense—an awfully creative theory considering Wilson and several other Cubs had crossed into the grandstand to confront Young.[23]

HACK WILSON: PROFESSIONAL PRIZEFIGHTER?

On December 14, 1929, news broke that Hack Wilson had agreed to face White Sox first baseman Art "The Great" Shires in a four-round fight. The bout would pay Wilson a guaranteed $10,000 and training expenses.[24] He finally appeared poised to cash in on his pugilistic prowess, which had brought him "nothing but fines and suspensions," plus pending civil litigation up to this point.[25]

Art Shires' amateur "record" included a pair of fistfights with his White Sox manager, Lena Blackburne, during the 1929 season.[26] Shires also had an official professional bout under his belt, having knocked out "Dangerous" Dan Daly in 21 seconds—a fight that ultimately brought Shires a suspension by the National Boxing Association due to accusations it had been fixed.[27,28]

Shires ridiculed Wilson for having lost a ball or two in the sun during the 1929 World Series, "Hack will think he is looking into the sun again, when I start throwing them at him. The fact he belongs to the National League, which really is a minor league, doesn't prod my Major League pride."[29] Even Ray Kolp weighed in on the Wilson-Shires saga, "Hack is a pushover for me any way you take it. He can't get a hit off my pitching in a month, and he wouldn't do any better with his fists."[30]

In a match billed as a tune up for the Wilson bout, Shires squared off against Chicago Bears center George Trafton on December 16. Trafton knocked Shires down twice in the first round and again in the second. The remainder of the five-round fight exposed the pair for their lack of conditioning, and Trafton eventually won by decision. Following Shires' embarrassing loss, Wilson decided to pass on the fight, "if Shires had beaten Trafton I might have gone to Chicago and tried to talk president Veeck of the Cubs into letting me go through with it. But there is no use in bucking the Cubs and making my wife mad just to floor a guy who has already been licked."[31]

Regardless, Art Shires kept fighting.[32] On January 10, 1930, Shires scored a four-round technical knockout against Braves catcher Al Spohrer in Boston. Following his victory, Shires bellowed, "I didn't want Al Spohrer. I wanted Hack Wilson!" to the 18,000 fans in attendance.[33]

"I want Shires twice as bad as he wants me," Wilson replied as he reconsidered travelling to Chicago to plead for the Cubs' blessing to pursue the fight.[34] That Wilson's guarantee had been increased to $15,000 (nearly $270,000 today) may have also played a factor.[35]

National League president Heydler weighed in on the matter, "We don't want to interfere with the off-season activities of our men any more than we can help, but when these activities threaten our investment in the man and the man, himself, it is time to call a halt...it has taken them so long to get where they are and yet they want to jeopardize this position for a few dollars."[36] This was rich, considering Wilson's expected payday nearly equaled his $16,000 salary for 1929. On January 25, however, Judge Kenesaw Mountain Landis dealt the death blow to any potential Wilson-Shires match, "Hereafter any person connected with any club in this organization who engages in professional boxing will be regarded by this office as having permanently retired from baseball. The two activities do not mix."[37] Though the Shires fight (and payday) was no longer in the cards for Wilson, he still had one battle to attend to before leaving for spring training at Catalina Island.

THE MILKMAN (FINALLY) HAS HIS DAY IN COURT

Trial in the case of *Edward Young v. Hack Wilson* was called on February 11, 1930, in front of Superior Court Judge William Fulton and a twelve-man jury in Chicago. Wilson seemed unconcerned, "It'll be a surprise if he wins the suit and an even bigger surprise if he collects it."[38]

When it finally came time for Young to testify, he admitted he heckled Wilson, "You big tub! Why don't you bench yourself?"[39] Wilson then leapt into the stands, knocked him down, and tossed him over a seat. As a result of the attack, Young suffered facial injuries requiring stitches and back pain so severe he was unable to work for several weeks.[40] Young, however, confessed that he had consumed a "few seidels of beer" (while Prohibition was in full swing), and—under examination by his own attorney—admitted he "could not say whether [he] was drunk or sober at the time."[41,42]

Hack Wilson took the stand and testified, "the vile names [Young] shouted at me were unbearable and

Hack Wilson trains in his basement at Martinsburg, West Virginia, January 1932. Wire services ran this photo with the caption "Hack emulates a pugilist."

my fighting blood naturally reached a boiling point, but I did not hit him."[43] Instead, Wilson described how he fell en route to confronting Young when his spikes slipped on the concrete—and that it was Young who actually lunged at and landed on top of him.[44] Seven witnesses testified for the defense, including Gabby Hartnett, each of whom corroborated Wilson's version of events.

The trial lasted five hours and a courtroom packed with baseball fans heard Wilson portrayed alternately as a "240-pound wild animal charging into baseball boxes" and as a "peace loving citizen."[45] It took the jury just 25 minutes to side with Wilson.[46] If the Young case had weighed on Wilson at all, he was now free to embark on the most amazing season he would ever have.

TOP OF THE WORLD

Hack Wilson put together a season for the ages in 1930. With 56 home runs, he set a National League record that would stand for 68 years. He was the second player ever to hit more than 50 in a season, after Babe Ruth. Wilson slashed .356/.454/.723 and led the NL with 105 walks. He is probably best remembered, however, for knocking in 191 runs, a major league record that still stands today—and may never be broken.

If a National League MVP Award had been presented in 1930, Wilson would have won. The same committee of the Baseball Writers' Association of America that bestowed NL MVP honors on Wilson's teammate Rogers Hornsby in 1929 conducted a vote following the 1930 season. Hack Wilson edged out Cardinals second baseman Frankie Frisch by six votes, 70–64.[47] Unfortunately for Wilson, the NL had abandoned the award (and the $1000 prize) following the vote in 1929 so his win is not officially recognized.[48]

PERSONA NON GRATA

In spring training in 1931, Cubs player-manager Rogers Hornsby announced Wilson would be moved from center field (the only position he had ever played as a Cub) to right field so that Kiki Cuyler could play center. The NL also introduced a new ball with raised stitches and a thicker cover, hoping to shift some balance back to the pitchers.[49]

Whether his fall from grace for the Cubs in 1931 (.261/.362/.435, 13 home runs) resulted from being forced to change positions, the new baseball, nighttime galivanting, or some combination thereof, Wilson thoroughly destroyed the goodwill he had earned as a Cub from 1926 through his triumphant 1930 season. In those five seasons, Wilson led the NL in home runs four times, runs batted in twice, and walks twice. His 1.177 OPS in 1930 is still a Cubs record.

On September 1, 1931, club owner William Wrigley Jr. declared, "I hope Hack Wilson is not in a Cub uniform next year."[50] That same day, it was revealed the Phillies had spurned an offer of "$150,000, Hack Wilson, and two other players" in exchange for Chuck Klein.[51] Days later, reports surfaced that the Cubs had offered to trade Wilson to the American Association Milwaukee Brewers—for Art Shires—but were rejected.[52]

The Cubs had hired private detectives to tail Wilson (and pitcher Pat Malone) to verify whether they were complying with curfew rules. The pair was caught breaking training on September 3 in Cincinnati. The next day, Hornsby started pitcher Bud Teachout in right field instead of Wilson.

Before the team returned from Cincinnati to Chicago on September 5, Hornsby instructed Wilson to report to Veeck the next morning, but would not tell him why.[53] While at the train station that same night, Malone got into a fight with a pair of mouthy reporters in Wilson's presence. Apparently, tensions were so high Hornsby would not disembark the train once back in Chicago until provided with a "special bodyguard."[54]

On September 6, Cubs management presented Wilson with evidence of numerous curfew infractions dating back to spring training, and then—ironically—condemned him for not getting involved the Malone fight. Wilson was suspended without pay for the remainder of the season. For his "disorderly conduct and roistering," aggressor Malone was fined, but not suspended.[55]

Wilson was nonplussed, "All I know is that when I did something wrong when Joe McCarthy was manager of the team, he told me to cut it out, and when I did anything wrong this year, Hornsby told me to report to the front office and they always plastered a big fine on me."[56] Unceremoniously, Hack's Cubs career was over.

FIGHTING FOR HIS CAREER

Motivated to prove he was still a valuable slugger, Wilson trained in his Martinsburg, West Virginia, basement prior to the 1932. It worked: Wilson had a resurgent 1932 season as the starting right fielder for the Brooklyn Dodgers, slashing .297/.366/.538 with 23 home runs and 123 RBIs. Sadly, 1932 would be his last truly productive major league season.

Wilson's final start in a big-league uniform came as a member of the Phillies at Wrigley Field on August 18, 1934. He struck out twice and grounded into a double play in three at-bats off his old pal Pat Malone. When asked in 1938 if he would have done anything differently if given an opportunity to do all over, Wilson replied, "I wouldn't change one minute of it—not a single minute."[57] ∎

Notes

1. Edward Burns, "Who Are These Cubs?," *Omaha World-Herald*, September 19, 1929. (The first of the "fistic encounters" recounted by Burns involved Wilson's arrest on May 23, 1926, at a Chicago speakeasy where Wilson challenged the arresting officers and claimed he was present simply to sign autographs. Others reported Wilson was nabbed trying to climb out a back window and that the tip for the raid actually came from Cubs management. Wilson was arraigned on a charge of disorderly conduct and ordered to buy a $1 charity tag as punishment.)
2. "Even in Death, Hack's Record Grows," *The* (Moline) *Dispatch*, June 23, 1999. Wilson's RBI total was reported as 190 throughout his lifetime, until it was officially changed to 191 in 1999.
3. Bud Teachout pitched a single inning for St. Louis in 1932. Hack Wilson hit his first career major league home run off Burleigh Grimes on June 25, 1924.
4. "Wilson Refuses Cards' $7500 Contract," *Chicago Tribune*, January 9, 1932. (Wilson's 1931 salary with the Cubs was $33,000. Cardinals general manager Branch Rickey offered $7500.)
5. Edward Burns, "Hack Wilson Attacks Fan as Cubs and Cards Divide," *Chicago Tribune*, June 22, 1928.
6. Burns.
7. Burns.
8. "Sues Slugger for Slugging Him," *Belvidere* (Illinois) *Daily Republican*, July 25, 1928.
9. "Chicago Fan Loses Razzberry Rights," *Reading* (Pennsylvania) *Times*, June 25, 1928.

10. *Edward Young v. Chicago National League Ball Club*, Case No. 481272, Complaint, Cook County Superior Court, 1928.
11. https://www.usinflationcalculator.com used for all such calculations throughout.
12. Clifton Blue Parker, *Fouled Away* (Jefferson, North Carolina: McFarland & Company, Inc., 2000), 74. (Wilson was born to unmarried parents.)
13. "Hack Wilson as Pugilist Has Big Day," *Chicago Tribune*, July 5, 1929.
14. "First Tilt," *Cincinnati Enquirer*, July 5, 1929.
15. "Hack Wilson as Pugilist Has Big Day," *Chicago Tribune*, July 5, 1929.
16. Irving Vaughan, "Warns Reds He's Set to Fight Again," *Chicago Tribune*, July 6, 1929.
17. Vaughan.
18. "Hack Wilson Adds Two Fights to List," *Alton* (Illinois) *Evening Telegraph*, July 5, 1929.
19. "Hack Wilson Anxious for Return Bout," *Omaha World-Herald*, July 6, 1929.
20. "Cubs Will Back Hack Wilson," *Wilkes-Barre* (Pennsylvania) *Record*, July 6, 1929.
21. "Hack Wilson Adds Two Fights to List," *Alton* (Illinois) *Evening Telegraph*, July 5, 1929.
22. *Edward Young v. Chicago National League Ball Club*, Amended Declaration, 1929. (No explanation for dismissing the Chicago National League Ball Club was given.)
23. *Edward Young v. Chicago National League Ball Club*, Plea of General Issue, 1929.
24. William Weekes, "Cub Outfielder to Get $10,000 for Short Bout," *The* (Moline) *Dispatch*, December 14, 1929.
25. William Weekes, "Great Shires to Meet Sunny Boy Wilson in Arena," *Freeport* (Illinois) *Journal-Standard*, December 14, 1929.
26. On May 15, 1929, Shires and Blackburne faced off in the White Sox clubhouse because Shires got lippy after being told he should not have donned a fashionable "red felt cap" during pre-game batting practice. Irving Vaughan, "Fight Follows Suspension of White Sox Star," *Chicago Tribune*, May 16, 1929. The pair came to blows again following a White Sox loss in Philadelphia on September 13, 1929 when Shires "almost chewed [White Sox] Traveling Secretary Lou Barbour's finger off and blackened manager Lena Blackburne's eyes" in an altercation in Shires' hotel room. "Police Called When Sox Star Runs Amuck," *Chicago Tribune*, September 14, 1929.
27. William Weekes, "Great Shires to Meet Sunny Boy Wilson in Arena," *Freeport* (Illinois) *Journal-Standard*, December 14, 1929.
28. "Baseball Star Now Under Ban in All States," *Detroit Free Press*, January 8, 1930.
29. William Weekes, "Hack Wilson is Signed for Four-Round Match with the Great Shires," *Chippewa Herald-Telegram* (Chippewa Falls, Wisconsin), December 14, 1929.
30. Tom Swope, "Kolp Ready to Fight 'Em All," *Cincinnati Post*, December 17, 1929. (In 71 career plate appearances, Wilson hit .259/.394/.500 against Kolp, with 13 walks and 4 home runs.)
31. "Hack Wilson Will Not Fight Shires," *Sterling* (Illinois) *Daily Gazette*, December 17, 1929.
32. "First Baseman Signs to Box 'Hack' Wilson," *Tampa Times*, December 14, 1929.
33. "Shires May Engage in One More Fight," *Rock Island* (Illinois) *Argus*, January 11, 1930.
34. "Wilson Aroused Seeking Permit to Fight Shires," *Freeport* (Illinois) *Journal-Standard*, January 13, 1930.
35. "Hack Aroused by Shires' Remarks," *The* (Moline) *Dispatch*, January 13, 1930.
36. Davis Walsh, "Clubs Aim to Stop Players from Boxing," *The* (Streator, Illinois) *Times*, January 14, 1930.
37. "Landis and Shires," *Collyer's Eye* (Chicago, Illinois) January 25, 1930.
38. "'Hack' Wilson Faces Court Case Today in Chicago," *Pittsburgh Press*, February 11, 1930.
39. "Tells Jury of Hack Wilson's Attack on Him," *Belvidere* (Illinois) *Daily Republican*, February 11, 1930.
40. "$20,000 Claim Filed by Bruin Fan Dismissed," *The* (Moline, Illinois) *Dispatch*, February 12, 1930.
41. Irving Vaughan, "Jury Unmoved by Milkman's Story of Fight," *Chicago Tribune*, February 12, 1930.
42. Paul Mickelson, "Wilson is Cleared on Assault Charge," *Nebraska State Journal* (Lincoln, Nebraska) February 12, 1930.
43. "$20,000 Claim Filed by Bruin Fan Dismissed," *The* (Moline, Illinois) *Dispatch*, February 12, 1930.
44. Irving Vaughan, "Jury Unmoved by Milkman's Story of Fight," *Chicago Tribune*, February 12, 1930.
45. Paul Mickelson, "Wilson is Cleared on Assault Charge," *Nebraska State Journal* (Lincoln, Nebraska) February 12, 1930. (After the verdict was entered, Wilson quipped, "The only crack I didn't like was that about being a 240-pound wild animal, if the Cubs think I weigh 240 pounds, they will make me carry bats.")
46. "Hack Wilson Given Verdict in Damage Suit with Milkman," *Corsicana* (Texas) *Daily Sun*, February 12, 1930.
47. "1930 Home Run King is Voted 'Most Valuable'," *Messenger-Inquirer* (Owensboro, Kentucky) October 8, 1930.
48. "Hack Wilson Will Get $1000 Just the Same," *Boston Globe*, October 8, 1930. (The Cubs voluntarily agreed to pay Wilson the $1000 prize he would have received if the award was still official.)
49. Orlo Robertson, "New Ball Fails to Scare Babe and Hack," *The* (Belleville, Illinois) *Daily Advocate*, February 10, 1931. (In 1930 the National League collectively hit .303/.360/.448 with 892 home runs, after the introduction of the new ball the league hit .277/.334/.387 with 493 home runs in 1931.)
50. "'Hack' Wilson is No Longer Wanted on Club," *The* (Woodstock, Illinois) *Daily Sentinel*, September 1, 1931.
51. "Phillies Refuse Cubs' $150,000 Offer for Klein," *Chicago Tribune*, September 1, 1931. (Wrigley's wish came true posthumously when the Cubs acquired Klein via trade with the Phillies on November 21, 1933 in exchange for Harvey Hendrick, Ted Kleinhans, Mark Koenig, and $65,000.)
52. George Kirksey, "Hack Dropped Without Pay by Hornsby," *Minneapolis Star*, September 7, 1931. (Shires ended the 1931 season with a .385 batting average for the AA Brewers.)
53. Frank Klein, "Demand Veeck and Hornsby be Removed," *Collyer's Eye* and *The Baseball World*, September 12, 1931.
54. Klein.
55. George Kirksey, "Hack Dropped Without Pay by Hornsby," *Minneapolis Star*, September 7, 1931.
56. George Kirksey, "Hack Wilson Returns to His West Virginia Home," *Decatur Daily Review*, September 11, 1931.
57. Bob Considine, "Old Times," *Cincinnati Enquirer*, October 26, 1938.

Smiling Stan Hack

Leadoff Batter Extraordinaire

Herm Krabbenhoft

Ross Barnes was the first principal leadoff batter (PLB) for the Chicago National League club. A PLB is defined as the player who is a team's game-starting leadoff batter for the most games in a given season, and Barnes was at the top of the lineup for all 66 games Chicago played in the NL's inaugural 1876 campaign. In the ensuing 146 years (through the 2022 season), 71 other players (including five Hall of Famers) have served as Chicago's PLB in one or more seasons. Tables A1–3 (see Appendix on pages 83–85) provide a complete list of the PLBs for the Chicago NL club. Although the club was known by various nicknames—White Stockings (1876–89), Colts (1890–97), Orphans (1898–1901)—before officially becoming the Cubs in 1907, "Cubs" will be used throughout the article for simplicity's sake.

Do any of the Cubs PLBs rank in the upper echelon of MLB's career leadoff batters? To be regarded a career leadoff batter, a player must have been a PLB for at least five seasons. Inspection of Tables A1–3 reveals the following seven players were career leadoff batters with the Cubs:

- Abner Dalrymple (8 PLB seasons)
- Jimmy Ryan (8)
- Jimmy Slagle (7)
- Max Flack (5)
- Stan Hack (11)
- Don Kessinger (8)
- Ivan DeJesus (5)

With regard to evaluating leadoff batter performance, it is generally (if not universally) agreed that the primary responsibility of a leadoff batter is to get on base in order to "set the table" (create RBI opportunities) for the hitters in the heart of the batting order. Thus, the most practical metric for evaluating leadoff batter performance is On Base Average (OBA), defined as the number of times a player gets on base divided by his total number of plate appearances.[1] Officially, there are three ways in which a batter can get on base safely: by getting a base hit, by drawing a base on balls, and by being hit by a pitched ball. Not included (officially) in getting on base safely are plays involving catcher's interference, dropped third strikes, safe on fielder's choices, and safe on fielding errors. Officially, total plate appearances include at bats, walks, times hit by pitches, and sacrifice flies (but not sacrifice bunts).

$$OBA = [H + W + HBP] / [AB + W + HBP + SF]$$

RESEARCH PROCEDURE

For the period from 1876 through 1900, the box scores provided in newspapers—principally The *Chicago Tribune* and *The Inter Ocean*—were used to identify Chicago's game-starting leadoff batter for each game. After determining the Cubs player with the most game-starting leadoff games, the box scores and game accounts were re-examined to obtain the player's at bats, hits, and walks in his leadoff batter games. With regard to getting on base via being hit by pitched balls (which commenced in the NL in 1887), the requisite HBP numbers for the 1887–1900 PLBs were obtained from Pete Palmer's detailed HBP list. The leadoff batter OBAs for the 1876–1900 PLBs were then calculated. For the period from 1901 through 2022, the Stathead search engine on Baseball-Reference.com was employed to

Stan Hack in Cubs uniform.

ascertain the number of leadoff batter games and the corresponding OBA for each Cubs player. The players with the most leadoff games in a given season (the PLBs) are listed in the Tables A1–3. Also included are the PLB's OBA—i.e., his OBA exclusively in games in which he was the leadoff batter. It is noted that the number of leadoff games shown includes games in which the player did not start the game but entered the game by replacing the player occupying the number-one position in the batting order. Typically, the number of non-starting leadoff batter games for PLBs is zero and usually no more than one or two games. For example, in 1989 Jerome Walton played in 115 games in which he batted leadoff; he was the game-starting leadoff batter in 114 of those games. In the game on May 7, Walton replaced game-starting leadoff batter, Dwight Smith, in the top of the seventh inning. Walton subsequently had one hit in one at bat, which are included in his leadoff batter statistics.

RESULTS

[A] Comparative Performance Among the Cubs Career PLBs

Table 1 presents the composite leadoff batter statistics for the aforementioned Dalrymple, Ryan, Slagle, Flack, Hack, Kessinger, and DeJesus. As can be seen, the Cubs principal leadoff batter who compiled the highest composite OBA—.402—is Stan Hack, who had the nickname Smiling Stan (see sidebar). Next in line is Jimmy Ryan, with a .390 OBA. The other five players listed in Table 1 assembled rather pedestrian OBAs—ranging from .353 down to .318. So, Stan Hack was found to be the Cubs best all-time PLB.

[B] Comparative Performance Among Contemporary Major League PLBs

How well did Stan Hack perform as the Cubs PLB compared to his contemporaries? Table 2 provides

relevant PLB OBA information for each season during Hack's ML career (1932–47). For each season the PLB with the highest OBA is listed for both the NL and AL. In order to qualify for the symbolic PLB OBA title, the player must have had at least 477 plate appearances (PA) as a leadoff batter—i.e., 3.1 plate appearances per team scheduled game. This is the same requirement in Major League Baseball's official rules for qualifying for a batting crown or OBA title.

For the first six years of his ML career (1932–37) Hack was a leadoff batter some of the time—23 games in his rookie season, 17 games the next year, followed by 52, zero, 54, and 41 leadoff batter games. His leadoff batter OBAs ranged from .311 to .451.

Beginning with the 1938 campaign, Smiling Stan was the PLB for the Cubs for ten consecutive seasons. Significantly, as shown in Table 2 (page 80), Hack won the symbolic leadoff batter OBA crown six times. It is also noted that in each of those six seasons his leadoff batter OBA was greater than that of the Junior Circuit's leadoff batter OBA leader.

In 1938 Hack won his first symbolic leadoff batter OBA crown with a nifty .408, easily outdistancing runner-up Goody Rosen's .376 leadoff batter OBA. However, Smiling Stan had a relatively off-year in 1939, producing a .376 leadoff batter OBA while Cincinnati's Billy Werber manufactured a .392 leadoff batter OBA to take over the throne. In 1940, Hack responded with a more typical .396 leadoff batter OBA to regain the crown. (Runner-up Werber had a .371.)

Hack repeated as the leadoff batter OBA champion in 1941, turning in a lustrous .424 leadoff OBA. Hack then made it a three-peat in 1942 when his .399 leadoff batter OBA was 48 points higher than silver medalist Tommy Holmes's .351. Hack's leadoff OBA dropped to .385 in 1943, but was still 27 points higher than second-place finisher Danny Murtaugh's .358.

Table 1. Composite Leadoff Batter Statistics for Cubs Career Principal Leadoff Batters

Player	PLB Seasons (First-Last)	G	LOG (%)	OBA
Abner Dalrymple	8 (1879-86)	709	645 (91)	.328
Jimmy Ryan	8 (1888-99)	954	867 (91)	.390
Jimmy Slagle	7 (1902-08)	898	743 (83)	.353
Max Flack	5 (1917-21)	638	570 (89)	.347
Stan Hack	**11 (1936-47)**	**1368**	**1231 (90)**	**.402**
Don Kessinger	8 (1967-75)	1228	1062 (86)	.318
Ivan DeJesus	5 (1977-81)	738	590 (80)	.335

NOTES: (1) The "G" column gives the total number of games played by the player during his principal leadoff batter seasons. (2) The "LOG (%)" column gives the total number of the player's principal leadoff games and corresponding %.

So, in 1943, Hack had picked up his fifth overall and fourth consecutive leadoff batter OBA trophy. But, that appeared to be his last one. As described in Eric Hanauer's SABR biography of Stan Hack, "Although Stan kept smiling, the losing was getting to him. At the end of 1943 he'd had enough. He didn't get along with [Cubs manager Jimmy] Wilson, and retired at the age of 33. Wilson's Cubs won their [1944] opener without Hack at third, but then lost 13 in a row. General manager Jim Gallagher fired Wilson, replacing him with Mr. Cub of that time, Charlie Grimm. One of the first things Grimm did was to call his old infield buddy and talk him out of retirement. Hack debuted on June 18. He was a bit rusty, played in only 98 games, and batted .282."[2] Hack was the Cubs leadoff batter in 93 of those games and put together a decent leadoff batter OBA of .369, a value which would have afforded him the trophy if he had played a dozen or so more games at leadoff. Pittsburgh's Pete Coscarart was able to claim the 1944 trophy with a relatively low .336 mark. Hack was 42 plate appearances shy of qualifying for the symbolic crown.

Table 2. Principal Leadoff Batters with the Highest OBA Each Season from 1932–47

National League				Year	American League			
Player (Team)	LOG (%)	PA	OBA		Player (Team)	LOG (%)	PA	OBA
Lloyd Waner (PIT)	129 (84)	592	.363	1932	Max Bishop (PHA)	106 (93)	512	.417
Stan Hack (CHC)	23 (32)	105	.324					
Pepper Martin (SLC)	132 (86)	622	.394	1933	Max Bishop (PHA)	112 (96)	501	.447
Stan Hack (CHC)	17 (85)	71	.451					
Buzz Boyle (BRK)	109 (71)	503	.380	1934	Harlond Clift (SLB)	137 (93)	642	.360
Stan Hack (CHC)	52 (47)	230	.311					
Augie Galan (CHC)	154 (100)	748	.399	1935	Rip Radcliff (CWS)	142 (97)	679	.347
Stan Hack (CHC)	0 (0)	— —	— —					
Jo-Jo Moore (NYG)	137 (89)	652	.362	1936	Lyn Lary (SLB)	155 (100)	745	.404
Stan Hack (CHC)	54 (36)	259	.408					
Lloyd Waner (PIT)	102 (66)	482	.370	1937	Lyn Lary (CLE)	156 (100)	741	.378
Stan Hack (CHC)	41 (27)	198	.414					
Stan Hack (CHC)	116 (75)	544	**.408**	1938	Frankie Crosetti (NYY)	157 (100)	757	.382
Billy Weber (CIN)	144 (92)	692	.392	1939	Barney McCosky (DET)	145 (99)	690	.383
Stan Hack (CHC)	144 (92)	664	.376					
Stan Hack (CHC)	147 (95)	680	**.396**	1940	George Case (WAS)	152 (99)	713	.348
Stan Hack (CHC)	140 (90)	649	**.424**	1941	Dom DiMaggio (BOS)	131 (91)	637	.394
Stan Hack (CHC)	126 (81)	591	**.399**	1942	George Case (WAS)	138 (93)	558	.378
Stan Hack (CHC)	113 (73)	515	**.385**	1943	George Case (WAS)	103 (73)	487	.347
Pete Coscarart (PIT)	108 (68)	505	.336	1944	George Stirnweiss (NYY)	150 (97)	706	.390
Stan Hack (CHC)	93 (95)	435	.369					
Stan Hack (CHC)	149 (96)	701	**.421**	1945	Eddie Lake (BOS)	114 (86)	518	.407
Eddie Stanky (BRK)	137 (87)	627	.435	1946	Eddie Lake (DET)	155 (100)	705	.371
Stan Hack (CHC)	90 (98)	407	.435					
Eddie Stanky (BRK)	145 (94)	678	.372	1947	Bob Dillinger (SLB)	137 (100)	635	.361
Stan Hack (CHC)	63 (83)	268	.391					

REFLECTING ON SMILING STAN

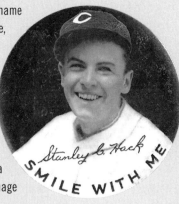

According to a 1932 newspaper article, Stan Hack had his "Smiling Stan" nickname before he began his major-league career with the Cubs. "In the Pacific Coast League, where young Mr. Hack was a star last year, his first season in professional baseball, he was known as 'Smiling Stan.' No matter how hard the coaches rode the rookie, Stanley would beam his contagious smile."[1]

Sometime during Hack's Cubs career (1932–47) souvenir pocket mirrors were produced by the Parisian Novelty Co. of Chicago. According to the description in a 2016 auction, the mirrors measured 2.25 inches in diameter. On the opposite side of the mirror was a black and white photo of Stan Hack with a facsimile autograph (Stanley C. Hack) and the slogan, "Smile With Me." "The image is printed on fabric substance with a very fine texture."[2]

In his autobiography, Bill Veeck wrote the following in Chapter 10 ("The Name of the Game is Gamesmanship"): "During my days with the Cubs, we had a great third baseman, Smiling Stan Hack. I well recall that in 1935, the sale of 'Smile-with-Stan-Hack' mirrors was exceptionally brisk to the bleacherites. Now that I think of it, it was rather strange how the makeup of female bleacherites seemed to need attention when the opposition was hitting." Veeck's tongue planted firmly in cheek, he continued, "And if a beam of light occasionally shone in the batter's eye on a particularly important pitch…well, what better pitch to choose? Unladylike? Of course. Unsporting? Perhaps. Ineffective? Oh no. Awfully, awfully effective. And, until it happened too often perfectly legal."[3] This account also appeared verbatim in a newspaper article published three and a half months after his book came out.[4]

In a 1979 newspaper article the day after Stan Hack passed away, Bill Veeck was quoted as follows: "Right now I see Stan's smile. It inspired one of my first zany ideas in baseball. I think it was the year after the 1932 World Series and I was determined to capitalize on Hack's popularity and smile. I believe it was after we'd sent him to the minors for a short spell. Anyhow, I thought up the slogan 'Smile With Stan Hack' and had a concessionaire make some mirrors with a grinning picture of Stan on the back. They were sold, on target day, in the bleachers. We still [felt?] that fans should not only enjoy Stan's smile, but they should take advantage of the sunshine and reflect the mirrors in the faces of the opposing batsmen. I believe we were playing Pittsburgh. Anyhow, the other team was furious. Umpires confiscated the mirrors, and threatened a forfeit if any more turned up. I've always hoped Stan saved one of those mirrors so he could occasionally look at it and enjoy his own smile, as so many of us did."[5]

Notes

1. Edward Burns, "Hack, Cubs' Rookie Infielder, Plucked Out of Bank on Coast," *Democrat and Chronicle* (Rochester, NY), January 10, 1932, 27.
2. The winning bid was $370.98. "Stanley C. Hack/SMILE WITH ME" pocket mirror, Hake's Auctions, hakes.com/Auction/ItemDetail/201987/STANLEY-C-HACKSMILE-WITH-ME-POCKET-MIRROR, March 15, 2016 (accessed December 18, 2022).
3. Bill Veeck and Ed Linn, *Veeck as in Wreck*, (New York: G.P. Putnam's Sons, 1962), 158.
4. Bill Veeck, "Gamesmanship Helped Indians Win 1948 AL Pennant," *News-Journal* (Mansfield, OH), September 14, 1962, 14.
5. David Condon, "Cub Fans, Smile if You Loved Stan Hack," *Chicago Tribune*, December 16, 1979, 86.

Table 3. Players with the Top Twelve Lifetime Leadoff Batter On Base Averages (1901-2022)

Player	ML Years	Games	LOG (%)	GS-LOG	OBA Titles	OBA
Max Bishop	1924-1935	1338	1220 (91)	1201	5	.424
Roy Thomas	1901-1910	1180	1120 (95)	1119	6	.409
Rickey Henderson	1979-2003	3081	2886 (94)	2875	10	.401
Earle Combs	1924-1935	1455	1072 (74)	1059	2	.399
Richie Ashburn	1948-1962	2189	1418 (65)	1412	6	.399
Stan Hack	1932-1947	1938	1368 (71)	1363	6	.398
Eddie Yost	1944-1962	2109	1741 (83)	1731	7	.396
Miller Huggins	1904-1916	1594	1325 (83)	1321	3	.3878
Topsy Hartsel	1901-1911	1287	1195 (93)	1189	3	.3876
Tony Phillips	1982-1999	2161	1390 (64)	1381	1	.386
Tim Raines	1979-2002	2502	1415 (57)	1397	4	.385
Dom DiMaggio	1940-1953	1399	1038 (74)	1035	1	.384

NOTES: (1) Players with at least 1000 leadoff batter games during 1901–2022 period. (2) Roy Thomas also played in 1899 (150 G; 67 LOG) and 1900 (140 G; 139 LOG). (3) Topsy Hartsel also played in 1898 (22 G; 0 LOG), 1899 (30 G; 6 LOG), and 1900 (18 G; 0 LOG).

Hack continued his un-retirement in 1945 by turning in another superb performance. He compiled an impressive .421 leadoff batter OBA, which outdistanced second placer Eddie Stanky's .416. Hack was competing for yet another leadoff batter OBA crown in 1946. But, in his 80th game (with a .412 leadoff OBA) he suffered a fractured bone in his left hand trying to knock down an eighth-inning line drive single by Don Padgett. He was out of the starting lineup until September 21, returning for the last ten games of the season. He upped his OBA to .435, but was edged out by Eddie Stanky, who beat him by a few percentage points (.4349 to .4346). Finally, in 1947, which turned out to be his final season, Hack played in just 77 games, compiling a .391 leadoff batter OBA in 63 first-batter appearances.

DISCUSSION

Stan Hack played major league baseball for 16 years (1932–47), entirely with the Chicago Cubs. He was their principal leadoff batter in eleven of those seasons (1936 and 1938–47). With the requirement of 477 leadoff batter plate appearances, Smiling Stan captured the NL's symbolic leadoff batter OBA throne six times—1938, 1940–43, and 1945. That's the most by any of the PLBs during the 1932–47 period, five other players having achieved multiple leadoff batter OBA crowns: Max Bishop (2), Lloyd Waner (2), Lyn Lary (2), George Case (3), Eddie Lake (2), and Eddie Stanky (2). Expanding the period to the 1901–2022 seasons, there have been only nine players who were leadoff batter OBA kings in five or more seasons—Roy Thomas (6),

George Burns (5), Bishop (6), Hack (6), Stanky (5), Eddie Yost (7), Richie Ashburn (6), Pete Rose (7), Rickey Henderson (10), and Ichiro Suzuki (5). From the perspective of composite leadoff batter OBA, during the 1901–2022 period there have been 55 players who accumulated one thousand or more career leadoff batter games. Stan Hack is one of those—altogether he was the Cubs leadoff batter in 1363 games. In those games he fabricated a composite .398 leadoff batter OBA, a figure which ranks number six in the top dozen of all-time—see Table 3.

Clearly, Smiling Stan Hack was a leadoff batter extraordinaire for the Chicago Cubs franchise and in the upper echelon of career leadoff batters for the entirety of Major League Baseball. ∎

Acknowledgments

I gratefully thank Pete Palmer for providing photocopies of the 1891–1900 ICI Day-By-Day sheets for Jimmy Ryan and detailed Hit-By-Pitch information for the 1887–1900 period. I also thank Larry Annis, Jack Bales, Cliff Blau, Bill Deane, Jim Drnek, Stanford Hack, Eric Hanauer, Ed Hartig, Richard Hershberger, Bill Hickman, Cassidy Lent, Gary Livacari, David McDonald, Alan Nathan, Dave Newman, Pete Palmer, John Racanelli, Jeff Robbins, Tom Shieber, Caleb Simonds, Richard Smiley, Cary Smith, Richard Stephens, Don Stokes, Gary Stone, Patrick Todgham, Mike Veeck, and Al Yellon for valuable help and/or discussions. And, I am grateful to Baseball-Reference.com and Retrosheet for their superb baseball-research-enabling websites.

Notes

1. Branch Rickey, "Goodby to Some Old Baseball Ideas," *Life*, August 2, 1954, 78–89.
2. Eric Hanauer, "Stan Hack," SABR Bio-Project (accessed December 12, 2022).

APPENDICES A, B, C

Appendix A (Tables A1–A3): Principal Leadoff Batters for the Chicago National League Teams (1876–2022)

Table A1. Principal Leadoff Batters for the Chicago National League Teams (1876–1925)

Year	Player	LOG (%)	OBA	Year	Player	LOG (%)	OBA
1876	Ross Barnes	66 (100)	.462	1901	Topsy Hartsel	124 (89)	.410
1877	Ross Barnes	22 (100)	.323	1902	Jimmy Slagle	90 (77)	.393
1878	Bill Harbridge	40 (74)	.335	1903	Jimmy Slagle	87 (63)	.415
1879	Abner Dalrymple	68 (96)	.302	1904	Jimmy Slagle	109 (91)	.337
1880	Abner Dalrymple	76 (88)	.331	1905	Jimmy Slagle	123 (79)	.385
1881	Abner Dalrymple	54 (66)	.364	1906	Jimmy Slagle	127 (100)	.327
1882	Abner Dalrymple	84 (100)	.319	1907	Jimmy Slagle	135 (99)	.370
1883	Abner Dalrymple	78 (98)	.322	1908	Jimmy Slagle	76 (73)	.296
1884	Abner Dalrymple	111 (100)	.327	1909	Johnny Evers	126 (99)	.369
1885	Abner Dalrymple	109 (96)	.344	1910	Johnny Evers	125 (100)	.412
1886	Abner Dalrymple	66 (80)	.315	1911	Jimmy Sheckard	109 (70)	.418
1887	Billy Sunday	50 (100)	.362	1912	Jimmy Sheckard	139 (95)	.387
1888	Jimmy Ryan	129 (100)	.377	1913	Tommy Leach	113 (86)	.384
1889	Jimmy Ryan	135 (100)	.403	1914	Tommy Leach	153 (100)	.352
1890	Jimmy Cooney	135 (100)	.360	1915	Wilbur Good	122 (95)	.309
1891	Jimmy Ryan	118 (100)	.355	1916	Rollie Zeider	73 (74)	.281
1892	Walt Wilmot	73 (79)	.288	1917	Max Flack	99 (76)	.329
1893	Jimmy Ryan	82 (99)	.409	1918	Max Flack	101 (82)	.337
1894	Jimmy Ryan	110 (100)	.422	1919	Max Flack	111 (96)	.343
1895	Jimmy Ryan	58 (54)	.401	1920	Max Flack	131 (97)	.374
1896	Bill Everitt	132 (100)	.367	1921	Max Flack	130 (98)	.342
1897	Bill Everitt	83 (90)	.375	1922	Arnold Statz	105 (95)	.350
1898	Jimmy Ryan	107 (74)	.410	1923	Arnold Statz	154 (100)	.376
1899	Jimmy Ryan	125 (100)	.357	1924	Arnold Statz	104 (77)	.330
1900	Jack McCarthy	66 (53)	.357	1925	Sparky Adams	126 (85)	.347

NOTE: The LOG (%) column gives the number of leadoff games the player had and the percentage of his leadoff games relative to the total number of games he played.

Table A2. Principal Leadoff Batters for the Chicago National League Teams (1926–75)

Year	Player	LOG (%)	OBA	Year	Player	LOG (%)	OBA
1926	Sparky Adams	152 (99)	.368	1951	Eddie Miksis	80 (80)	.317
1927	Sparky Adams	146 (100)	.335	1952	Eddie Miksis	75 (81)	.279
1928	Woody English	90 (78)	.345	1953	Frank Baumholtz	114 (86)	.378
1929	Woody English	70 (49)	.326	1954	Bob Talbot	87 (76)	.280
1930	Footsie Blair	111 (83)	.313	1955	Dee Fondy	55 (37)	.353
1931	Kiki Cuyler	49 (32)	.436	1956	Eddie Miksis	53 (46)	.308
1932	Billy Herman	82 (53)	.364	1957	Bobby Morgan	50 (40)	.293
1933	Woody English	54 (51)	.350	1958	Tony Taylor	124 (89)	.303
1934	Billy Herman	71 (63)	.352	1959	Tony Taylor	149 (99)	.331
1935	Augie Galan	154 (100)	.399	1960	Richie Ashburn	117 (77)	.425
1936	Stan Hack	54 (36)	.408	1961	Richie Ashburn	73 (67)	.369
1937	Augie Galan	112 (76)	.336	1962	Lou Brock	83 (67)	.338
1938	Stan Hack	116 (76)	.408	1963	Lou Brock	102 (69)	.305
1939	Stan Hack	144 (92)	.376	1964	Jimmy Stewart	81 (61)	.334
1940	Stan Hack	147 (99)	.396	1965	Don Landrum	60 (46)	.276
1941	Stan Hack	140 (93)	.424	1966	Adolfo Phillips	92 (79)	.344
1942	Stan Hack	126 (90)	.399	1967	Don Kessinger	135 (93)	.275
1943	Stan Hack	113 (78)	.385	1968	Don Kessinger	154 (96)	.276
1944	Stan Hack	93 (95)	.369	1969	Don Kessinger	157 (99)	.333
1945	Stan Hack	149 (99)	.421	1970	Don Kessinger	152 (99)	.334
1946	Stan Hack	90 (98)	.435	1971	Don Kessinger	136 (88)	.313
1947	Stan Hack	63 (83)	.391	1972	Don Kessinger	108 (72)	.357
1948	Hank Schenz	72 (75)	.315	1973	Rick Monday	114 (77)	.389
1949	Emil Verban	37 (38)	.302	1974	Don Kessinger	86 (56)	.349
1950	Wayne Terwilliger	92 (69)	.308	1975	Don Kessinger	138 (90)	.321

Table A3. Principal Leadoff Batters for the Chicago National League Teams (1976-2022)

Year	Player	LOG (%)	OBA	Year	Player	LOG (%)	OBA
1976	Rick Monday	131 (96)	.346	2000	Eric Young	147 (96)	.370
1977	Ivan DeJesus	149 (96)	.330	2001	Eric Young	145 (97)	.334
1978	Ivan DeJesus	124 (78)	.347	2002	Cory Patterson	56 (37)	.311
1979	Ivan DeJesus	152 (95)	.349	2003	Mark Grudzielanek	69 (57)	.358
1980	Ivan DeJesus	107 (68)	.338	2004	Todd Walker	60 (47)	.370
1981	Ivan DeJesus	59 (56)	.272	2005	Jerry Hairston	78 (68)	.344
1982	Bump Wills	90 (70)	.337	2006	Juan Pierre	159 (98)	.333
1983	Mel Hall	59 (53)	.352	2007	Alfonso Soriano	125 (93)	.345
1984	Bob Dernier	136 (95)	.355	2008	Alfonso Soriano	105 (96)	.350
1985	Bob Dernier	113 (93)	.318	2009	Alfonso Soriano	70 (60)	.295
1986	Bob Dernier	52 (48)	.272	2010	Ryan Theriot	56 (58)	.310
1987	Dave Martinez	89 (63)	.370	2011	Starlin Castro	72 (46)	.370
1988	Mitch Webster	44 (63)	.303	2012	David DeJesus	116 (78)	.358
1989	Jerome Walton	115 (99)	.334	2013	David DeJesus	69 (82)	.341
1990	Jerome Walton	97 (96)	.347	2014	Emilio Bonifacio	63 (91)	.319
1991	Chico Walker	68 (55)	.306	2015	Dexter Fowler	146 (94)	.350
1992	Doug Dascenzo	44 (32)	.285	2016	Dexter Fowler	119 (95)	.393
1993	Dwight Smith	65 (59)	.349	2017	Jon Jay	53 (38)	.325
1994	Tuffy Rhodes	50 (53)	.342	2018	Albert Almora	50 (33)	.368
1995	Brian McRae	136 (99)	.349	2019	Kyle Schwarber	56 (36)	.304
1996	Brian McRae	154 (98)	.361	2020	Ian Happ	37 (65)	.333
1997	Brian McRae	70 (65)	.303	2021	Rafael Ortega	54 (52)	.378
1998	Lance Johnson	65 (76)	.333	2022	Rafael Ortega	54 (46)	.288
1999	Lance Johnson	77 (81)	.327	——	——————————	————	——

NOTES: (1) Ryne Sandberg also had 59 leadoff batter games in 1983; his leadoff batter OBA was .271. (2) Shawon Dunston also had 44 leadoff games in 1988; his leadoff batter OBA was .260. :

Appendix B (Tables B1–B2): Leadoff Batter On Base Averages for Selected Cubs Principal Leadoff Batters

Table B1. Jimmy Ryan—Chicago National League Seasons with Leadoff Batter Games

Year	G	LOG (%)	Leadoff Batter OBA
1885	3	0	– – –
1886	84	7 (8)	.429
1887	126	0	– – –
1888	131	131 (100)	.377
1889	135	135 (100)	.403
1891	118	118 (100)	.355
1892	128	72 (56)	.378
1893	83	82 (99)	.409
1894	110	110 (100)	.422
1895	108	59 (50)	.401
1896	128	0	– – –
1897	136	22 (16)	.440
1898	144	107 (74)	.410
1899	125	125 (100)	.357
1900	105	21 (20)	.415
Composite	**1662**	**986 (59)**	**.390**

NOTES: (1) Ryne Sandberg also had 59 leadoff batter games in 1983; his leadoff batter OBA was .271. (2) Shawon Dunston also had 44 leadoff games in 1988; his leadoff batter OBA was .260.

Table B2. Stan Hack—Chicago National League Seasons with Leadoff Batter Games

Year	G	LOG (%)	Leadoff Batter OBA
1932	72	23 (32)	.323
1933	20	17 (85)	.451
1934	111	52 (47)	.311
1935	124	0	— — —
1936	149	54 (36)	.408
1937	154	41 (27)	.414
1938	152	116 (76)	.408
1939	156	144 (92)	.376
1940	149	147 (99)	.396
1941	151	140 (93)	.424
1942	140	126 (90)	.399
1943	144	106 (74)	.392
1944	98	93 (95)	.369
1945	150	149 (99)	.421
1946	92	90 (98)	.435
1947	76	63 (83)	.391
Composite	**1938**	**1368 (71)**	**.398**

NOTE: See Note, Table A-1.

Appendix C (Table C): Principal Leadoff Batter OBA Kings for Chicago's ML Teams (1901–2022)

Table C-1. Principal Leadoff Batter OBA Kings for Chicago's Major League Teams (1901-2022)

Year	Player	Team	LOG (%)	OBA
1901	Billy Hoy	White Sox	132 (96)	.403
1909	Johnny Evers	Cubs	126 (81)	.369
1910	Johnny Evers	Cubs	125 (81)	.412
1919	Nemo Leibold	White Sox	119 (85)	.404
1920	Max Flack	Cubs	131 (85)	.374
1925	Johnny Mostil	White Sox	145 (94)	.392
1935	Augie Galan	Cubs	154 (100)	.399
1935	Rip Radcliff	White Sox	142 (97)	.347
1938	Stan Hack	Cubs	116 (75)	.408
1940	Stan Hack	Cubs	147 (95)	.396
1941	Stan Hack	Cubs	140 (90)	.424
1942	Stan Hack	Cubs	126 (81)	.399
1943	Stan Hack	Cubs	113 (73)	.385
1945	Stan Hack	Cubs	149 (96)	.421
1960	Richie Ashburn	Cubs	117 (75)	.425
1984	Bob Dernier	Cubs	136 (84)	.355
2012	David DeJesus	Cubs	116 (72)	.358
2014	Adam Eaton	White Sox	123 (76)	.362
2016	Dexter Fowler	Cubs	119 (73)	.393

NOTES: (1) Ryne Sandberg also had 59 leadoff batter games in 1983; his leadoff batter OBA was .271. (2) Shawon Dunston also had 44 leadoff games in 1988; his leadoff batter OBA was .260.

Handy Andy Pafko

A Wisconsin-Born Player Succeeds in Chicago and Milwaukee

Steve Krevisky

Andy "Pruschka" Pafko was born to Czech parents in Boyceville, Wisconsin, in 1921. The Wisconsin native enjoyed a quick rise to major league success. By 1943, at the tender age of 22, he won the Pacific Coast League MVP Award, playing with the Los Angeles Angels. He then appeared in 13 games for the 1943 Chicago Cubs, batting .379 in only 61 plate appearances. He became established as a regular in 1944, playing center field and batting .269 with occasional power. His rookie performance earned him the approval of Billy Southworth, manager of the rival Cardinals.

Pruschka became a star in 1945. He posted 4.4 WAR and slashed .298/.361/.455, with 12 home runs and 110 RBIs. This breakout performance earned him his first All-Star berth. He finished a good fourth in the National League MVP voting, behind Phil Cavarretta, Tommy Holmes, and Red Barrett. He also enjoyed the first of four World Series appearances, though the Cubs couldn't match the heroics of Hank Greenberg, falling to the Tigers in seven games. Although he struggled in the Series, Pafko managed two doubles and a triple.

1946 marked a season of substantial injuries. Pafko batted .282 in only 65 games, recovering from a June ankle injury only to lose the remainder of the season to a fractured arm in August. Despite missing three weeks due to a kidney infection, he bounced back in 1947, batting .302 and launching 13 home runs in 129 games. He also returned to the All-Star Game, marking the first of four consecutive appearances.

Pafko moved to third base in 1948, but the change didn't stop him from excelling at the plate. He posted 6.1 WAR, batting .312 with 26 homers, 101 RBIs, and an OPS of .891. He received MVP votes for the third time in four years. Pafko returned to the outfield for most of 1949, also logging 49 games at third. He batted .281, and although his power was down, he posted his third straight three-win season. Unfortunately for the Wrigley faithful, the Cubs were sliding down in the standings, posting the third of five consecutive losing seasons.

1950 might have been the Wisconsin-born Pafko's best season. He made his fourth consecutive All-Star

team and received MVP votes for the fourth time. He drilled 36 homers, with 92 RBIs. He slashed .304/.397/.591, leading the Cubs and finishing in the top 10 in the National League in all three categories. The 6.4 WAR stood out as the high point of Pafko's career.

Long-simmering trade rumors about Pruschka were finally substantiated in June 1951, when the Cubs sent him to the Brooklyn Dodgers. The Chicago fans were rather upset about losing one of their favorites, especially a native Midwesterner. Pafko hit 30 home runs and knocked in 93 RBIs for the Cubs and Dodgers. He watched from left field when Bobby Thomson belted the famous "Shot Heard 'Round the World" to end the three-game playoff series and Brooklyn's season on October 3.

Pafko had a solid 1952 with "Dem Bums." He drilled 19 homers and drove in 85 while batting .287 with a .805 OPS. He also played in a career-high 150 games. The Dodgers faced the Yankees in the World Series, but for the second time in Pafko's career, his team would lose in seven games.

In 1953, the Dodgers traded Pafko to the Milwaukee Braves, in their first season after moving from Boston. The hometown favorite was still a regular player with solid power numbers in 1953 and '54. When Henry Aaron moved to right field in 1955, Pafko lost most of his playing time. The late-'50s Braves were a powerhouse, featuring stars like Aaron, Eddie Mathews, Joe Adcock, Warren Spahn, and Lew Burdette. Pafko played

Andy Pafko

in both the 1957 and '58 World Series, as his career wound down. 1959 was his last season as a player, and he subsequently went on to manage in the minors and scout.

Pafko's outstanding career featured some truly memorable games:

- On July 3, 1945, the Cubs demolished the Braves, 24–2. Andy went 4-for-6 a walk, a double, and 5 RBIs.

- On May 16, 1948, Pafko went 5-for-5 with a double and two home runs. He both scored and knocked in four runs in a losing effort against the Reds.

- Just over a month later, on June 19, Pafko lit up Ebbets Field with yet another 5-for-5 performance. All five hits were singles, and Pafko's three RBIs made the difference in the 5–2 win over the Dodgers.

- On August 2, 1950, at the Polo Grounds, Andy went 3-for-3 in a losing cause against the Giants. Pafko drilled three homers in the game, all off Sal Maglie.

Even without the single-game heroics, Andy "Pruschka" Pafko had a very solid career. He received MVP votes in four seasons, finishing fourth in 1945. He made five All-Star teams, including four in a row from 1947 through 1950. He posted an OPS of at least .800 in 11 different seasons, including a stretch of seven in a row. Although he was a career outfielder, he didn't just transition smoothly when the club needed him to move to the infield, he put up one of the best seasons of his career. He was a solid performer on four pennant-winners and one World Series champion, and his great play along with his Wisconsin background made him a fan favorite in both Chicago and Milwaukee. ■

References

Baseball-Reference.com, "Andy Pafko Stats, Height, Weight, Position, Rookie Status & More," https://www.baseball-reference.com/players/p/pafkoan01.shtml.

Retrosheet.org.

Dale Voiss, "Andy Pafko," SABR BioProject, https://sabr.org/bioproj/person/andy-pafko.

A Fox in White Sox

Joseph Wancho

In the modern game, a team's fortune or failure is often the burden of the general manager. The GM hires the field manager, signs or passes on available free agents, makes transactions with teams, and, with the farm director and his legion of scouts, oversees the amateur free agent draft.

Out of all that activity, it is the trades that many fans remember the longest. Every franchise in the major leagues can lay claim to moves where their GM hoodwinked the opposing front office, as well as those deals that have every fan asking the rhetorical question "What the hell were you thinking?"

In 1948, the White Sox finished in last place in the American League with a 51–101–2 record, 44½ games behind pennant-winner Cleveland. It was the fifth straight losing season for the South Siders. Chicago vice president Chuck Comiskey named Frank Lane as the general manager of the Sox in October 1948, replacing Leslie O'Connor. Previously, Frank Lane served as president of the Triple-A American Association from 1946 to 1948.

Over the years there has been much scrutiny of Lane and the deals he made, but these naysayers did not deter him. "Don't cry about a bad deal," said Lane. "Walk away from it and go on to the next one. The worst thing a general manager can do after a bad deal is to stand pat."[1]

It should be noted that while the White Sox never won a pennant during Lane's reign, they were in much better shape when he left in 1955 than they were when he arrived. He doesn't get the credit he deserves for building the foundation of the "Go-Go Sox" of the 1950s. The Sox broke through and won the American League pennant in 1959.[2]

Lane got right to work improving the team for the 1949 season. His first deal, on November 10, 1948, was acquiring pitcher Billy Pierce and $10,000 from Detroit in exchange for catcher Aaron Robinson. For the next 13 seasons, Pierce was a starting pitcher for the Sox, winning 20 games twice, and winning at least 14 nine times. As of 2023, Pierce ranks fourth all-time in wins for the Sox, with 186. He is also the team's all-time leader in strikeouts with 1,796.

Less then a year later, Lane added another critical piece to the Sox. Like the deal for Pierce, he gave up very little while acquiring a cornerstone of Sox history. "When I was still president of the American Association, I stopped off one night in Lincoln, Nebraska and saw their ballclub," said Lane. "And they had two little guys that I loved as soon as I saw them. A left-handed pitcher and a second baseman with a huge chaw of tobacco in his left cheek. They were Bobby Shantz and Nellie Fox. 'If I ever get to the big leagues, these are the two guys I'm going to get.' Well, I never got Shantz, but I did get Fox."[3]

Indeed, he did. On October 8, 1949, Connie Mack, the owner and manager of the A's, dealt catcher Buddy Rosar to the Boston Red Sox for utility infielder Billy Hitchcock. With the A's now in the market for a catcher, Lane was only too happy to help them. On October 19, Lane traded catcher Joe Tipton to the Philadelphia Athletics for Fox.

In his biography of Connie Mack, author Norman Macht wrote that White Sox vice-president Chuck Comiskey had initially asked for infielder Pete Suder as compensation for Tipton. Since Suder was a favorite of Connie Mack, Fox was offered instead. The Athletics did not foresee Fox rising above the status of a utility player.[4] In hindsight, Mack rated the Tipton-Fox deal as the worst transaction he ever made, supplanting selling pitcher Herb Pennock to Boston in 1915.

Suder was blocking Fox's path to a starting job at second base in Philadelphia. The Aliquippa, Pennsylvania, native was the A's starting second sacker in 1947 and 1948. In 1949, Suder (right-handed batter) and Fox (left-handed) shared duties at the keystone, sometimes Fox playing second while Suder handled third. Suder showed a greater ability to provide the A's offense, hitting 10 home runs, driving in 75 runs and batting .267. Fox's line was less impressive: 0 home runs, 21 RBIs, and a .255 average. In the field, Suder played 100 more innings, committing 12 errors to Fox's seven.

Stan Baumgartner of the *Philadelphia Inquirer* noted that Fox was five years younger than Tipton,

SABR/THE RUCKER ARCHIVE

Nellie Fox turning the double play.

the way he was dragging his foot across the bag."[7] Richards brought in Joe Gordon to tutor Fox.[8] Gordon had retired from the majors after the 1950 season and was beginning a new chapter in his life as a player-manager for the Sacramento Salons of the Pacific Coast League.

While Gordon worked on his glove and footwork, Chicago coach Doc Cramer tutored Fox on the finer points of hitting. This included Fox changing his bat from one with a thin handle to one with a thicker handle. Cramer also worked on reducing Fox's habit of lunging at pitches.[9]

Like a sponge, Fox absorbed the extra tutelage. He batted .285 or better every season from 1951 to 1960. Within the decade, he led the American League in hits four different seasons. Fox had a steady eye at the plate. In his 19-year career, he only struck out 216 times in 9,232 at-bats.

In the field, he led AL second baseman in fielding average six times, and from 1952 to 1961 he led the league in putouts by a second baseman every year. Fox also led the league in assists in six seasons. He was selected as the American League's Most Valuable Player in 1959. He was the recipient of the Gold Glove in 1957, 1959, and 1960.

As for Joe Tipton, he played seven seasons with four different teams, all in the AL. His career batting average was .236 with 29 home runs and 125 RBI. He also fielded his catching position at an average of .984.

Fox played 19 years in the big leagues. He compiled a lifetime batting average of .288 and fielded his second base position at a .984 clip. Fox was selected to the most All-Star Games in White Sox history with 15. He was elected to the National Baseball Hall of Fame in 1997, 22 years after he passed away from cancer. ∎

and outhit the catcher, .255 to .204. But while Fox was a "singles hitter," Tipton had "plenty of power" in his bat. He hit three home runs. Fox also drove in 21 runs compared to Tipton's total of 19.[5]

One has to wonder what the A's considered a power hitter. In 1941, Tipton's first season in professional baseball, he stroked 13 round-trippers. That was the high-water mark in his career.

"We were short of capable infield reserves," said Lane. "Especially, we needed a replacement for Cass Michaels. Fox has tremendous promise and fits in with our plan of rebuilding the Sox with youth."[6]

It was a curious comment. Michaels batted .308 in 1949 and was selected to his first All-Star Game. But more importantly, at the time of the Fox-Tipton deal, Michaels was still on the Chisox roster. If there was one similarity shared by both Tipton and Michaels, it was that both players had their difficulties getting along with Chicago manager Jack Onslow. Although Lane and Onslow disagreed at times as GMs and managers will do, they were on the same page regarding Tipton and Michaels: Both players had to go. Michaels started the 1950 season at second base. Despite batting .312, he was traded to Washington on May 31 as part of a six-player swap. The deal opened the door for Fox to become the starting second baseman.

The new second-sacker of the Sox, however, was hardly a finished product. As Chicago worked out in spring training in Pasadena in 1951, it was apparent that Fox would need instruction with the bat, and his glove. "It was brutal the way Fox was pivoting (at second base)," said new Chisox manager Paul Richards. "I was surprised he didn't get hurt making the pivot

Notes

1. *The Sporting News*, June 15, 1960: 9.
2. Ironically, Lane helped the White Sox win the 1959 pennant from afar. While the GM of Cleveland, Lane traded Early Wynn and infielder-outfielder Al Smith to Chicago for Minnie Miñoso and Fred Hatfield in 1957.
3. Bob Vanderburg, *Frantic Frank Lane: Baseball's Ultimate Wheeler-Dealer* (Jefferson, NC: McFarland & Co., 2013), 14.
4. Norman Macht, *Connie Mack: The Grand Old Man of Baseball* (Lincoln, Nebraska: University of Nebraska Press, 2015), 446.
5. Stan Baumgartner, "A's Get Tipton in Trade for Fox," *Philadelphia Inquirer*, October 19, 1949: 47.
6. "White Sox Trade Tipton for Fox," *Chicago Daily News*, October 18, 1949: 29.
7. Robert W. Bigelow: SABR Biography Project: Nellie Fox. https://sabr.org/bioproj/person/Nellie-Fox. Accessed April 1, 2023.
8. Bigelow.
9. Bigelow.

The Path to the Cubs and White Sox from the Negro Leagues

17 Barrier Breakers

Alan Cohen

Numerous talents from the Negro Leagues made their way into the employ of the American and National League franchises in Chicago. Integration did not come to these clubs until four seasons after the debut of Jackie Robinson with the Dodgers on April 15, 1947, and even then, the pace of integration was frightfully slow. This article details the journeys of 17 pioneers.

MINNIE MIÑOSO

On May 1, 1951, Minnie Miñoso became first Black player to play in Chicago for either the Cubs or White Sox. The White Sox were the third American League team to integrate, sixth overall.

Miñoso, from Cuba, had first played professionally in the United States with the New York Cubans in 1946. He spent three years with the Cubans and in 1948 batted .344. Late in the 1948 season, he was sold to the Indians and spent the latter part of that season at Dayton in the Central League. At Dayton, he played second base and third base and went 21-for-40 at the plate. When he made his debut with the Indians on April 19, 1949, he was the seventh Black player in the big leagues after Jackie Robinson and the first from outside the United States.

He played nine games with the Indians before being sent to the minors. Cleveland sought to convert

Minnie Miñoso was the first Black player to cross the color line for a big-league team in Chicago.

him to the role of an outfielder, and they positioned him in the outfield with San Diego. In his first game with the PCL Padres, he was charged with two errors. When he made it to the majors to stay, nobody questioned his ability in the outfield. During the late 1950s, he was the preeminent left-fielder in the American League, leading the league in games played at that position for six consecutive seasons and garnering three Gold Gloves. With the bat, there was never any question. With San Diego in 1949, he batted .297 with 22 home runs and 75 RBI in 137 games. His average rose to .339 in 1950, with 20 homers and 115 RBIs.

Miñoso began 1951 with the Indians and appeared in eight games before Cleveland traded him to the White Sox on April 30, 1951. He had his best seasons in Chicago. During his first seven years with the White Sox, he was on five All-Star teams and received the first ever Gold Glove (1957). He led the league in being hit by a pitch six times. After the 1957 season, he was traded back to the Indians, where his stellar performance continued. During two years with Cleveland, he batted .302, continued to lead the league in being hit by a pitch, was named to his sixth All-Star team (1959), and garnered his second gold glove (1959).

By 1959, Bill Veeck—the owner who had signed Miñoso to his first Indians contract—had taken over at Chicago, and he traded for Miñoso prior to the 1960 season. Minnie was ecstatic about the return to Chicago and got off to a great start with a pair of homers (including a grand slam) in a 10–9 win over Kansas City. In 1961, at the age of 37, he played in 152 games.

The White Sox brought the ever-smiling Miñoso back for token appearances in 1976 and 1980, giving him the distinction of having played in five decades. Miñoso was a happy man. As he said, "When you come from nowhere—cutting sugarcane in Cuba—and get somewhere, you have to be happy."[1]

SAM HAIRSTON

Sam Hairston got his start in the Negro Leagues with the Indianapolis Clowns in 1944 and was with them through 1949. In 1948, he led his team in batting with a .357 average. In July 1950, during the midst of another banner season with the Clowns, he was acquired by the White Sox and sent to Colorado Springs in the Western League, for whom he played in parts of six seasons. In 1951, he had a cup of coffee with the White Sox, appearing in four games, during which he went 2-for-5 with a pair of walks, before returning to the minors. When he debuted on July 21, 1951, he became the second Black player to play for the White Sox. In 1955 at Colorado Springs, he posted a .350 batting average with 48 extra-base hits and 91 RBIs, but he never got a return call to the White Sox.

Hairston's legacy in Chicago goes far beyond those few games, however. He was with the White Sox organization for 48 years as player, scout, and coach. Two of his sons played major league baseball in Chicago. John Hairston played with the Cubs, and Jerry Hairston played for the White Sox, after Sam scouted him. Two of his grandsons also played for Chicago teams. Scott Hairston, in 11 major league seasons, spent one season with the Cubs. Jerry Hairston, Jr., in 16 major league seasons, spent two seasons with the Cubs.

AL SMITH

One of the players for whom Miñoso (and Fred Hatfield) was traded when he left the White Sox at the end of the 1957 season was Al Smith, a teammate with the San Diego Padres in 1950. Smith first played in the Negro Leagues in 1946 with the Cleveland Buckeyes. The Indians obtained him in 1948, and he was sent to Wilkes-Barre in the Eastern League. He batted a team-leading .316 in 1948 and .311 in 1949. In 1950, he was promoted to San Diego of the PCL and debuted with Cleveland in 1953. In his best season with Cleveland, 1955, Smith was named to the American League All-Star team and finished third in MVP balloting. When he joined the White Sox in 1958, he became their eighth Black player—seven of those eight having spent time in the Negro Leagues. He was a big part of their pennant-winning team in 1959 and was again named to the All-Star team in 1960, when he batted a career-high .315.

HECTOR RODRIGUEZ

Hector Rodriguez spent all but one of his early years in the Mexican League. In 1944, he played with the New York Cubans. On October 1, 1944, he played in an All-Star game in New Orleans and went 4-for-5 with one double and an RBI as his Northern All-Stars defeated the Southern All-Stars 6–1. Against Satchel Paige, who pitched the first five innings, he went 3-for-3 with a double and an RBI single. He signed with the Brooklyn

Hector Rodriguez came to the United States with the New York Cubans in 1944 and played third base for the White Sox in 1952.

Dodgers organization prior to the 1951 season and was traded to the White Sox after batting .302 at Montreal in 1951. With Chicago in 1952, he played in 124 games and batted .265.

CONNIE JOHNSON

The first Black pitcher for the White Sox was Connie Johnson who debuted on April 17, 1953. He had first pitched in the Negro Leagues with the Toledo Crawfords in 1940, and he was named to the East-West game in his very first season. The following year, he joined the pitching-rich Kansas City Monarchs where he pitched alongside Hall-of-Famers Satchel Paige and Hilton Smith. In 1946, he had his best season with the Monarchs, winning 12 games (5 championship games) and striking out 10 or more batters in four games. He made his second East-West appearance in 1950 and was named the winning pitcher. In his first game with the White Sox, he came in to relieve in the eighth

Connie Johnson from Stone Mountain, Georgia, was a Negro League All-Star who played with the White Sox and Orioles.

inning against the St. Louis Browns. Pitching in relief for the Browns was Satchel Paige. The matchup marked the first time that Black pitchers had ever faced each other in an American League game.

SAM JONES

Pitcher Sam Jones was with the Buckeyes in 1947 and 1948 and hurled in the Negro League World Series in 1947, making one appearance in relief. After the 1948 season, when the Negro Leagues were consolidated to one 10-team Negro American League, the Buckeyes split their time between Louisville and Cleveland. Jones remained with them until the Indians obtained him in 1950. In one of his least glorious NAL appearances, he entered a game in relief, on May 22, 1949, and did not retire a single batter, walking two, hitting one, and allowing a base-hit to the fourth. He was charged with four runs in an 18–8 loss to Birmingham.[2]

His first stop in the Indians minor-league system was at Wilkes-Barre where he went 17–8. The next season, he was with San Diego, going 16–13. He had brief stints with Cleveland in 1951 and 1952 before being traded to the Cubs prior to the 1955 season. When he made his debut on April 11, 1955, he became the Cubs' fourth Black player—after Ernie Banks, Gene Baker, and Luis Marquez—each of whom who had played in the Negro Leagues. He continued to have control problems in his days with the Cubs. In his rookie season, he lost 20 games and led the league in walks with 185. However, he also led the league in strikeouts (198). His best season was with the Giants in 1959, when he led the league in wins with 21.

MONTE IRVIN

Although Monte Irvin is best remembered for his years with the Giants—he and Hank Thompson had broken their color line in 1949—he joined the Cubs in 1956, becoming their fifth Black player.

While playing with the Newark Eagles in 1941, Irvin once homered in three games on the same day: August 17. A doubleheader was played in the afternoon at Columbus, Ohio, and a night game was played at Dayton, Ohio. The Newark Eagles defeated the Homestead Grays in each game. He was 22 years old at the time.[3]

LARRY DOBY

Another notable player known for his career with another team, in this case the Indians, was Larry Doby, who debuted with the White Sox on April 17, 1956. He had previously starred with the Newark Eagles, appearing in both East-West games in 1946. On July 5, 1947, he had become the first openly Black player in

Larry Doby starred with the Newark Eagles before breaking the American League color barrier with the Indians in 1947. He not only played with the White Sox but later, in 1978, became their first Black manager.

the AL when he joined Cleveland. He remained in baseball after his playing days and became the second Black manager in the history of the AL when he took over as White Sox manager during the 1978 season.

SCOUTS: JOHN MORRIS AND JOHN DONALDSON

A discussion about the early Black players with the Cubs and White Sox is incomplete without reference to the Black scouts who came to work with the clubs. The Cubs hired their first Black scout, John "Yellow Horse" Morris in 1949.[4] He had pitched for Kansas City, Detroit, and Chicago in the Negro Leagues from 1924 through 1930. Although the Cubs would not integrate at the major-league level until 1953, Black players appeared on minor league rosters well before then, and some made it to Wrigley Field. The White Sox hired their first Black scout, John Donaldson, in 1949. Donaldson had played for the Kansas City Monarchs from 1920 through 1924. During his time with the White Sox, a few Black players were signed. His first discovery, made while he was traveling on the team bus with the Memphis Red Sox, was Bob Boyd.

BOB BOYD

Bob Boyd was with Memphis 1949 and the early part of 1950. He had first played with the NAL team in 1947 and appeared in the East-West Game from 1947 through 1949. On Opening Day in 1949, Memphis faced the Chicago American Giants at Comiskey Park, and Boyd homered. When he homered with the White Sox on August 8, 1953, he became the first player to homer at Comiskey Park in both the Negro Leagues and the American League.

The White Sox obtained Boyd during the 1950 season, and he went to Colorado Springs, batting .373 in 42 games. In 1951, he batted .342 at Sacramento in the PCL and was a late season call-up by the White Sox.

When he debuted on September 8, 1951, he was the third Black player in White Sox history. He did not have much success with Chicago, appearing in 96 games in parts of three seasons, batting only .259. He was sold to the Cardinals and then drafted by Baltimore prior to the 1956 season and, in five seasons with Baltimore, batted .301. In his best season, 1957, he batted .318 and finished 16th in MVP balloting.

HARRY SIMPSON

The Philadelphia Stars were not a preeminent Negro League team. They had few star players and sent only a couple to the American and National leagues in the years following integration. The first player from the Stars to crash the barrier was Harry Simpson. After batting .300 with the Stars in 1948, he joined the Cleveland organization and made his AL debut in 1951. When he joined the White Sox on May 5, 1959— becoming their ninth Black player and the eighth Negro Leaguer to play with the team—Simpson had already played with the Indians, Athletics, and Yankees. In all, he played for five AL/NL teams, earning his singular nickname: "Suitcase."

BOOKER MCDANIEL

Although the Cubs did not integrate until 1953, they had Black players in their minor league system as early as 1949, when Booker McDaniel, who started with the Monarchs in 1941, played with the Los Angeles Angels of the PCL. He was the first Black player with the Angels and was with them for two seasons, posting a combined record of 11–13, but, at age 36, he was considered too old to advance any further.

ERNIE BANKS

Ernie Banks and Gene Baker arrived with the Cubs on September 14, 1953. Each had played shortstop with the Kansas City Monarchs. When Baker went to the Cubs organization in 1950, Banks was still in high school. After graduation, Banks went to the Monarchs and played for the first time on June 4, 1950, getting three hits in seven at-bats in a doubleheader against Memphis.[5]

Banks was on a fast track to integrated baseball when he got his draft notice from the United States Army. He re-joined the Monarchs when he came out of the service in 1953 and was clearly the top player in what was left of the NAL. He played in the East-West Game at Comiskey Park on August 16, 1953. John Donaldson suggested that the White Sox sign Banks, but they passed on the opportunity. Banks was sold to the Cubs on Tuesday September 8 and reported on

Ernie Banks: It's a Beautiful Day For Baseball—Let's Play Two!

Monday September 14.[6] In his last Negro League at-bat, on September 13, he singled, stole second base, and scored the winning run in a 2–1 win over Birmingham at Pittsburgh's Forbes Field.[7] In his first batting practice swing with the Cubs the next day, he hit a ball over the fence at Wrigley Field.[8]

He made his Cubs debut on September 17, 1953. By the time he had finished playing with the Cubs in 1971, more than 30 Black players had been with the team, nine of whom had played in the Negro Leagues.

GENE BAKER

Baker spent four seasons in the Cubs' minor-league system after playing with the Monarchs in 1948 and 1949. After beginning the 1950 season with Springfield in the International League, he was sent down to Des Moines in May, breaking the color line in the Western League. In the beginning of July, after batting .321 in 49 games in Class A, he was promoted to the Los Angeles Angels in the PCL, where he batted .280 in 100 games. His first game with the Cubs was on September 20, 1953.

SAMMY DRAKE

One of Banks's teammates on the 1953 Monarchs was Sammy Drake. Drake joined the Cubs organization in 1954 but did not get to the big leagues until 1960. He was the 13th Black player for the Cubs and the eighth whose path to the Big Leagues included a stint in the Negro Leagues. Most of the Black players that joined the Cubs had played in the Negro Leagues prior to 1949, the only exceptions being Drake and Banks.

LUIS MARQUEZ

Joining Banks and Baker with the Cubs in 1954 was Luis Marquez. Marquez starred in Puerto Rico and played in the Negro Leagues from 1946 through 1948, batting .324 in 1947. In 1949, he broke the color line with the Portland Beavers of the PCL, and, in 1951, joined the Boston Braves, becoming their second Black player. He was the first colored Puerto Rican player to make it to the AL/NL major leagues. On April 13, 1954, when he entered the game as a defensive replacement in the seventh inning, he became the third Black player in the history of the Cubs.

THE FINAL THREE: GEORGE ALTMAN, LOU JOHNSON, AND WILLIE SMITH

In the last years of the Negro Leagues there were as few as four teams at the top echelon. Three players from this era joined the Cubs. On August 25, 1955, the Cubs bought three players from the Kansas City Monarchs, two of whom made it to the Cubs roster. George Altman played with the Monarchs for three months in 1955 before joining the Cubs organization. He made his Cubs debut on April 11, 1959, and played nine seasons in the majors. He was an All-Star in 1961 and 1962. Lou Johnson also played for the Monarchs in 1955. He first signed with the Yankees organization in 1953 and took a circuitous route to fame. After leaving the Pirates organization in 1955, he went to the Monarchs. He finally got to the majors with the Cubs on April 17, 1960, but is best remembered for his time with the World Champion Dodgers in 1965.

The last of the three was Willie Smith, known as Wonderful Willie Smith. He played in the Negro American League with the Detroit Stars and Birmingham Black Barons from 1957 through 1960 and played in the 1958 East-West All-Star Game. He was signed by the Detroit organization during the 1960 season and made it to the majors with the Tigers in 1963. He had his best years with the Angels and joined the Cubs in 1968. He played in parts of three seasons for the Cubs.

BUCK O'NEIL

One more name must be mentioned. In Kansas City, Altman and Johnson were managed by Buck O'Neil. After the 1955 season, O'Neil, who had brought Banks to the Monarchs in 1950, joined the Cubs as a scout, and later coached for the team. In 2022, O'Neil and Minnie Miñoso were inducted into the National Baseball Hall of Fame in Cooperstown, joining Banks and Doby. ∎

Sources

In addition to the sources shown in the notes, the author used Baseball-Reference.com, Retrosheet.org, Seamheads.com and:

Costello, Rory. Sam Hairston biography on SABR Bio-Project.

Lester, Larry and Wayne Stivers. *The Negro Leagues Book: Volume 2* (Kansas City, Noir-Tech Research, 2020).

Rives, Bob. Bob Boyd biography on SABR Bio-Project.

Notes

1. Danny Peary, *We Played the Game* (New York, Hyperion, 1994), 101.
2. "Black Barons Win Two, Play Wednesday," *Birmingham News*, May 23, 1949: 14.
3. "Eagles Whip Grays Twice to Extend League," *Columbus Dispatch*, August 18, 1941: B-3, "Satchel Paige and Mates Coming Back; Grays Lose," *Dayton Daily News*, August 18, 1941: 17.
4. "Cubs Sign Negro Scout," *Pittsburgh Courier*, April 2, 1949: 24.
5. "KayCee Monarchs, Memphis Red Sox Split Doubleheader," *Pittsburgh Courier*, June 10, 1950: 23.
6. "Two Negro Stars Bought by Cubs," *Boston Globe*, September 8, 1953: 39.
7. "Monarchs Top Barons Twice," *Pittsburgh Sun-Telegraph*, September 14, 1953: 18.
8. "Four Recruits Joins Cubs for Fall Workout," *Chicago Tribune*, September 15, 1953: F-3.

Michigan City White Caps

Bob Webster

In the early 1950s, minor league baseball was in a decline. Televisions were fairly new and air conditioning became more affordable, giving people reasons to stay home. More recreational activities became available. Going to a ballpark in the evening for entertainment and to cool off wasn't as necessary as it had been in the past. With many people moving to the suburbs, ballparks were no longer close by. There were 59 leagues and more than 400 minor league teams in the late 1940s. By the end of the '50s, 300 cities had lost their minor league teams.[1] Independent teams were the first to go. They did not have the financial backing to stay afloat on their own. The Mississippi-Ohio Valley League was a Class-D league, which had its beginnings as the Illinois State League in 1947. Following the 1955 season, the league expanded and changed its name to the Midwest League. Since the geographical footprint of the league now reached into Illinois, Iowa, and Indiana, the old name did not fit well anymore.

The Hannibal Citizens were in trouble. Known as the Cardinals in 1953 and 1954, the Hannibal, Missouri, team lost their affiliation with the St. Louis Cardinals in 1955. Even though attendance at Clemens Field (named after Hannibal native Samuel Clemens, also known as Mark Twain) increased from 33,065 in 1954 to 40,977 in 1955, the newly independent team's existence was in jeopardy without the financial backing that came from affiliation with a major league team.

Al Shinn, a 20-year-old first baseman for the Citizens, took over as player-manager during the 1955 season. On January 29, 1955, he married Georgiana Lewis in Chicago. Georgiana's family lived in Long Beach, Indiana, which borders Michigan City on the north/northeast side. Michigan City and Long Beach are located on the southern shores of Lake Michigan. Whenever games in Kokomo and Lafayette (Indiana) were rained out, he would visit his in-laws in Long Beach. Knowing that baseball in Hannibal was in trouble, Shinn and his brother-in-law, Bob Hood, talked about bringing baseball to Michigan City.[2] Shinn and Hood took a "man on the street" poll and determined that Michigan City was open to supporting minor league baseball.[3] On November 28, 1955, league directors met in Columbus, Ohio. They voted to change the name of the Mississippi-Ohio Valley League to the Midwest League, and granted Michigan City a franchise for the 1956 season, with Opening Day scheduled for April 29.[4] The "White Caps," a reference to nearby Lake Michigan and its breaking waves, became a minor league affiliate of the New York Giants. Michigan City already had a ballpark. Ames Field, a 4,000-seat park, was completed in 1939. There was room to add more seats if necessary, with a parking lot beyond the right field wall and a grassy area with playground equipment, a fountain, and tennis courts beyond the center and left field walls.

There were obstacles to playing in Michigan City. Ames Field was already scheduled heavily by youth baseball. The team's ownership group, which was led by Shinn, hired Ralph Waterhouse as club president. Waterhouse already headed up the youth baseball leagues and only agreed to the position with the minor league club provided the new team's schedule didn't interfere with the youth leagues.[5] There were also concerns that two big-league teams played in Chicago, only 54 miles away. It wasn't certain that fans would attend Class-D games when the Cubs and White Sox were so close. Just two miles from the ballpark, Lake Michigan presented its own obstacle. Washington Park, at the northern edge of Michigan City, was a great place to swim, and it featured an amusement park and a zoo. The concern was that the townspeople might prefer cooling off at the lake to putting up with the heat at a ballpark.[6] The attendance goal for the inaugural season was 50,000, or approximately 800 people for each of the 63 home games. Former Notre Dame football coach Frank Leahy, who lived in Long Beach, was brought in to head up advanced ticket sales.[7] As promotional stunts, the team set aside certain days for citizens of various cities in the area to attend games as a group. The cities included: St. Joseph, Benton Harbor, and Niles, Michigan, along with Gary, Hammond, Valparaiso, LaPorte, and South Bend, Indiana.[8] Ames

SABR/THE RUCKER ARCHIVE

Future Hall of Famer Juan Marichal was one of the most significant players to wear a White Caps uniform.

Field was approaching 20 years old, and needed some sprucing up in preparation for the White Caps. It received a complete paint job, a new press box, and a screen to protect fans from foul balls. A new, covered dugout down the first base side would house the visiting team. A large board down the right field line listed the standings, and a new scoreboard, operated from the press box, sat atop the left field wall.[9] Opening Day, April 29, 1956, had an interesting twist. The White Caps opened the Midwest League season in an afternoon game at Kokomo, then traveled back to Michigan City for an 8:00 rematch that same evening. Approximately 6,000 were expected to attend Opening Day at Ames Field. Mayor Fedder tossed the first pitch. Four bands were scheduled to be in a parade that escorted the team to Ames Field. A color guard raised the flag and orchids were handed out to the first 500 ladies in attendance.[10] Attendance for the 1956 season totaled 48,765, or 774 per game, so they came very close to meeting their attendance goals for their inaugural season.

Twenty-one-year-old player-manager Al Shinn led the White Caps to a 55–71 record in 1956, good for seventh place. Charlie Alsop's 14–7 record and league-leading 2.64 ERA earned him a spot on the All-Star team. He was the only White Caps player to make the All-Star team in 1956. Bill Redfield, sports editor for the *Michigan City Post-Dispatch* said in July that the club "stood a good chance of finishing on the right side of the financial ledger." Redfield also said, "the galleries seldom have been below 600 and have surpassed 1,200 on occasions.[11] 1956, the Al Shinn-led ownership group sold the team to a group headed by M.B. Bergerson. Bergerson was president of B & K Products, the firm that ran root beer stand franchises in the Midwest.[12] The 1957 club improved to 68–57. John Orsino

and Manny Mota earned spots on the All-Star team. Future major leaguer Bobby Bolin led the team with 15 wins. Orsino, Mota, Bolin, Matty Alou, and Bob Farley all eventually played in the majors.

The White Caps' best year was 1958. Former major leaguer Buddy Kerr managed the team. The shortstop had amassed a .249 batting average in his nine-year major-league career, the first seven with the New York Giants and the final two with the Boston Braves. Jose Tartabull joined Juan Marichal as the two future-major leaguers on the club. Marichal's 21 wins and 1.87 ERA led the Midwest League. He was Rookie of the Year as well as an All-Star, and Buddy Kerr was named the league's Manager of the Year. The White Caps won the first half of the season and Waterloo took the second half. Waterloo won the five-game championship series, 3–2.

Marichal, who would go on to a Hall-of-Fame career, was the most famous player to ever wear a White Caps uniform. Michigan City was his first assignment after being signed by the Giants. He credits White Caps manager Buddy Kerr with his early success.[13] When spring training camp broke in 1958, a bus headed for Michigan City. Among the players were three Latinos and four blacks. Marichal was not introduced to racism in the farming communities of the Dominican Republic and was quite surprised to see that when the bus stopped to eat, they had to check to see if the seven dark-skinned players could eat inside with the White players. He said that Kerr always made sure that the seven were served their meal before he would eat. In addition to his sparkling record and ERA, Marichal struck out 246 batters in 245 innings, and was the winning pitcher in both of Michigan City's championship series victories. Despite their success, by 1958 it was apparent that the White Caps, averaging only about 500 fans per game, were not a profitable team. It was estimated that they needed around 700 fans per game to break even. According to Bill Redfield, the Michigan City newsman, the franchise was churning out some decent prospects, enough to keep the Giants happy. Much of their success in 1958 was because of the way Kerr handled the young players.[14] Things fell apart for the White Caps in 1959. On the field, their 51–74 record was good for eighth and last place in the

Table 1. White Caps Year-by-Year Results

Year	Position	GB	W	L	Pct	Attendance
1956	Seventh	18.5	55	71	.437	48,765
1957	Fourth	8	68	57	.544	25,484
1958	Second	1.5	69	55	.556	30,562
1959	Eighth	25.5	51	74	.408	28,775

At age 18 in 1957, Matty Alou played in Michigan City in his first stint in the minor leagues.

not represented at a league meeting held in Davenport, Iowa, in November and did not submit the dues. The four-year run for the Michigan City White Caps was over.[15] ∎

league. Jose Tartabull did however lead the Midwest League with 106 runs scored. Rick Joseph and Wayne Schurr joined Tartabull as future-major leaguers to play for the White Caps that year.

Off the field, the Giants changed their Midwest League affiliation from Michigan City to Quincy, Illinois, for the 1960 season. Without major league affiliation, Michigan City could no longer field a team. There was a deadline of January 15, 1960, for teams to post a league membership dues of $1,000. Michigan City was

Notes

1. Lloyd Johnson and Miles Wolff, "The Decline: 1952–1962," *The Encyclopedia of Minor League Baseball*, Second Edition (Durham: Baseball America, 1997), 411.
2. Allan D. Shinn Obituary, https://www.legacy.com/us/obituaries/dailyjournalonline/name/allan-shinnobituary?id=14343775. Accessed February 2, 2023.
3. Dick Micell, "Michigan City in 'Pro' Debut," *South Bend Tribune*, March 25, 1956, 39.
4. Bob Ford, "Midwest Baseball League is Formed," *Kokomo Tribune*, November 29, 1955, 32.
5. Micell.
6. Micell.
7. Micell.
8. Paul S. Peterson, "The Sports Scene," *The Herald Press* (St. Joseph, Michigan), April 26, 1956, 8.
9. "Michigan City Prepares for Baseball Team," *Vidette-Messenger of Porter County*, March 10, 1956, 5.
10. Peterson.
11. Bob Barnet, "'D' Baseball Flourishes at Michigan City," *Muncie Star*, July 3, 1956, 16.
12. "Michigan City Group Buys Baseball Club," *Decatur Sunday Herald and Review*, July 22, 1956, 19.
13. Juan Marichal and Lew Freedman, *Juan Marichal* (Minneapolis: MVP Books, 2011), 35–39.
14. Dick Micell, "Sideline Slants," *South Bend Tribune*, July 27, 1958, 34.
15. Al Ney, "Midwest League 10 Teams Now, Probably 8 Soon," *The Courier* (Waterloo, Iowa), November 23, 1959, 15.

1967: A Perfect Season for Ken Holtzman

A Cubs Weekend Wonder in the Summer of Love

Jeff Allan Howard

The flip side of Ken Holtzman's 1968 Topps baseball card speaks to the 22-year-old's accomplishments in 1967, his sophomore season in The Show: "While fulfilling his military obligations. Ken pitched for Chicago whenever he was able to get a weekend pass."

Conscription was a real factor in young people's lives in 1967. As the Vietnam War escalated, some were drafted, others waited to be drafted, and some enlisted. Ken Holtzman enlisted in the Illinois National Guard in January 1967. The call to active service ultimately came with an order to report on May 22, 1967.[1] Holtzman's saga was not unique for the times. In fact, *Sports Illustrated* observed, "For the first time since World War II, both major league pennant races could be determined by military obligations."[2] The young Cubs roster endured more absences than most teams, though none was quite as drastic as Holtzman's.[3] Holtzman started just 12 games in 1967. The first three inconspicuously ended up as no-decisions. On Saturday night, April 29, Holtzman logged his first victory, a nine-inning, six-hit, complete game performance against the fledging Houston Astros. The Cubs triumphed, 4–1, at the Astrodome.

On May 5, back at Wrigley Field, Holtzman scored his second win against his hometown team, the St. Louis Cardinals. The feat was not without some drama. Holtzman was lifted for a pinch-hitter in the bottom of the seventh inning, with the Cubs trailing, 3–1. A three-run rally sparked by four consecutive two-out-singles by Billy Williams, Lee Thomas, Ron Santo, and Ernie Banks salvaged a 5–3 triumph. Said Holtzman, "First time, I've ever won a game up here after leaving it."[4] Holtzman won his third game in a row on Wednesday, May 10, before just 2,176 fans on a rugged 48-degree Chicago afternoon. Luck was on his side again during the 5–4 victory over the San Francisco Giants. Holtzman's rocky pitching line in the adverse conditions included 7⅔ innings, eight hits, and eight walks. He loaded the bases in the second, third, and fourth innings, but the Giants left 14

men on base in the game. Dick Radatz came in from the pen to retire Willie Mays with two outs in the eighth, and survived a shaky ninth inning to secure the win.

Holtzman's fourth win came against the Dodgers in the City of Angels. Holtzman pitched a complete game in an epic, 11-inning, three-hour and 24-minute affair. It was the nightcap of a marathon Sunday doubleheader in which both games went to extras. Holtzman himself began a rally with a one-out single off Dodger reliver Ron Perranoski in the top of the eleventh inning. The Cubs won, 6–3, after subsequent singles by Popovich, Beckert, and Billy Williams, who further supported the win with a perfect 5–5 day at the plate.[5] A May 20 game at Wrigley Field was Holtzman's last start before reporting for duty. The Cubs honored him with a 20–3 shellacking of the Dodgers, including home runs by Adolpho Phillips, Randy Hundley, and Beckert. The defense chipped in with three double plays. Holtzman pitched a complete game, yielding seven hits and striking out three.

Holtzman began service with the 108th US Army National Guard Medical Battalion in Fort Polk, Louisiana. A June 17 Associated Press photo documented his training experience. It was captioned, "Baseball Pro in New Training," and quoted Holtzman as saying, "Actually, I kind of like it."[6] Holtzman graduated basic training on July 22 and continued service obligations with medic training in San Antonio, Texas, at the Brooke Army Medical Center on Fort Sam Houston.[7] Holtzman discovered he could fly to a game destination, start a

Ken Holtzman

baseball game, and return to military service all while on a weekend pass. To properly prepare for that event, the Cubs dispatched Elvin Tappe to Texas. The two spent about two weeks gradually working Holtzman's arm back into shape.[8]

On August 13, after 85 days without throwing a big-league pitch, Holtzman came home to Chicago for the first game of a Sunday doubleheader. Some 32,750 fans saw Holtzman go $5\frac{1}{3}$ innings before running out of gas.[9] "When Mr. Durocher came in the sixth and asked me if I was struggling," Holtzman said, "I said I was and that was it." Bill Stoneman saved the 6–2 victory against the Phillies.[10]

On Saturday, August 19, Holtzman missed a flight connection but eventually arrived in the Liberty Bell City after stops in Atlanta and Baltimore.[11] The next day, he notched his seventh straight win, going eight innings against the Phillies. The Cubs won, 6–1, and Stoneman once again provided relief help. The offense provided a 14-hit barrage with a home run from Ernie Banks.[12]

It took two weeks for Holtzman to get another weekend pass. He faced the Mets in the nightcap of a Sunday doubleheader on September 3, the day before Labor Day. It was the seventh straight game between the two teams in just four days.[13] Holtzman threw $7\frac{2}{3}$ innings for the 6–3 victory.

Holtzman flew to Cincinnati for the penultimate game of the regular season. On Saturday, September 30, the Cubs welcomed their teammate by rocking Reds starter Milt Pappas with an eight-spot in the first inning. That made Holtzman's work easy, and he coasted to a 9–4 victory at Crosley Field. His six-inning stint helped the secure a third-place finish. Holtzman ended the season with a perfect 9–0 record.

In the game of baseball, perfection rarely happens. The game is not designed for perfect performance, but it is occasionally accentuated by such acts of noteworthy achievement. There have been perfect days at the plate by batters. There have been rare perfect games thrown by pitchers. Perfect seasons thrown by pitchers are even rarer.

You will not find Holtzman in Cooperstown, but he has been inducted into the Chicago Cubs Hall of Fame, the National Jewish Sports Hall of Fame, and the St. Louis Sports Hall of Fame. In a 2018 interview upon his induction the St. Louis Sports Hall of Fame, Holtzman reflected on the 1967 season, "The military and the Major Leagues allowed me to travel, and it seemed like every time I showed up, the Cubs would score eight or ten runs and I wound up 9-0. It was just one of those magical years."[14]

Holtzman did have run support as he supported his country. In the four "leave games," the Cubs scored six runs three times and nine runs once, for a total of 27. In all, they rang up 67 runs for Holtzman's nine wins.

On August 14, reflecting on Holtzman's first start after military training, *Chicago Tribune* reporter Robert Markus wrote, "More than 30,000 turned out yesterday to cheer for Kenny Holtzman. It's not that Ken Holtzman has done more than millions of other young men before him. It's just that when they called his name he answered. He marched off to do his duty and perhaps it's a reflection of our times that a man can be a hero for doing no more that than— his duty."[15] ∎

Notes

1. Robert Markus. "Must Serve at Least 6 Months: Cubs lost Holtzman to Active Duty," *Chicago Tribune*, May 7, 1967, B1.
2. "Scoreboard. Secret Weapon," *Sports Illustrated*, June 26, 1967, 14. https://vault.si.com/vault/1967/06/26/42991#&gid= ci0258bdee400226ef&pid=42991---016---image. The article cites multiple teams and players affected by military service in 1967, including Jim Lonborg, Joe Morgan, Rod Carew, and Mickey Lolich.
3. "Cubs Regain Popovich, Lose Ellis," *Chicago Tribune*, August 15, 1967, C2. Paul Popovich spent two weeks with the West Virginia National Guard and had returned just as pitcher Jim Ellis started a two-week stint with the Marines. Cubs infielders Glenn Beckert, Don Kessinger and Paul Popovich also served intermittent military obligations that season.
4. Edward Prell. "3-Run rally in 7th Brings 5–3 triumph," *Chicago Tribune*, May 6, 1967, E1.
5. Game 1 also went to extra innings, with the Dodgers winning, 2–1, on a two-out, walk-off single by Willie Davis in the tenth. Don Drysdale logged the win.
6. The AP Photo caption also stated that he was "the only pitcher in the National League with a perfect record."
7. Richard Dozer. "Cubs Triumph in 12: Beat Giants, 5–4." *Chicago Tribune*, July 22, 1967, F1.
8. "The Pitcher is a Private." July 26, 1967 AP Wire photo. Photo with Holtzman (in Army fatigues) and Tappe with caption that reads, "Cubs pitcher Ken Holtzman puts on a glove for a workout with Cub coach Elvin Tappe. Holtzman…Tappe is here to give the young pitcher daily workouts after the Army work day is over." Tappe, a former catcher and member of the College-of-Coaches was a current scout in the Cubs organization.
9. George Langford, "Ken Gives blood to Hurl for Cubs," *Chicago Tribune*, August 13, 1967, B1. In the article, Holtzman said, "The only reason I was assured of being here was because I donated a couple pints of blood for Viet Nam. Which automatically gets you a pass."
10. George Langford, "Holtzman Gets Answers," *Chicago Tribune*, August 14, 1967. C2.
11. "Holtzman Will Pitch Against the Phillies Today." *Chicago Tribune*. August 20, 1967, B1.
12. Richard Dozer, "Cubs Rout Phillies, 6–1," *Chicago Tribune*, August 21, 1967. C1. "Holtzman could have gone the distance but to do so, it risked him being AWOL on his return to camp. As it was, he pitched 8 innings, exited the game, showered, left the ballpark with suitcase in hand, grabbed a cab at 5:30 to make his 6:25 flight to San Antonio."
13. It marked the third successive doubleheader between the two teams on Labor Day weekend, due to the need to make up four rainouts. A Thursday makeup game from a June 10 Chicago rainout started the series. The three doubleheaders allowed the teams to make up three straight rainouts in New York City in August (with a rare site change). The Cubs won five of the seven contests.
14. St. Louis Sports Hall of Fame 2018 Induction interview. https://www.stlshof.com/ken-holtzman, 6:28.
15. Robert Markus, "When Kenny Comes Marching Home," *Chicago Tribune*, August 14, 1967, C3.

The South Side's First Home-Run King

Joseph Wancho

" Now it's even. It's neck and neck. We'll start from here and see who's boss."
—Reggie Jackson[1]

There have been two players in Chicago White Sox history that led the American League in home runs. Only two over the first 123 seasons of baseball on the south side of Chicago. The second of those two players led the league in two different seasons. The first did not accomplish the feat until 1971, 70 years after the American League went major in 1901.

It might seem like a low number, but the White Sox built their greatest teams on fielding, speed, and pitching. As of 2022, there have been seven players for the franchise that have hit 40 or more home runs in a season. However, none of them led the league in home runs.

Bill Melton is not one of those seven. But the California native, who became to be known as "Beltin' Melton" to the Comiskey Park faithful, broke through the 71-year drought by finishing on top of the AL heap with 33 home runs in 1971.[2]

Melton showed an aptitude for hitting early on. At Citrus College, he batted .300 and hit nine home runs. It was his good fortune that Chicago White Sox scout Hollis Thurston was on hand to witness his exploits. "The reason I signed was because I primarily needed the money to go to school," said Melton. "At that particular time, there was not a draft and the most they could offer me was $8,000. I remember hitting a couple of home runs over 400 feet at Brookside Park, the day Hollis Thurston was there. He offered me something like $2,000, $5,000, and then $8,000 after the last home run which was about 450 feet."[3]

In 1964, Melton began the long and winding road to the big leagues in the Sarasota Rookie League as a second baseman and outfielder. From there, he made stops in Appleton, Wisconsin (1966) with the Class A Fox Cities and in Evansville, Indiana (1967) with the AA White Sox.

He began the 1968 season at AAA Hawaii of the Pacific Coast League. Melton was called up to the White Sox, making his major league debut on May 4,

1968, against the New York Yankees at Comiskey Park. Playing third base and batting seventh, Melton knocked in a run by way of a sacrifice fly in the bottom of the second inning. Chicago won the game 4–1. "I wasn't even shaky," said Melton. "I guess I was too tired to be scared. I've only had about five hours sleep in the last 50 after they called me up."[4]

As for playing third base, Melton was getting a crash course from Chicago manager Eddie Stanky's coaching staff. "Most of my instructions on how to play third base were done on a plane," said Melton. "I will never forget Eddie Stanky's coaches, they were drawing on an airplane napkin, on a bunt situation you want to play here."[5]

Chicago sent Melton back down to Hawaii on May 22. Melton returned to the White Sox in September 1968. Stanky had been fired after the Sox started the season with a 34–45 record. He was eventually replaced with Al Lopez.[6] Stanky had taken over for Lopez after 1965 due to Lopez dealing with an illness. Now, Lopez was replacing "The Brat" three years later.

In that final month, Melton appeared in seventeen games and batted .317. He swatted two home runs and drove in thirteen runs. As a result, Lopez all but handed Melton the third base job for 1969. "But where I look for the biggest lift is at third base, with our rookie Bill Melton," said Lopez. "This kid really swings a good bat. He knocked in some big runs for us after we brought him up late in the season."[7]

Pete Ward was one of seven players who started at third base for Chicago in 1968. Ward started 77 games at the hot corner, more than the others. Ward was a versatile player who also saw playing time at first base and the corner outfield positions. However, Ward batted .216 in 1968 and Lopez felt that there must be a be a better solution.

Melton's first big moment came on June 24, 1969. Chicago beat the Seattle Pilots 7–6 in the nightcap of a doubleheader at Sicks' Stadium. In the that second

103

Bill Melton

game, Melton went four-for-five with three home runs and a double, becoming the fifth player in White Sox history to hit three home runs in one game. Melton victimized Seattle starter Fred Talbot with solo home runs in the second and fourth innings. In the sixth, Melton connected off Pilots' reliever John O'Donoghue. All three home runs were hit over the left field wall. In the ninth, he smoked a line-drive double to left field that fell several feet short of the outfield wall. "What has helped me is leveling my bat," said Melton. "Originally, I held my bat straight up. Then last fall in the Instructional League, Al Lopez suggested I go even farther. He had me hold the bat back, even with the ground. Well, it worked well until recently when I began dropping my right shoulder with the result I was uppercutting again. I've gone back to a 45-degree angle."[8]

The adjustments Melton made at the plate paid off. In his first full season he led the Sox in home runs (23), doubles (26), and RBI (87) while batting .255. In the AL, only expansion Kansas City (Ed Kirkpatrick with 14) and California (Rick Reichardt with 13) had home run leaders with a lesser total than Melton. "Bill Melton has done better than anybody has a right to expect," said Sox shortstop Luis Aparicio. "But he needs help."[9]

In spite of the new infusion of talent, the White Sox were not a competitive team. Their drop in the standings was astounding. In 1967 under Stanky, the White Sox were in a pennant race with Detroit, Boston, and Minnesota until the final week of the season. They finished in fourth place with an 89–73 record. But in 1968 they plummeted to eighth place with a 67–95 mark, 36 games behind pennant-winning Detroit. The following year with expansion came the realignment into two divisions. Chicago fared no better, finishing in fifth place of the six-team AL West division with a 68–94 record.

Lopez resigned due to health reasons seventeen games into the 1969 season. He was replaced with long-time coach Don Gutteridge. The revolving managerial

door continued in 1970 when Gutteridge was let go on September 1 after the Sox plummeted to the AL West cellar with a 49–87 record. Ultimately, he was replaced with Chuck Tanner.

Melton continued to smash home runs at a record pace. On September 21, 1970, Melton became the first player in White Sox history to hit 30 or more home runs in a season. In the first game of a doubleheader against Kansas City, Melton smacked a solo shot off Royals' relief pitcher Aurelio Monteagudo. The home run was Melton's 22nd smash hit at home. The previous mark was 21 set by Zeke Bonura in 1934.

The spider webs on the Comiskey Park turnstiles were hardly disturbed as only 672 tickets were sold. Many more will swear they were there to witness the record-breaking night.

Melton eclipsed the previous record of 29 home runs set by Gus Zernial (1950) and Ed Robinson (1951). Melton ended the season with 33 round-trippers, finishing sixth in the league.

The year was not all glory for Melton, who split time with Syd O'Brien at third base. When he wasn't in the hot corner, Melton was patrolling right field. Gutteridge did not view Melton much as a third baseman, but Tanner felt otherwise.

One big change for the White Sox was the insertion of Wilbur Wood into the starting rotation. The southpaw knuckleballer had mostly pitched in relief with some spot starting assignments sprinkled during his ten seasons. Chicago's team ERA shrank from 4.54 in 1970 to 3.12 in 1971.

Two key additions came via the trade route. Chicago obtained outfielders Jay Johnstone from California and Rick Reichardt from Washington, which added some pop to their lineup and solidified its outfield.

Melton was inserted into the cleanup spot of the White Sox lineup with Carlos May either before him or in the five-hole. The rest of the lineup was adjusted as Tanner sought the right combination.

At the beginning of the year, Melton swatted only six home runs through May 31. But in June he caught fire. Strengthened by a stretch of four games (June 14–17) "Beltin' Melton" clubbed four home runs and totaled eleven RBI. In all, he hit twelve homers, drove in 26 runs and batted .311 in June. It was easily the most productive month of his career to date.

At the All-Star break on July 11, 1971, Melton was batting .286 with 20 home runs and 52 RBI. Melton and Detroit's Norm Cash shared the AL home run leaderboard with 20 apiece. Boston's Reggie Smith and Minnesota's Tony Oliva were right behind with eighteen.

Melton was passed over for the All-Star game, held July 13 at Tiger Stadium. The AL were victorious, 6–4, breaking an eight-game losing slump against the senior circuit. The bottom of the third inning was indeed historic. Oakland's Reggie Jackson smashed a ball that banged off a light tower on top of the ballpark. Later in the inning, Baltimore's Frank Robinson also homered, becoming the first player to hit a home run for each league.

As the final month of the season approached, Cash, Smith, and Melton were all tied with 27 home runs. Jackson trailed by two with 25 dingers. The home run race may have tightened, but the same could not be said for the AL West division championship. Oakland (87–47) flexed its muscles and held a sixteen-game lead over second-place Kansas City (70–62). Chicago (63–70), although it showed improvement in the standings, were in third place, 23½ games out.

On September 23, with a week left in the season, Cash, Jackson, and Melton were all even with 30 home runs. On September 28, Cash swatted two solo home runs off Steve Hargan at Cleveland. Jackson, who had led by one, also hit a solo homer against Mike Hedlund of Kansas City.

Melton had yet to have a multi-homer game in 1971. Tanner inserted Melton into the leadoff position to potentially give the slugger more at bats. On September 29, he broke through for his first. The White Sox won 2–1 over Milwaukee at Comiskey Park. Both runs came off single shot home runs by Melton off the Brewers' Jim Slaton. "I spread myself out more in the batter's box, moved closer to the plate, choked two inches on the bat—a Mike Andrews model that I tried earlier in the season," said Melton. "And I went up there guessing on the pitches. I guessed at a pitch and if I didn't get it, I let it go by. But I wasn't about to walk. Sure, I was going for the home run. I have been for three weeks."[10]

On Thursday, September 30, 1971, Melton made White Sox history, clubbing a home run off Brewers' pitcher Bill Parsons in the third inning. The miniscule crowd of an announced 2,814 fans cheered loudly in cavernous Comiskey Park. "I was so happy today, I didn't know what to do," said Melton. "When I got to the dugout, I threw my batting helmet into the crowd. Then I went back into the clubhouse because Tanner told me he would take me out of the game if I got the 33rd. But Rich Morales came back and told me the fans were still standing and cheering for me to come back so I did."

When Melton eventually got back to the clubhouse, the fan who caught the historic ball was waiting for him. "I gave him $50 for it," said Melton. "He said it was the 490th ball he had gotten here and Wrigley Field. I asked him if he ever worked."[11]

In the off-season, Chicago traded Tommy John and infielder Steve Huntz to Los Angeles for first baseman Dick Allen. That season Allen became the second, and last, White Sox player to lead the league in home runs. He hit 37 home runs in 1972 and 32 home runs in 1974.

Melton suffered a back injury in October 1971. He fell from the roof of his house and landed on his tailbone. He returned to the Sox lineup in 1972, but was lost for the rest of the season after back surgery in July.[12] Over the next three years Melton averaged 18 home runs, 73 RBI, and batted .254.

Chicago traded Melton on December 11, 1975, to the California Angels. One year later he was traded to Cleveland. Melton retired in 1977. He hit 160 home runs, drove in 591 runs, and batted .253 for his career. After his playing career, he would return to the White Sox in 1992 as a community relations representative. In 1993–94 he worked with Michael Jordan daily on his swing, helping the basketball star transition to baseball.[13] Then in 1998, Melton moved to WGN television as a White Sox pre- and postgame commentator. ∎

Notes

1. Ron Bergman, "Athletics Set One Record, Want Another—100 Wins," *Oakland Tribune*, September 20, 1971, 35.
2. Although born in Gulfsport, Mississippi in 1945, Melton considers himself a native of California.
3. Mark Fletcher, "Former Chisox slugger Bill Melton interviewed," *Sports Collectors Digest*, July 30, 1993, 241.
4. George Langford, "'Cisco Kid' Wins for the White, Sox, 4–1," *Chicago Tribune*, May 5, 1968, 2–2.
5. Fletcher.
6. Assistant coach Less Moss twice took over as the White Sox manager on an interim basis.
7. Edgar Munzel, "Lopez Sees Chisox in Thick of Western Title Fight" *The Sporting News*, January 11, 1969, 43.
8. Edgar Munzel, "Melton Barely Misses a 4-HR Salvo," *The Sporting News*, July 12, 1969, 25.
9. Dave Nightingale, "Exit McGraw, Berry, Ward: 3 Sox sure they'll depart," *Chicago Daily News*, September 26, 1969, 39.
10. George Langford, "Wood, Melton Combine," *Chicago Tribune*, September 30, 1971, 2–3.
11. George Langford, "Melton A.L. Home Run King," *Chicago Tribune*, October 1, 1971, 3–6.
12. *The New York Times*, "Melton Lost for Season; Has Rare Back Treatment," July 28, 1972. https://www.nytimes.com/1972/07/28/archives/melton-lost-for-season-has-rare-back-treatment.html.
13. Curtis Koch, "Here's How Bill Melton Helped Michael Jordan Play Baseball with the White Sox," May 9, 2020, WGNRadio.com, https://wgnradio.com/sports-central/heres-how-bill-melton-helped-michael-jordan-play-baseball-with-the-white-sox.

Bill Veeck

The Second Time Around

Dan Helpingstine

Bill Veeck had a decades-long baseball career. He was known for bringing a little person up to bat with the sole intention of getting a walk because his strike zone was impossibly small. He was the first big-league owner to put names on the backs of uniforms. He erected a huge center field scoreboard in between the upper decks of Comiskey Park that became known as "The Monster." "The Monster" exploded with noise and fireworks when a White Sox player hit a home run. He tweaked the baseball establishment with other gimmicks and promotions. Eventually—at least in Chicago—Bill Veeck became known as the man "who saved the Sox." But Veeck's latter stint in the White Sox front office didn't go quite as swimmingly as some might have hoped.

After a losing 1975 season, it appeared that the Chicago White Sox, a charter member of the American League, would move from Chicago to Seattle after a 76-year run. The team had an old ballpark, an eroding fan base, and John Allyn's Artnell Co. had cash flow problems. (Former White Sox catcher Ed Herrmann would tell this writer, that, on one occasion, three dozen bats had been shipped to the White Sox when six dozen had been expected. According to Herrmann, team president Allyn told his players that "things were a little short."[1])

Veeck, who had first owned the White Sox with CBC Corp. from 1959 through 1961, stepped in with a group of investors to purchase the team and keep the franchise in Chicago. At first, the American League owners told Veeck he had to restructure his offer and finances in order to buy the club.[2] For a time, it appeared that the White Sox might still head to Seattle. However, Veeck raised an additional $1.2 million, and the league approved his purchase.[3] He was given the keys to Comiskey Park and the franchise.

Veeck's first move was to try to evoke memories of a better era of White Sox history, by hiring 67-year-old Paul Richards to manage the 1976 club. Richards, a solid baseball man, had managed the White Sox to four winning seasons in the early 1950s, including a 94–60 finish in 1954, part of an incredible string of 17 straight winning seasons, 1951–67. During that run, they managed seven seasons of 90 wins or more, five second place finishes, and—under Veeck's leadership—won the American League pennant in 1959, their first since the 1919 Black Sox.

To Veeck, there was nothing better than a big crowd at a major league ballpark. For the April 9 opener against Kansas City, a crowd that would total somewhere over 40,000 made its way into Comiskey Park. The early spring day was cool and crisp, but the sun shone like mid-summer. The distinct smell of marijuana emanated from the left-center upper deck.[4]

About an hour before game time, Veeck walked through the stands down the lower left field corner. Fans left their seats to shake his hand, pat his back, and give him hugs, showing their gratitude.[5] They knew Comiskey Park could have sat empty that day.

The opener couldn't have gone better for the White Sox. They won, 4–0, behind the complete-game, six-hit pitching performance of left-handed knuckleballer Wilbur Wood. The only glitch came in the bottom of the fifth inning when first baseman Jim Spencer hit a two-run homer and "The Monster" malfunctioned, sounding like a car engine failing to turn over. But everything else had gone so well that Veeck would later joke about the fireworks show that didn't happen, and fans went home happy.[6]

There was more fun at Comiskey on May 31 when the White Sox played the Texas Rangers. In the home first, the White Sox had the bases loaded with two out. Center fielder Chet Lemon lifted a routine fly ball to medium left. Rangers outfielder Tom Grieve took a couple steps in and then stopped. A dense fog had engulfed the stadium, and with arms helplessly extended, Grieve searched in vain for the ball that hid in the mist.

The outfield had been soaked by some recent rainy and damp weather. When the ball landed, its whiteness sank into the wet, deep green grass without the slightest bounce. The fans saw it, the Rangers infielders finally saw it, but Grieve still hadn't located it. By the time Grieve finally spotted the ball, the bases had been cleared, and Lemon slid into third with a three-RBI triple. The White Sox won the game, 9–4, and with the help of a nine-game winning streak earlier in the month, stood just three games behind first place Kansas City. Could this team, once thought to be leaving Chicago, now actually contend for the Western Division title?

Well, no. The team's weak hitting and porous outfield defense were eventually exposed. Furthermore, the sentimental hiring of Richards, who had not acted as a field manager since 1961, turned out to be a public relations debacle. By the end of August, the White Sox had sunk to last place and *Chicago Sun-Times* beat reporter Joe Goddard wrote that Richards was out of touch with his younger club. A photo accompanying his August 31 story showed Richards huddled in the corner of the dugout with his warm-up jacket zipped up to his neck. He looked lonely and cold.[7]

The story, mostly documented with anonymous sources, told of Richards acting detached and uninterested. He had stopped taking lineup cards to the umpires, instead letting players do the chore. One time a player noticed that Richards didn't have a third baseman in the lineup. Richards told the player to pencil himself in.

An incensed Veeck held a news conference to respond to the Goddard story and demanded the anonymous sources come forward.[8] None did, and Veeck had to know they wouldn't. They were anonymous for a reason. If any of these players wanted to play for the White Sox or any other team in 1977, they couldn't admit they had ratted on their manager. Meanwhile, the Goddard story was never truly discredited.

The final month of the season was a disaster. The White Sox dropped 16 of their last 17. In a three-game series against the Twins, the Sox sold a combined total of 9,762 tickets and were outscored, 22–9, in a Minnesota sweep. They finished last, 25½ games behind division-winning Kansas City, and they barely avoided losing 100 games. It was the team's second worst season since 1950. A baseball season, that had begun with good cheer, newfound hope, and evoked memories of winning campaigns, ended with disgusted fans believing their team had quit on them.

Enter the Rent-a-Player strategy. Since Veeck couldn't compete with George Steinbrenner or other well-monied owners when it came to signing free agents or keeping star players, he came up with a tactic that he hoped would help in the short run. He would trade a player or players he knew he would not be able to sign, in exchange for another player he knew would not be able to sign. In essence, he was "renting" a player for a season before that player would move on elsewhere.

Veeck began by sending left-handed Terry Forster and future Hall of Famer Rich Gossage to Pittsburgh for power-hitting right fielder Richie Zisk. Then, right before the 1977 season began, slick fielding shortstop Bucky Dent was traded to the Yankees for Oscar Gamble. Because of the strong years Zisk and Gamble put up, the transactions succeeded. But in the long run, they also failed.

With Zisk and Gamble leading the way, the 1977 team became one of the most popular in franchise history. Because of a revamped and suddenly potent offense, the 1977 White Sox became known as the "South Side Hitmen." No lead was safe against them. One hit led to another and another, and the devastating Hitmen offense annihilated their opposition.

Comiskey Park rocked with noise and emotion that summer. Fans sitting in the left field seats held up banners that read, "Pitch at Risk to Zisk." The stadium would echo with the refrain from Queen's "We Will Rock You" during rallies. And fans would cheer loud and long after home runs, demanding that players do "curtain calls." The home-run hitter felt the obligation to step out of the dugout to tip his hat. By the end of July, the White Sox sat in first place, 5½ games ahead of Kansas City and Minnesota.

But despite all the excitement and fun, there were newspaper stories circulating that Zisk and Gamble would not return in 1978. After all, they were "rent-a-players." (Gamble told this writer that Veeck did make an offer to him but that it didn't come close to what San Diego would offer.)[9]

In the end, Kansas City went on a tear during the last two months of the season. The Royals ended up

Orestes "Minnie" Miñoso and Bill Veeck had a longstanding friendship that spanned multiple decades in baseball.

Bill Veeck once replied to a fan letter, stating the motto he found most inspiring was "Success comes in cans, failure comes in can'ts."

winning 102 games and took their second division title in a row.

But the Sox fans still loved their Hitmen. After a meaningless 3–2 loss in the final game of the season against Seattle, fans wouldn't leave Comiskey. They remained in the old stadium for about an hour and a half, wanting to hold onto the memories of 1977. But the dismantling of the team would lead to one of the most infamous incidents in team history: Disco Demolition.

Drawing fans had grown tough as the memories of the Hitmen faded. The dropping attendance only made things worse for the financially strapped franchise. The White Sox were on their way to their sixth losing season of the decade. The front office was looking for innovative ways to draw a crowd. They succeeded on July 12, 1979.

Mike Veeck, Bill's son, cooked up the idea. He approached Chicago radio personality Steve Dahl with it. Dahl had been let go from WDAI-FM when the station switched its programming to Disco. Dahl was able to catch on with WLUP-FM, but he still hated Disco and remained angry about his dismissal.

The concept of Disco Demolition was simple. Fans could gain entry to Comiskey for a doubleheader against Detroit with a Disco record and $.98. (98 was the frequency of WLUP.) The records would then be collected and blown up on the field in between games. It seemed like a winning proposition. WLUP would promote it, the White Sox would get a decent crowd, and Rock and Roll fans could vent about the hated Disco music they thought was destroying American culture.

The White Sox got more than a decent crowd. Over 47,000 jammed into the old ballpark with more outside wanting to get in on the fun. A thick haze of marijuana smoke hung over the upper deck like the fog during the May 31, 1976, game. Anyone could see that the atmosphere was menacing.

Steve Dahl went onto the field and the disco records were blown up on cue. Then everything blew up.

An AP photo by Fred Jewell tells a great deal of the story.[10] Instead of a "Pitch at Risk to Zisk" banner, a "Disco Sucks" flag hangs from upper deck. Smoke rises up in center field close to the warning track. "Fans" swarm over the field with more on the way. A scoreboard message asking people to return to their seats glows ineffectually.

There was so much damage to the field that the second game was forfeited to the Tigers. Veeck's critics piled on. His gimmicks and tricks had finally caught up with him, they crowed. His franchise and reputation were truly going up in smoke, and, shamefully, no one in baseball came to his defense.

The problem with Disco Demolition wasn't the resulting chaos and destruction on the field. It was merely symbolic of the wreck that was the Chicago White Sox franchise. The year 1979 marked the twentieth year since the team's last appearance in the World Series, but another appearance was not on the horizon. If the team had an interesting present and bright future, it wouldn't have needed a zany promotion to draw fans, and it certainly wouldn't have needed anything like Disco Demolition, a stunt that ultimately drew people who were not baseball fans and who did not care what they did to a historic baseball stadium. To build a future for a club in the free-agent era required one thing that Veeck didn't have: deep pockets.

A year and a half later, Veeck sold the White Sox to an investment group headed by Jerry Reinsdorf and Eddie Einhorn.

But Veeck had inherited a bad situation. The team had little talent, attendance remained a chronic problem, and the White Sox weren't coming close to contending for a division title. For a few years, the club was overshadowed by a more talented and popular Cubs team. The truth was the franchise had been on shaky ground since 1967 when they blew a chance to go to the World Series by losing the last five games of the season. On September 29, for the game in which they faced elimination from the pennant race, the White Sox sold only 12,665 tickets. Despite staying in the pennant race until the 160th game of the season, ticket sales dropped slightly from the previous year. The White Sox, because of a weak offense, were considered "boring."[11] (Then they lost the first ten of the 1968 campaign.)

But there had been the 1977 South Side Hitmen. There next time there was that much excitement at Comiskey Park was when White Sox won their first division title in 1983. LaMarr Hoyt, Richard Dotson, Ron Kittle, Britt Burns and Harold Baines were the core of that 1983 team which won 99 games. Those players had all come to the White Sox in various ways when Veeck was the owner.

A packed house of an announced 50,412 attended the July 31, 1977, doubleheader against Kansas City. The day was the high point of the season, when it appeared the slugging hitmen might have what it took to make the playoffs. Part of the draw that day was a promotion that allowed any fan with a banner to go on the field in between games. A large parade formed and made its way around the field. Unlike Disco Demolition, there was no riot or chaos. Just fans feeling like they were a part of their team. And Bill Veeck made that happen. ∎

Notes

1. Ed Herrmann, telephone interview, February 10, 2000
2. Gregory H. Wolf, "1975 Winter Meetings: The Threat of Free Agency and the Return of the Master Showman," *Baseball's Business: The Winter Meetings*, Vol. 2 (SABR: Phoenix, AZ, 2017). Also at https://sabr.org/journal/article/1975-winter-meetings-the-threat-of-free-agency-and-the-return-of-the-master-showman. Accessed June 12, 2023.
3. Joseph Durso, "Veeck Has the Funds to Pay White Sox Price Today," *The New York Times*, December 10, 1975, https://www.nytimes.com/1975/12/10/archives/veeck-has-funds-to-pay-white-sox-price-today-veeck-set-to-buy-white.html. Accessed June 12, 2023.
4. Phil Hersh, "Veeck Was the Life of Comiskey Party," *Chicago Tribune*, September 28, 1990.
5. Mike Trueblood, "Veeck Insures Fan Good Time With Sox," *Belvedere Daily Record*, April 10, 1976, 6.
6. "Holy Cow! Sox win 4–0," Bob Verdi, *Chicago Tribune*, April 10, 1976. Section 2, 1, 5.
7. Joe Goddard, telephone interview, January 9, 2009.
8. Bob Logan, "Sox chiefs refute gripes," *Chicago Tribune*, September 1, 1976, Section 6, 1, 3.
9. Oscar Gamble, telephone interview, October 15, 2004.
10. Floyd Sullivan (Editor), *Old Comiskey Park—Essays and Memories of the Historic Home of the Chicago White Sox 1910–1991* (Jefferson, NC: McFarland & Co., 2014), 110.
11. "Stanky Blasts Critics, Says Team Will Win on Guts, Determination," *Chicago Tribune*, August 25, 1967, Section C, 1.

Belle of the Ballclub

Marla Collins's Unusual Path from Cubs Ballgirl to Playboy Model

Dan VanDeMortel

Smile. Tilt your head. Lean back. A little more. You've got it. Right there. Beautiful! *Snap!*

With each pose, each shutter click, Marla Collins crossed the line from Chicago Cubs ballgirl to *Playboy* model. Both paying roles relied on sexuality: one teased and implied, the other overt. And before you hyperventilate about "pornography," know this: If Collins had it to do all over again, she would—*no* regrets. Her journey from Wrigley Field grass to *Playboy*'s glossy print proved to be a textbook case of life's serendipity.

Born in 1958 in Evergreen Park, Illinois, and raised in nearby Oak Lawn, Collins grew up shy and quiet in the Chicago suburbs. Attractive but not outgoing, she became a high school pom-pom girl and did some pageant modeling, including a Miss Illinois contest, to help crack her shell.

As part of a "mixed family" of White Sox and Cubs supporters, Collins chose the latter, vigorously tracking the team and her favorite player, all-star shortstop Don Kessinger. She took her passion to the sandlots, too, playing games with her brothers and sisters.

Upon graduation, Collins searched for her true direction. She attended Marine Valley Community College in nearby Palos Hills for two years, earning a liberal arts degree, then entered Chicago's Columbia College for courses in radio broadcasting and other subjects. "I was dabbling, jumping around, trying to figure out what I really wanted to do," she recalled.[1]

Then, unexpectedly, Collins entered the White Sox's orbit via her mother's friend, Comiskey Park concession stands head John Studnicka, whose union sought a woman to run a beer and wine stand. After successfully interviewing, she began working there during and after her school term. As the only woman alcohol vendor, she became popular, raking in considerable profit from selling 12 kegs of beer per game.

Meanwhile, changes were underway with the crosstown Cubs that would capture Collins. In 1977, longtime owner Philip Wrigley died. His son, William, took over, stressing his family had no intention of selling the team or installing light towers atop Wrigley, baseball's sole unlit venue. The "not for sale" sign fell in 1981, however, when he sold his franchise share to the *Chicago Tribune*, ending his family's 65-year reign. With Wrigley out, former Philadelphia Phillies manager Dallas Green took over as executive VP. "Building a New Tradition" became the team's marketing slogan, supported by frenetic action. Green abrasively declared lights necessary for the club's survival and quickly remade the Cubs in his image—one that had propelled the Phillies to the 1980 World Series. He imported Philadelphia bench coach Lee Elia to manage and sportswriter Ned Colletti for public relations, and traded for rookie standout (and future Hall of Famer) Ryne Sandberg, shortstop Larry Bowa, and other players. This thorough house-cleaning sparked some fans' hopes but made more cynical, tradition-bound ones cringe.

Sometime in 1981, Cubs administrative personnel visited Comiskey, where they approached Collins about becoming a ballgirl when the White Sox were out of town. Soon afterward, she met with the team's director of stadium operations, Tom Cooper. Assured she could continue her vending job, she agreed to start in 1982 on a one-year deal for about $100 ($310 in 2023 dollars) per game.[2]

Collins, then and now, is unsure why the Cubs switched from using ballboys to hiring a ballgirl, but Green's mission to freshen a musty organization was a likely factor. Oddly, the heretofore historically conservative club was following in the wake of one of baseball's most iconoclastic owners, Charles Finley of the Oakland A's. Always open to any promotion that would irritate his fellow owners and sell tickets, in 1971 he had stationed two comely, curvaceous, female high school students along the foul lines. They fielded foul balls and, between innings, served lemonade and cookies to the umpires. Clad in tight white shorts, green or gold fitting shirts, gold knee socks, and white shoes, Finley's charges mixed baseball practicality with sex appeal, capturing the eyes of fans, players, and photographers.[3] "I wanted to get the female interested in baseball," he once expressed, although winking that it didn't hurt that most interest came from men.[4]

In April 1982, Collins made history by becoming the first major league ballgirl to work between the dugouts. Her responsibilities—good weather or bad—included chasing foul balls that dropped near the screens, handing extra baseballs to the home plate umpire, and retrieving rejected ones the umpires rolled toward her. Her "office" was a nearby stool, where she awaited the umpire's signal to handle four or five dozen balls per game.

In all, it was a confined, unremarkable job. But Collins dramatically captured attention far exceeding her tasks. First, she was the *only* woman on the field. Second, the Cubs, a team historically impervious to on-field success, demonstrated better skill at selling cheesecake. Per guidelines, Collins was outfitted in a snug, pin-striped, team uniform-replica pullover shirt, even tighter, extremely high shorts, and socks and sneakers over her trim, 5"6' athletic frame.[5] Consequently, she provided a curious and sexy diversion for fans suffering through an abysmal fifth-place finish in the National League's Eastern Division.

In essence, Collins went viral. Not just with ballpark fans but with iconic WGN-TV (cable television) announcer Harry Caray, a bespectacled bon vivant—part walking baseball encyclopedia, part carnival barker—with unparalleled skill in promoting the game, the Cubs, and himself. "He really got my name out there and got me noticed. He would ask, 'Where's that ballgirl? Let's see what she's doing.' The Cubs weren't doing well, so he'd say, 'Let's look over and see what Marla's doing.' Then he started doing it more frequently," she explained.[6] Noticed, indeed. WGN-TV's national reach ensured coast-to-coast attention, resulting in better visual and name recognition than that of some Cubs. The station soon moved her closer to the visiting dugout: a better camera angle to feature her in the background when action focused on the plate.

With Collins's exploits standing out like a diamond in a pile of coal, a mutual marketing no-brainer decision ensued to continue her role for another year, and two more after that. And so did a slew of endorsements, public appearances, and interviews, including one with local rising star Oprah Winfrey. She joined the Cubs Caravan, a collection of players, coaches, and executives who toured Illinois and spring training locations to sign autographs, take pictures, wine and dine, and otherwise connect with fans.

Amidst this building adoration, Collins juggled many jobs. "I was young and still trying to figure out what I wanted to do. I had a *lot* going on," she laughed years later.[7] She was a cocktail waitress at the Park West music venue. A Chicago Italian restaurant hired her to do lunchtime coat-checks, where she made $200–$300 ($576–$864 today) per shift. Meanwhile, she sampled college courses, pondering a potential career in radio. And she continued working at Comiskey until schedule overload led her to end the four-year position.

Collins's income increased, but the connections were worth even more, transcending those with fans. "I got to know a lot of the players fairly well since I came through the aisles where they were and would hang out around the dugouts, especially when it rained. I talked and joked around with them," she remembered.[8] She met Cubs alumni such as Ernie Banks, Ron Santo, and her hero, Kessinger. And, being single, she accepted social invitations from George Brett, Keith Hernandez, Steve Sax, and Duane Kuiper.[9] Nothing romantically serious developed, but her time with Hernandez proved invaluable as he introduced her to Jack Childers and his son, Mark, of Talent Network Inc., who became her agent in 1984.

Meanwhile, Caray remained Collins's consistent promoter, even conducting interviews of her in the dugout during rain delays. "He asked all sorts of random questions. One time, he noticed my tattoo, a small rose on my right thigh. Not a lot of people had them at the time. He said, 'Can we see your tattoo?' I don't know how he found out, but I ended up showing it to him," she recollected.[10] Living a block apart in Chicago's historic Gold Coast district, she and Caray occasionally shared rides home and she met his wife, Dutchie.[11]

During the 1985 season, Caray went full tabloid. Learning that Collins was wearing an engagement ring, he hosted her on his "Tenth Inning" postgame show, requesting "All right, show America that ring of yours."[12] Which is how America—and Marla's mother—found out she was engaged to Joe Evans, a real estate developer she met through a mutual friend while on a Cubs promotional assignment. Much like her fame, the engagement materialized unpredictably, happening weeks after they had met. Proving love can be blind, Evans was a die-hard St. Louis Cardinals fan who hated the rival Cubs.

The engagement put Collins at the crossroads. And so did the Cubs blanket pass to pursue non-baseball related promotional activities. At age 27 in 1985, she was time-limited as a ballgirl and, in an era before women sideline reporters or announcers, had no foreseeable future with the Cubs. Consequently, she decided to renew the role for 1986 at $150 ($409) per game, then move on. Looking for The Next Big Thing professionally and personally, and after refusing previous offers, she decided, without asking the Cubs' permission, to pose for *Playboy* magazine. "My dad and Joe were okay with it. And my mom said, 'Why not? You're young. You'll regret it if you don't,'" she explained.[13]

Playboy had been founded in 1953 in Chicago—the "Third Coast" that "most genuinely expresses America as a whole,"—by Hugh Hefner, an unhappily married former *Esquire* copywriter.[14] It eventually defined new standards of femininity via sexualized pictorials that also portrayed women in everyday life: the kind of woman *you* could encounter in your daily routine. *Playboy* redefined masculinity, too, gearing its content and philosophy to urbane, affluent bachelors (or those who aspired to be) with a taste for life's delicacies: the forerunner of yuppies and metrosexuals.

The magazine played an important role in America's decades-long sexual revolution, eventually growing into Playboy Enterprises, Inc., a cultural institution and empire of print and video enterprises, recreational clubs, charitable activities, and merchandise. Its interviews and occasionally nude photos of celebrities made headlines. Its name adorned the top of the Playboy Building, an Art Deco Chicago skyscraper that housed editorial and business offices.[15]

Nervously but bravely, Collins travelled alone to her June 1985 two-hour test shoot at Playboy's headquarters. She was given scarves and skimpy clothing, "strategically placed, to pose in," she chuckled retrospectively.[16] Once she passed the audition, Childers helped her sign a $20,000 ($55,608) contract with incentives based on magazine sales and other considerations.[17]

Then came five days of photo-shoots. Each session introduced new color themes and staff-selected make-up and outfits, each filmed on different sets with strobe lights. Was she intimidated? You bet. "I started off shy because I'd never done anything like that. I'd go into a dressing room and come out to a room that had few curtains, so I'd wonder if people in nearby buildings could see me, but I was told that wasn't the case."[18] Eventually, her comfort increased, especially since photographer James Schnepf and the 30-odd crew treated her respectfully and gave her final picture approval. Later, shots were taken of her while working at a Cubs game. A September 1986 end-of-season publication date was set.

But *Playboy* quick-pitched, releasing its September-dated issue in July. The magazine first appeared on the West Coast, where some Cubs saw it during a team road trip, reporting it to Collins upon their July 17 return. Consequently, she was apprehensive throughout the homestand, waiting for the hammer to fall. Her fears were well-founded. Upon arriving at Wrigley on July 22, she was whisked into meetings with Cooper and operations VP Don Grenesko, possibly Green. "Don't you think it's embarrassing for the organization," Grenesko asked.[19] Collins disagreed, replying that the photo spread was tastefully done. Her argument fell on deaf ears. Discussions continued without resolution before she was dismissed and walked to the door.

As game time neared, unsuspecting cameramen perched behind Collins's seating area to get close up shots, waiting fruitlessly for her entrance. Finally, the Cubs announced her departure, tersely noting that the club did "not authorize nor does it condone or approve of [her] appearing in *Playboy*."[20] Cooper and Colletti referred to Collins's firing as a mutual separation. Green and Commissioner Peter Ueberroth avoided commenting like a batter ducking a head-hunting fastball.

Playboy's pre-publication predictions that its issue would supply a "little spice" and "get the Cubs some headlines about something other than their playing" were prescient.[21] Reporters buzzed about, pursuing a story too titillating to ignore. Players, some of whom had asked for autographed copies, were generally supportive. "Everybody takes their clothes off now and then. That's the best thing I've seen out of uniform all year," Caray quipped.[22] Knowing Collins's situation, he relayed that she had been misinformed about the release date, intimating that *Playboy* knew the value of publicity and that a release after the season would capture less interest.[23] He advised her to hire an attorney to fight for her job.

Collins had no employment contract with the Cubs. She also had no intention of pursuing litigation, but—per Childers's recommendation—she defended herself in the court of public opinion. She camped out at Sluggers sports bar, a block from Wrigley, to field questions as deftly as Kessinger. "[Childers] said this was going to make a lot of publicity, and it sure did for a couple of days straight. The more issues sold, the more you made, so this was the best thing for *Playboy* and me. I talked with lots of fans and did tons of interviews. It was a crazy time," she enthusiastically recalled.[24] She insisted she wasn't angry with the Cubs, had planned on leaving her position, was getting married in September, and did the *Playboy* shoot for business and personal fulfillment. She chalked up the Cubs' objections to their "conservative ways" and the fact that she had sometimes captured more attention than the team.[25]

She also found the Cubs attitude "hypocritical."[26] "They said they didn't want me as a sex object. I didn't think that was true. They were the ones who told me to cut my shorts shorter and my tops tighter."[27] Newspaper opinion pieces—written by men, replete with double entendres and sexist drivel—differed on the Cubs' decision, but agreed with Collins's complaint. Pulitzer Prize-winning *Tribune* columnist Mike Royko summed it up best: "Of course it's hypocritical. But hypocrisy is the very backbone of our sexual moral standards. Many of our outstanding bluenoses are secret lechers."[28]

Collins and the press drew comparison to publicized cocaine abuse by players, for which no one was banned. They also made a more direct linkage to Caray's broadcasting partner, Steve Stone, who had appeared semi-nude in *Playgirl*'s July 1983 issue. He had asked for and been given team permission to do so: an unlikely approval for Collins to have received for *Playboy*. And he was never reprimanded, let alone fired, a "double standard" Collins still finds confusing.[29]

Stone supported Collins keeping her job. His call went unanswered, though, as fully clothed grounds crew member Roger Baird, greeted by boos, was inserted as her temporary replacement. Two weeks later, the team introduced two young women, attired like Collins, to rotate as ballgirls until the season's end.[30] They were required to sign a Code of Conduct to prevent future indelicate developments.

Meanwhile, Collins was besieged with offers for interviews, autographs, positions at radio stations, and even full-time ballgirl employment. She accepted some invitations, signed Cubs memorabilia and, yes, *Playboy* issues. As for a full-time ballgirl position, no thanks. In August, she did, however, make a guest ballgirl appearance for the Class A Midwest League Madison (Wisconsin) Muskies. She received a warm welcome from the team's president and 2,593 patrons, then sat near the Madison dugout, clad in tight white shorts and a green satin team jacket.[31] Afterwards, approximately 100 attendees followed her for autograph and photo catches at the cleverly named Muskie Bait Shop souvenir stand.

Collins took interior design courses, obtained a two-year art degree, and eventually settled in suburban Barrington Hills. Her first daughter, Autumn, was born in 1989, followed by her second, Callan, in 1992. While raising her children, she trained for a career as an ultrasound sonographer. For almost 25 years, she has conducted gynecological and infant echocardiograms at a private doctor's office. She and Joe divorced, but they remained friends and she was a caregiver when he died in 2012. She is on good terms with the Cubs and still a die-hard fan, although her attendance has dwindled over the years. She still honors baseball memorabilia autograph requests. *Playboy*, too, including a rare, seductive, fold-out poster contained in early

EBAY

Marla Collins still makes occasional autograph appearances and her Cubs publicity shots and a rare *Playboy* poster are still bought and sold by collectors.

editions, one of which she framed and hung in her basement bar for many years.

Collins's outlook remains open-minded. "I go with the flow. One thing led to another. I'm not sure how, but everything fell into place. I believe 'Do it now.' If there's something you want to do, you should just do it," she replied contentedly when asked to explain her unpredictable journey across the baseball landscape.[32]

With modern eyes, Collins's journey across *Playboy*'s landscape is equally intriguing. Objectively examining the 13 pictures contained in her "Belle of the Ball Club" eight-page layout, eight were taken at Wrigley, featuring Caray, an umpire, players, and her departure from the park. They are tame enough to be featured in a team yearbook. As for the other five, three reveal breasts and four pubic hair, all mixed with soft lighting, black lingerie, sparkling jewelry, and a permed mane of *Flashdance*-inspired 1980s hair that makes Collins laugh retrospectively. "I know this is nudity, but you almost see that much when I have a bathing suit on…. The string bikinis…on the market barely cover anything," she said in 1986.[33] True then and now.

Viewpoints on "pornography" are rarely objective, however, but rather engulfed in a swirl of political bickering, sexual mores and hang ups, religious dogma, body objectification, differing assumptions of women's role, alleged harmful effects on children, the legacy of our Puritan and Pilgrim settlers, and the amorphous definition of "obscene." *Playboy* has been part of this debate for seven decades.

Playboy's circulation peaked at seven million (approximately three million of whom were women) in the early 1970s. But over the next few years, sales declined due to competition from more risqué magazines and mass market, sexually oriented videotapes. *Playboy*'s brand and Hefner's hedonistic lifestyle at his Los Angeles mansion also became somewhat passé.

The 1980s brought a cultural and political rightward tilt, exemplified by President Ronald Reagan's administration, which viewed *Playboy* as a purveyor and symbol of moral decay. Collins's pictorial timing could not have been more inopportune. Attorney General Ed Meese led a commission to report on pornography's impact and make recommendations to the Department of Justice to curb it. He was supported by an unlikely alliance of religious organizations, focused on immorality and family values, and feminists alarmed by patriarchy and sexism.[34] In April 1986, before the final report was issued, the commission's director intimidated companies such as 7-Eleven and Rite Aid into removing *Playboy* and other soft-core magazines from their shelves. Playboy argued such conduct was forbidden under the First Amendment. In July, a federal district court agreed. Later that month, the "Meese Report" recommended several legal restrictions on pornography, but stopped short of listing *Playboy* among its cited pornographic titles.[35]

Hefner's daughter, Christie, who became Playboy president in 1982, remarked, "The magazine presents women in a lot of different ways, depending upon what pages you are reading."[36] And, pre-Collins, those pages had contained insightful *Playboy* Interviews with baseball luminaries Earl Weaver, Henry Aaron, and Steve Garvey. But when Collins elected to control and enhance her own sex appeal, the Cubs balked. They made no such move when ace pitcher Jake Arietta posed naked (private parts covered) for *ESPN: The Magazine*'s 2016 "Body Issue." Double standards persist.

The Cubs and America unknowingly whiffed on the real story in the September 1986 issue, hidden behind stylized images: 18-year-old centerfold Playmate Rebekka Armstrong. Likely HIV-positive since 16, she courageously announced her condition in 1994, led HIV/AIDS education efforts, came out as lesbian, and later claimed on 2022's *Secrets of Playboy* #MeToo-inspired docuseries that on promotional engagements she was deceivingly sent out on dates, including one in which she was drugged and sexually assaulted.

Collins never went to the Playboy Mansion or met Hefner. And she never experienced harassment or vilification via mail, phone calls, or personal interactions over her decision to pose. In an age before being ratioed or bullied on social media, her experience was safe, profitable, professional, and uplifting. "The Cubs did what they felt they had to do, no hard feelings," she reckons today.[37] Many Americans appreciated Collins's choice. Some shrugged. Others were offended. Where do you land on the spectrum? Your answer says more about you than it does about her. ■

Acknowledgment

Heartfelt thanks are extended to Marla Collins for graciously sharing her memories of the Cubs and *Playboy*, and to Ken Manyin for his contributions to the finished article.

Notes

1. Marla Collins, telephone interview, February 20, 2023.
2. Collins's starting yearly pay, assuming she worked all 81 games, was $8,100 ($25,112 in 2023 dollars). Under that same assumption, her 1986 annual pay was $12,150 ($33,165).
3. Debbie Stivyer's sister was a secretary in the Oakland A's office, which likely explains her hiring. She and Mary Barry were each paid $5 ($37) an hour. Their employment ended by 1975 because of several complaints from the A's players' wives. Stivyer went on to sell cookies locally, married the founder of the Fields Investment Group, and started her cookie business, Mrs. Fields Cookies, which grew to over 650 bakeries nationwide, 80 internationally.
4. Alessandra Stanley, "Among Baseball's Ballgirls, Fielding Skills Take 2d Place," *The New York Times*, July 5, 1991.
5. Collins's flattering measurements were widely reported but are, respectfully, not conveyed here. Her uniform number changed each season: 82, 83, 84, 85, and 86.
6. In inclement weather, Collins wore Cubs-themed jackets, and either pantyhose or blue-striped pants to match her top and keep her legs warm. Which led Caray to remark, "Marla's not wearing any pants," when she removed them. Marla Collins telephone interview, March 8, 2023.
7. Collins interview, February 20, 2023.
8. Collins interview, February 20, 2023.
9. Brett (third base, Kansas City Royals), Hernandez (first base, New York Mets), and Sax (second base, Los Angeles Dodgers) were all-stars. Kuiper (second base, Cleveland Indians) was an average player, but later became a Ford C. Frick finalist award announcer for the San Francisco Giants.
10. Collins interview, February 20, 2023.
11. Collins later dined at Caray's restaurants, attended his funeral, and spoke fondly of him years later. Collins interview, February 20, 2023.
12. "Belle of the Ball Club," *Playboy*, September 1986, 75.
13. Collins interview, February 20, 2023.
14. Thomas Dyja, *The Third Coast* (New York: Penguin Press), 2013, xxxiv.
15. The building is now known as the Palmolive Building. From 1959–74, Hefner resided in the Playboy Mansion in Chicago's Gold Coast district. He permanently relocated to the Playboy Mansion West, Los Angeles, in 1974.
16. Collins interview, February 20, 2023.
17. Collins estimates achieved incentives brought her total payment to $40,000 ($111,216), perhaps more.
18. Collins interview, February 20, 2023.
19. "Cubbies Let Ballgirl Go," *The Sun*, July 23, 1986.
20. "Cubbies Let Ballgirl Go."
21. "Chicago Ballgirl Wants to Pin Up Cub Hopes," *The New Mexican*, July 23, 1986. The Cubs were 39–51 when Collins departed.

22. "Nice to Have Seen You Marla," *Centre Daily Times*, July 23, 1986; Tony Weitzel, "Along The Trail," *Naples Daily News*, August 29, 1986.
23. Pete Ryan, "Missing Marla…," *Albuquerque Tribune*, July 28, 1986.
24. Collins interview, February 20, 2023.
25. Tom Friend, "The Naked Truth: Cub Front Office Finds It Can't, Uh, Bare to Look at Its Ballgirl Anymore," *Los Angeles Times*, July 23, 1986.
26. "People," *Maclean's*, August 4, 1986; Collins interview, February 20, 2023.
27. Brad Falduto, "Looking Good: Collins Wows 'Em in Her Warner Park Appearance," *Capital Times*, August 14, 1986; "So What's The Meaning of Marla," *Capital Times*, August 15, 1986; Collins interview, February 20, 2023.
28. Dave Wischnowsky, "Where's Marla Collins? Well, She's Right Here," *Kankakee Daily Journal*, August 29, 2009.
29. Collins interview, February 20, 2023.
30. Airline stewardess Mariellen Kopp, 22, and office worker Kathy Wolter alternated in the position. They were paid $50 ($136) per game. Baird was deployed in the event both were unavailable for a game(s).
31. Bad weather kept attendance below Warner Park's (also known as the "Fishbowl") 6,750-capacity. Still, the crowd size doubled that of average Muskies games. Before Collins arrived, the Muskie Boosters sponsored a "buns contest," in which fans cast votes for the unmarked photos of the backsides of 23 players. Infielder Tony Cabrera, the winner, received $25 ($68) and a trophy.
32. Collins interview, February 20, 2023.
33. Mike Fish, "National Pastime? Ex-Cub Ballgirl Now a Favorite Spectator Sport," *Kansas City Times*, July 29, 1986.
34. Feminism fell into two categories: equity feminism (the movement for women's legal and social equality) and gender feminism (contending women are prisoners of a patriarchal system and in a gender war with male oppressors). The former was milder and largely endorsed by Hefner; the latter drew his ire as they were more harshly critical. Although even Gloria Steinem, firmly in the equity camp, once wrote that "There are times when a woman reading *Playboy* feels a little like Jew reading a Nazi manual." Steven Watts, *Mr. Playboy: Hugh Hefner and the American Dream* (New York: Wiley), 2009, 241, 247, 372.
35. Meese released the report at a news conference held in the DOJ's Great Hall. Ironically, he spoke in front of the "Spirit of Justice": a 12-foot statue of a woman baring one breast.
36. Carrie Pitzulo, *Bachelors and Bunnies* (Chicago: University of Chicago), 2011, 126.
37. Collins telephone interview, March 8, 2023.

Field of Hollywood Dreams

Actors and Their Baseball Roles Beyond the World's Most Famous Cornfield

David Krell

Kevin Costner's place in the Hollywood-baseball paradigm is as evident as a thunderclap during an Iowa rainstorm. In four movies, Costner uses the national pastime as a cornerstone for stories about love and regret.

- He's a retired ballplayer hosting a sports radio show and pursuing love with Joan Allen's character in *The Upside of Anger*.

- He's an aging pitcher attempting a perfect game and pursuing love with Kelly Preston's character in *For Love of the Game*.

- He's a veteran minor-league catcher tutoring an undisciplined pitcher and pursuing love with Susan Sarandon's character in *Bull Durham*.

- He's a farmer transforming his cornfield into a baseball field for dead ballplayers who are somehow resurrected in *Field of Dreams*.

So ingrained is Costner in baseball's cultural fabric because of the Iowa-set movie that in 2021 he was invited to make a grand entrance before MLB's inaugural "Field of Dreams Game" at the shooting site in Dyersville. Costner watched from behind second base as the White Sox and Yankees emerged from the cornfield just as Ray Liotta and his fellow actors had while portraying Shoeless Joe Jackson and the Black Sox.

Field of Dreams and Costner's other baseball movies indicate a deep love of baseball. But the star is not the only cast member from *Field of Dreams* who had screen time in other movies with a baseball theme.

James Earl Jones plays Terence Mann, a revolutionary author whose work in the 1960s influenced a generation of Baby Boomers. In *Shoeless Joe*, W.P. Kinsella's 1982 novel that served as the source material for *Field of Dreams*, the author was J.D. Salinger. Mann is a fictional character whose monologue towards the end of the movie succinctly captures the romance, perseverance, and appeal of baseball: "The one constant through all the years, Ray, has been baseball. America has rolled by like an army of steamrollers. It's been erased like a blackboard, rebuilt, and erased again. But baseball has marked the time. This field, this game—it's a part of our past, Ray. It reminds us of all that once was good, and it could be again."

This brief discourse, with Jones' baritone voice exuding authority, is the heart of the movie. The actor known for being the voice of Darth Vader and CNN boasts a lengthy resumé heavy on roles reflecting an authoritative presence. Among them: Admiral Greer in *The Hunt for Red October*, Jack Jefferson in *The Great White Hope*, and Senator/President Douglass Dilman in *The Man*. Baseball fans, however, will also note Jones's roles in *The Bingo Long Traveling All-Stars & Motor Kings* and *The Sandlot*.

Bingo Long, a 1976 film, stars Billy Dee Williams and Jones as the pitching-catching battery of Bingo Long and Leon Carter. Long, star pitcher of the Negro National League's St. Louis Ebony Aces, a fictional club, creates Bingo Long's Traveling All-Stars and Motor Kings after Carter, a slugger with the Baltimore Elite Giants, talks about workers needing to seize the means of production from the owners. Aces owner and funeral home mogul Sallison Potter is the villain, a tightwad who mistreats his players on every day that ends in Y, inspiring Long to go his own way with the barnstorming squad.

Reviewers found Jones' performance notable. The Alexandria-Pineville (Louisiana) newspaper *Town Talk* called attention to the "noisy bravado" of the Carter character. United Press International described Williams and Jones as being "in peak form."[2] Jones also received praise in the *Macon News*: "[W]hat an incredible performance he gives as he moves from the joyous, scheming delight of forming a team, to depths of sadness as the team is threatened with extinction."[3] The *San Pedro News-Pilot* lauded, "He apparently can play any kind of comedy or drama with equal skill and veracity."[4]

In an interview concurrent with the film's release, Jones addressed the issue of characters performing as showmen in addition to ballplaying, including dancing in the streets when they go to a new town. He noted a basic reason for the tomfoolery that occurred in the Negro Leagues. "Because there are black people who are still sensitive about seeing black people clown around—and the sensitive ones, I have found, tend to travel in intellectual circles that I neither understand nor trust—doesn't mean you can't show a time when black people used clowning around as a survival technique."[5]

When *Bingo Long* premiered in 1976, the Negro Leagues were considered a curious footnote in baseball history, and only five players who spent either all or most of their careers in the Negro Leagues had been inducted into the National Baseball Hall of Fame in Cooperstown: Cool Papa Bell, Josh Gibson, Judy Johnson, Buck Leonard, and Satchel Paige. As of 2023, there are 34 such inductees, scholarship on the Negro Leagues is flourishing, and MLB itself is promoting Negro League history through a partnership with the Negro Leagues Baseball Museum in Kansas City, Missouri.

In *The Sandlot*, a 1993 film, Jones plays Mr. Mertle, who doesn't appear until a key scene at the end. A group of kids play on a southern California sandlot field separated from Mertle's property by a fence. They believe him to be a mean recluse with a dangerous animal known as "the beast." Scotty Smalls, new kid in the neighborhood, joins the games although his baseball knowledge is so deficient that he thinks Babe Ruth is a woman. This creates a problem when he takes his stepdad's Ruth-autographed baseball for the group to use, and it is hit over Mertle's fence. Smalls tells them about the autograph and gets a quick education about Ruth's icon status.

The kids attempt to retrieve the ball by means of various shenanigans, ultimately sending the fence crashing down on "the beast," which turns out to be an excitable but kind English mastiff named Hercules. Thankfully, the canine is okay. Benny "The Jet" Rodriguez and Smalls—respectively the best and worst players—apologize to Mertle. To their surprise, Mertle was a ballplayer who palled around with Babe Ruth and knew him as George. After learning about the ball, which Hercules has chewed up, Mertle offers one signed by all of the 1927 Yankees and proposes an exchange: "You guys come by once a week and talk baseball with me, we'll call it an even trade." The epilogue shows Smalls, now a Dodgers broadcaster, announcing Rodriguez as a pinch runner and calling his game-winning steal of home.

Many reviews of *The Sandlot* included critiques of Jones's scene, specifically his character's claim that he would have beaten the Babe's home-run record if he hadn't gone blind from getting beaned. Detractors

PUBLICITY SHOT COURTESY OF UNIVERSAL PICTURES

Before his memorable role in *Field of Dreams*, James Earl Jones received rave reviews for his portrayal of fictional Negro Leagues slugger, Leon Carter.

claimed that this was historically inaccurate because the dialogue implies that Mertle would have been the first Black player in the major leagues. They were too quick to judge. David Mickey Evans, the movie's screenwriter and director, has said that Mertle is referring to hitting more home runs than Ruth but while playing in the Negro Leagues.[6]

Jones also appeared in the sequel *The Sandlot 2*.

Art LaFleur is another alumnus of both *Field of Dreams* and *The Sandlot*. He played Chick Gandil, one of the eight Black Sox players, in *Field of Dreams*. He portrayed a more eminent role in *The Sandlot*: Babe Ruth himself. The Sultan of Swat appears to Benny in a dream and advises him to make the most of his gifts, beginning by hopping over the fence and retrieving the ball.

In 2011, LaFleur recalled the audition. "When I went to read for the part...I had just read *The Babe*, a biography of Babe Ruth. So when I went into the audition I went in 'as' Babe. I wore a newsboy kind of hat. I went in with a cigar...the Babe always had a cigar. Babe Ruth, when he would see kids, he would always say, 'hi keed.' He would always use the word 'keed' for kid. And he had a habit of slurring his words. When he would talk about baseball he would say 'baysh-baw.' I went to read for [writer/director] Mickey David Evans [*sic*] and about halfway through he said, 'he's the guy!'"[7]

LaFleur also appeared in 1992's *Mr. Baseball*, starring Tom Selleck. His film and television career began with a small role as a Russian villain in the 1978 TV-movie *Rescue from Gilligan's Island*, and included the sports movies *The Replacements* (football) and *Speed Racer* (auto racing). Art LaFleur suffered from Parkinson's disease and died in 2021.

PUBLICITY STILL COURTESY OF 20TH CENTURY FOX

Art LeFleur embodied Babe Ruth in *The Sandlot*.

In *Field of Dreams*, Timothy Busfield played Ray's brother-in-law, Mark, who wants Ray to sell the property before it goes into foreclosure. Busfield also took on the role of Minnesota Twins slugger Lou Collins in the 1994 film *Little Big League*. He informed his performance with real-life experience. Although he is most prominently known for his Emmy-winning portrayal of fun-loving artist and advertising executive Elliot Weston on *thirtysomething*—which ran on ABC from 1987 to 1991—Busfield played semipro baseball for the Sacramento Smokeys for nine seasons. His pitching record was 30–12.[8]

"Tim Busfield came in really late," explained screenwriter Adam Scheinman. "We had cast a guy [for the Lou Collins role] named Brad Johnson, who was about 6-foot-4 and just looked like a Mike Trout-type guy. In my mind, that character was always like Lou Gehrig. He didn't talk very much. If he spoke, it was a big deal. But [Johnson] couldn't get out of his commitment. He had a TV pilot and right at the last minute, they wouldn't let him out. We were really strapped."[9]

For Busfield, a Lansing, Michigan, native and devoted Tigers fan born in 1957, playing in a major-league ballpark fulfilled a fantasy. "It's a dream come true, really. Even in *Field of Dreams*, I didn't have to play ball. To be able to work out with a major-league team after spending my childhood wanting to play Major League Baseball [*sic*], and realizing I just wasn't good enough, to have that opportunity to play ball and to be at a pivotal moment in a movie that still plays, was a great experience."[10]

Little Big League includes cameos from 17 real-life MLB personalities as themselves, including Randy Johnson, Ken Griffey Jr., and Lou Piniella. *New York Times* film critic Stephen Holden praised the scenes filmed at the Metrodome. "Adding to the realism are the appearances of a number of major league players as the Twins' opponents. The glow and cleancut [*sic*] innocence of these scenes evokes the magic of the game as seen through the eyes of a youthful fan."[11]

The last entry in our cast list is Steve Eastin, a former high school pitcher, who played disgraced White Sox pitcher Eddie Cicotte in *Field of Dreams*. In *Austin Powers: The Spy Who Shagged Me*, the second film in the three-film series starring Mike Myers as the titular superspy, Eastin plays an umpire.

With its nostalgia and wish fulfillment, *Field of Dreams* has been a warm introduction to baseball for many people since its release in 1989 and it remains a perennial favorite. Hopefully, future screenings will prompt curiosity about baseball beyond the Black Sox Scandal, MLB's annual game in Dyersville, and Ray Liotta's inverted portrayal of Shoeless Joe Jackson as a southpaw in the field and a righty in the batter's box. The cast's interconnection with other baseball movies has allowed *Field of Dreams* to resonate further both in baseball and popular culture. ∎

Notes

1. David Foil, "'Bingo's Traveling All-Stars' Solid, Satisfying Showmanship," *Town Talk*, July 21, 1976: C-4.
2. David Dugas, "Black Baseball Comedy Gets Laughs," *Sacramento Bee*, July 18, 1976: 9.
3. Madeleine Hirsiger "'Bingo Long:' Interesting To Many Local Extras," *Macon Telegraph & News*, July 18, 1976: 8B.
4. Don Lechman, "'Bingo!' Universal has a winner," *San Pedro News-Pilot*, July 9, 1976: E1.
5. Susan Stark, "The Times Are Changing; So Is James Earl Jones," *Detroit Free Press*, July 25, 1976: 7C.
6. David Mickey Evans to David Krell, February 15, 2023.
7. Mike Smith, "Interview with Art LaFleur," Media Mikes, https://mediamikes.com/2011/01/interview-withart-lafleur, (last accessed February 13, 2023).
8. See "Timothy Busfield," Trivia inset, Internet Movie Database, https://www.imdb.com/name/nm0124079. Busfield was nominated for an Outstanding Actor in a Drama Series Emmy Award every season. He won for the final season.
9. Tom Dierberger quoting Adam Scheinman, "An oral history of *Little Big League*," Bally Sports, https://www.ballysports.com/north/news/an-oral-history-of-little-big-league-3709392, October 14, 2020, (last accessed February 14, 2023).
10. Tom Dierberger quoting Timothy Busfield, "An oral history of *Little Big League*," Bally Sports, https://www.ballysports.com/north/news/an-oral-history-of-little-big-league-3709392, October 14, 2020, (last accessed February 14, 2023).
11. Stephen Holden, "When a 12-Year-Old Fan Inherits a Baseball Team," *The New York Times*, June 29, 1994: C21.

Larry Fritsch, Card King

The First Full-time Dealer's Legacy Continues After 53 Years

Tom Alesia

In 1989, Larry Fritsch sat in a rural Wisconsin warehouse—big enough to fit a full-sized baseball field and filled with 35 million cards—searching for a player who best exemplified the hobby of card-collecting.

Honus Wagner? Mickey Mantle? Hank Aaron?

"No, no," said Fritsch, collector extraordinaire and pioneer of the baseball card business. Then his face lit up like he'd just hit a stand-up double. "Vic Raschi," he proclaimed. Raschi enjoyed an impressive 10-year career in the 1940s and '50s, playing on six World Series-winning teams with the New York Yankees. But there's nothing particularly notable about Raschi cards, aside from sentimental value. Fritsch was the sentimental one. "A real stopper," Fritsch beamed, noting that Raschi had died a few months earlier, in October 1988. "On my baseball card of him, he's eternally young; he's Vic Raschi in the '50s." Fritsch paused. "I guess the cards are another way of us trying to delay the inevitable."

Fritsch was 52 when he made those comments. The Stevens Point, Wisconsin, resident lived another 19 years, always collecting, always selling, always promoting the hobby. He created his company, Larry Fritsch Cards, on May 1, 1970. It marked the first time someone worked full-time buying and selling baseball cards.

During the late 1960s, Larry suffered health problems related to stress. A graduate of the University of Wisconsin-Stevens Point, where he studied history and political science, he held multiple part-time jobs. He spent 10 years as a train baggage handler. He did tax research for the Wisconsin Legislative Fiscal Bureau. He worked at a paper mill. And he collected cards. Always. "A doctor told him that he was doing too much and he needed to cut back," said Larry's grandson Jeremy. Then his doctor added some advice: Just do what makes you happy. "That," Jeremy said, "was a no brainer for [Larry]: Sell baseball cards."

Larry already had an elaborate collection and enough stock to support his wife and two children, then aged 11 and three. Collectors looked forward to receiving his nearly 200-page catalogues up to six times annually. Still, in 1974, Larry told the *Milwaukee Journal* that most of his customers were between ages 13 and 16. There was enough interest to maintain the business, but the early years were worrisome. "When we built the first [warehouse] addition in 1975, it cost $20,000. I thought, 'Holy Christ, how are we going to pay for this?'" Larry said in 1989. "Now I buy a collection for twice that amount and don't even think about it."

Fritsch Cards remains a major player in the card hobby business. Late in Fritsch's life, his son Jeff served as the company's general manager and unsung visionary. Listed as the company's warehouse manager at age 16, Jeff ran day-to-day operations for nearly 30 years, before his death in 2017 at age 58. Since then, Fritsch Cards' majority owner and clean-up hitter (business-wise) is Jeremy Fritsch, Larry's grandson and Jeff's son. At 38, Jeremy has 13 years of experience working at Fritsch Cards. In August 2020, he engineered the $1.8 million sale of 12 unopened boxes of 1986-1987 Fleer basketball cards, featuring then-rookie Michael Jordan.

Today, Fritsch Cards operates with seven employees from the same monstrous warehouse on a 26-acre former farm. Larry started expanding it in 1975, after operating the business out of his basement, which also sits on the same property. "I believe there's a 'collecting

Larry Fritsch

Jeremy Fritsch

119

Larry Fritsch in his younger days.

gene.' I believe that exists," Jeremy said, sitting at his office, where photos of his grandfather and father hang over his shoulder. "[Larry] definitely passed that gene on to my dad and me."

Larry's legacy looms as large as a retractable roof. In 1989, Steve Ellingboe, executive editor of *Sports Collectors Digest*, called Larry's collection "by far, the best baseball card collection in the world." At the time, Fritsch Cards also sold more than 200,000 mail-order cards per week.

Larry bought directly from manufacturers and countless other collectors. He bought just about everything, including thousands of Jell-O boxes with baseball cards on the package. "My grandfather was buying in such quantity that we had 10 people, most of them stay-at-home moms, come in to get a case of cards, take them home, pull them from the wrapping, sort and organize them then bring them back," said Jeremy. "There's still stuff in the warehouse we come across that we didn't know was back there."

Larry, Jeremy said, was a "borderline hoarder." His passion, and that of Jeremy's father Jeff, prevented them from quickly unloading cases. Although many sealed boxes were opened to form complete sets, Larry and Jeff had enough stock to keep many cases untouched. And any unopened case became lucrative—worth far more than the 21,000 cards Fritsch currently has listed on eBay.

Larry was married to Mollie Hendrickson for 27 years, until 1985. After the divorce, Larry still gave her credit for supporting the card sales. "I think of thousands and thousands of hours put in here by my wife and myself," Larry said in 1989. "This thing didn't get here by accident."

For more than three decades, Larry served as the face of the card business. Outlets ranging from *Time* magazine to talk show host Tom Snyder sought comments from him. Larry was also a familiar face at big card shows. "He was gruff," Jeremy said. "That's the exterior he had before he would let you in. It was his way. But once you got close to him or broke down that wall a bit he was kind and appreciative, especially of people who were collecting. He understood what they were going through to get complete sets put together or find that card that they wanted. It's something he went through himself. He could empathize with that."

Larry was a wily businessman with an encyclopedic knowledge of vintage baseball cards. He also had a nationwide network of scouts. He paid his "bird dogs" a commission when they discovered certain cards. The deals that Larry made with card companies were significant, but sometimes exaggerated, according to Jeremy. "I've heard people say there were full [train] boxcars sent to Stevens Point full of cards. Those are fun myths," Jeremy said. "He had deals with Topps when they had excess product. But the truth is he bought large quantities because he wanted to sell full sets. He never wanted to run out of stuff. He wanted to say, 'I have this in my collection,' or, 'I have this to sell.'"

Fritsch opened a Cooperstown baseball card museum in 1989. It featured a complete set of T206s from 1909, all in near-mint condition. The museum, which occupied the space of a former Ford dealership, lasted until 1992. Jeff didn't like to fly, and Larry couldn't provide enough on-site logistical support while living in Wisconsin. However, the museum made a distinct impression upon a pre-teen Jeremy. He recalled riding a bicycle through the museum when it was closed and stopping often to gaze. "Even then," Jeremy said, "I thought, 'This is cool. People come to see all this stuff and I'm around it all the time.'"

Not everything Larry and Jeff touched turned to gold. They bought cases of a football card series with candy canes in each pack. Over time, the candy canes melted and ruined many cards. And Fritsch Cards wasn't immune to the manufacturers' glut of products in the early 1990s. "In one of our warehouses," Jeremy said, "you think you see a wall, but it's just all the stuff stacked up—and it's 10 to 12 cases deep packed with early '90s cards! It's hard to overstate how much we have."

Fritsch Cards also created its own series, including cards featuring the All-American Girls Professional Baseball League, the Negro Leagues, and players who made the major leagues but didn't last long enough to have their own baseball card. Jeremy said Fritsch Cards, while maintaining a solid online presence, still publishes and mails more than 10,000 print catalogues twice annually. Because Larry's wide interests extended to non-sport cards, Fritsch Cards is also planning an entire catalogue devoted to them. The cards range from politicians to entertainers, from the late 1800s to the 1960s.

The COVID-19 lockdowns provided an unexpected boost for Fritsch Cards and the card collecting hobby in general, as many people dove into or rediscovered their love of cards during 2020, but it ended plans for the company's 50th anniversary celebration. "It went from doing something really big," Jeremy said, "to having a generic cake from the bakery."

Fritsch Cards still provides homespun service. With every purchase, whether it's an unopened box from the 1970s or a $1 card off eBay, they add a simple handwritten note: "Enjoy your card!" This tradition extends back to Larry. "My grandfather also would write a little note about how a card was acquired," Jeremy said, "or what it meant to him."

The flashy card variations that are so sought-after today wouldn't have impressed Larry. "He *did* say, 'It was better in my day,' when he opened something new," Jeremy said with a laugh. "A color border never meant much to him." ∎

Sources

Alesia, Tom, "Stevens Point collector is king of cards," *Wausau Daily Herald*, January 29, 1989.

Jeremy Fritsch, one-on-one interview, February 25, 2023.

"The Sultan of Swap," *Milwaukee Journal*, July 7, 1974.

"Larry Fritsch" Obituary, December, 2007. https://www.pisarskifuneralhome.com/guestbook/170319.

Reborn at 111 Years Old

Wisconsin's Glorious Neighborhood Park Plays with History

Tom Alesia

Wausau, Wisconsin's Athletic Park opened just three weeks after Fenway Park. Thanks to an eight-foot-tall, New Deal-era granite wall studded with ruby-red boulders, the stadium still stood proudly in 2012. Inside, however, the nearly 100-year-old ballpark groaned with age. Its old-time charm and broad shoulders couldn't withstand passing years and changing baseball economics. The grandstand was winter-beaten, with ragged benches for fans. The concession stand was tucked underneath with precious little space to serve as a main concourse. Even the costume of the team's mascot was a patchwork.

The park had weathered storms before. In 1950, half of its grandstand was destroyed by fire. But the Wausau Timberjacks, a Detroit Tigers minor-league affiliate, played there *the next day*. All told, four low-level minor league teams under 11 different names were scattered throughout the park's colorful past. Athletic Park was the longtime home to the Woodchucks, part of the relentless collegiate Northwoods League, which sandwiches 72 regular-season games in 2½ months.

Local ownership worked hard, but in 2012 the Woodchucks were up for sale, and Athletic Park seemed to have more quit than quaint remaining. Enter western Wisconsin native Mark Macdonald. Freshly retired

at 52, Macdonald had risen to co-owner of Los Angeles-based American Funds after 30 years in finance. Two months after seeing Athletic Park for the first time, Macdonald bought the club in February 2012 for the relatively low price of $750,000. "It was historic. I knew that," Macdonald said in the Woodchucks' conference room just beyond center field. "Historic sometimes is code for old and run down and that's what it was: old and run down."

Macdonald's pockets were overflowing, but his motivation meant as much as his money. Preserving Athletic Park's history means working within the confines of the granite wall. The Woodchucks offices boast an original trowel used to build that granite wall in the 1930s.

Macdonald's plan to revamp Athletic Park meant creating a new stadium inside an old one. He kept the ballpark's most notable feature—the wall—and remodeled the interior and an area adjacent to the field. It would take 10 years of construction. "That wall is very important to the people around here," Macdonald stated. "It's history. We've accentuated the history."

Two miles away, at the Marathon County Historical Society, archivist Ben Clark unveiled a three-foot wide and eight-inch tall picture from May 13, 1912. The panoramic photo was taken at the first game at what

In 1912, the outfield advertisements included a 17-foot-tall bull.

was then dubbed Yawkey Park, named after wealthy businessman and civic leader Cyrus Yawkey. On land deeded to the city by the Wisconsin Valley Electric Company, the Wausau Timberjacks beat the Aurora (Illinois) Blues, 4–0, in the Class C Wisconsin-Illinois League. The result is written on the photo. In left field, a 17-foot-tall bull advertises a tobacco company.

For its first 20 years, the park also served as a hockey rink in the winter. In the summer, the B.F. Schultz Brass Band led "baseball parades," Clark said, "and in between innings they would perform to keep fans engaged."

The ballfield's westward orientation means the setting sun can be blinding in the batters' box. Macdonald said, "I've had umps say to me, 'I didn't see a pitch in the sixth inning. I was guessing back there.'"

Clark said the wall arose from a precursor to the Works Progress Administration. It gave Wausau residents jobs off and on from 1933 to 1936. The project originated in part because the first parks director was a landscape architect, not a program director. "It's not a coincidence that a granite company was beyond center field," Clark said. "But, logistically, the wall was not something that could be built overnight." By the time the wall was completed, fans had grown used to it. No team celebrated its completion, and the new name, Athletic Park, took a couple of years to gain traction.

Over decades, Wausau was home to an insurance giant that advertised heavily on *60 Minutes*, but the city never had a four-year college. The Athletic Park grew in civic importance, and the wall gave Wausau a showcase. "It adds a very distinct quality," Clark said,

"to what otherwise would have been a very cookie cutter ballpark."

Athletic Park's minor league legacy is spotty. Seven years after his major league playing career ended, former Brooklyn Robins third baseman Wally Gilbert served as player-manager for the Wausau Lumberjacks, batting a team-leading .355 in 1939 and .360 in 1940. In 1956, the Lumberjacks featured Vada Pinson, who tallied 2,757 career hits in the major leagues, and in 1957 five-time All-Star Cookie Rojas.

For the next 18 years, Wausau had no minor league team, but Athletic Park remained busy. It was home to Wisconsin's high school baseball tournament and the Wausau Barons of the Dairyland League. It also hosted the Wausau Muskies, a semi-pro team in the Central State Professional Football League. A 99-yard touchdown run by Walt Schoonover at Athletic Park in 1949 remains the oldest record still in semi-pro football history.

Wausau's high school team supporters, the Lumberjack Dugout Club, booked a rising 21-year-old rock musician for a fundraising concert at Athletic Park on July 16, 1958. The act, Buddy Holly and the Crickets, was rained out, so they performed the scheduled second show that evening at an indoor facility. Less than seven months later, touring the Midwest during a brutal winter, Holly died in a plane crash.

Minor league baseball returned in 1975 in the form of the Wausau Mets of the Class A Midwest League. The team featured future big leaguers Ned Yost in 1975 and Mookie Wilson in 1977. The Seattle Mariners began a nine-year affiliation with Wausau in 1981. That next

Athletic Park as it appears today, home to the Wausau Woodchucks of the Northwoods League, a summer collegiate league.

WAUSAU WOODCHUCKS

The granite wall has been the ballpark's most enduring feature, seen here in a 2022 photo and in the team photo from 1941.

year, the Wausau Timbers featured eight future big leaguers, including Harold Reynolds, Ivan Calderon, Jim Presley, and Darnell Coles. In 1984, Hall of Famer Edgar Martinez spent his first full season of minor league baseball at Athletic Park.

Eventually, larger markets gobbled up Midwest League franchises. The Timbers were bought in 1990. They became the Kane County (Illinois) Cougars, and their crowds grew to over 500,000 fans per season, more than five times what Wausau drew. The Cougars took Athletic Park's scoreboard with them when they left.

The Woodchucks brought baseball back to Wausau in 1994. Today they draw more than 1,200 per game in the Northwoods League, more than many of their predecessors.

Chicago Cubs' 2016 World Series MVP, Ben Zobrist, is a Woodchucks alum. So is two-time All-Star pitcher Pat Neshek. And Milwaukee Brewers star Jim Gantner managed the 2007 squad, which included his son. Those who played in Wausau don't forget Athletic Park. When 11-time Gold Glove winner Omar Vizquel, a Wausau Timber in 1986, was asked what he remembered about the stadium, he didn't hesitate. "360 [feet] to center field," Vizquel said. "I was a power hitter in that park."

Due to renovations, the left field corner is only 304 feet away from home plate. To reduce the effects of the glaring sun, Macdonald and his architects reduced rows and angled seats along the first base line, dropping capacity to about 3,400. Most of it is covered

behind home plate, or along the third base line and right field.

This season, Macdonald has a spiffy new video board in right field and new clubhouses planned. "It was very cramped. In order to create space, we had to go up and toward the field to have enough space to make it big enough for remodeling," he said. "We took the grandstand off the granite wall. The grandstand now extends back over the wall, which gives opportunities for backlighting. It shows off the wall." Location in a residential neighborhood provides both charm and harm from Athletic Park. Houses, some as close as 100 feet from home plate, have been pelted with foul balls for more than a century, and the closest parking spaces require faith that your car will escape a foul-ball dent.

Ann Chilles has lived across the street from Athletic Park for 40-plus years. "We have house windows broken and garage windows broken," Chilles said. "And you've got to watch out when walking out your door or backing out your car." That said, Chilles is a Woodchucks fan and loves the park's renovations.

Macdonald worked with Wausau officials to create a playground outside the field along the first-base line. It required buying and demolishing two houses that had fallen into disrepair. It's now part of a concrete playground that the Woodchucks use four hours before game time, and the city operates at all other times.

The renovations cost Macdonald and a foundation that he operates about $10 million, more than he ever realized he would spend. "I've made a lot of investments in my life," Macdonald said. "This will not be the best one by far for [financial] gains."

Tom Magnuson grew up in the neighborhood and managed an American Legion team there for more than 40 years. He recalled how the park's sole caretaker let him and his childhood friends play on the field. He also remembered teams that paid a dime for returned foul balls. Cracked bats were given to kids, Magnuson said, and they pounded nails into the bats to reuse them. "I'm glad the granite wall remains," Magnuson said. "It kindles in my mind the ballpark of my youth. It was a high point of our 'Wonder Years.'"

At 64, lean and sandy-haired, Macdonald remains committed to Athletic Park, regularly putting in 14-hour work days. He anticipates installing artificial turf on the infield to help Wausau join a new summer women's collegiate softball league in 2024. A southern Oregon resident with a wife and four adult children, he spends early May through August each year in Wausau.

Before buying the Woodchucks, Macdonald had gone to Chattanooga, where the Los Angeles Dodgers' double-A team was for sale at $12 million. That team, he said, was losing $500,000 per year. He passed on it. A west coast broker knew Macdonald's Wisconsin roots and sent him to Wausau. It was a perfect match.

Other teams contact him frequently about purchasing another baseball club. He politely declines. Athletic Park and the Woodchucks have become his passion. "When I bought the team, I didn't realize the emotional investment I would be making. I'm the guardian and caretaker of a huge community asset." He paused. "I'm proud of that." ∎

Sources

"History," Wausau Woodchucks, https://northwoodsleague.com/wausau-woodchucks/history-2. Accessed June 12, 2023.

Mark Macdonald, in-person interview, January 27, 2023.

Ben Clark, in-person interview, January 27, 2023.

Glen Moberg, "Historic Wausau Ballpark To Be Renovated," Wisconsin Public Radio, April 16, 2013, https://www.wpr.org/historic-wausau-ballpark-be-renovated. Accessed June 12, 2023.

Tom Magnuson, online interview, February 6, 2023.

CONTRIBUTORS

TOM ALESIA spent his youth at pre-lights Wrigley Field. A longtime entertainment and features newspaper writer/editor, he is author of obscure HOFer Dave Bancroft's popular 2022 biography *Beauty at Short*. He won the National Music Journalism Award and wrote the acclaimed book *Then Garth Became Elvis* in 2021. Find his work at TomWriteTurns.com. A 35-time marathon finisher and a cancer survivor since 1998, he lives in Madison, Wisconsin, with his wife, Susan. They have a son, Mark.

ALAN COHEN chairs the BioProject fact-checking committee, serves as Vice President-Treasurer of the Connecticut Smoky Joe Wood Chapter, and is a datacaster (MiLB first pitch stringer) for the Hartford Yard Goats of the Class AA Eastern League. His biographies, game stories and essays have appeared in more than 65 SABR publications. He is currently involved with the Retrosheet project on Negro League Games from 1920 through 1949. His story on Willie Mays in Birmingham (1949–50) appeared in the recent SABR publication on Mays. He has four children, nine grandchildren, and one great grandchild and resides in Connecticut with wife Frances, their cats Ava, and Zoe, and their dog Buddy.

S.P. DONOHUE's poetry, fiction, and essays have appeared widely in journals, most recently in *Seneca Review* and *Michigan Quarterly Review*. On the Northwestern University faculty since 1998, she teaches in the undergraduate and graduate creative writing programs.

R.A.R. EDWARDS is a professor of history at the Rochester Institute of Technology in Rochester, New York. A native of Connecticut, she is a life-long Red Sox fan. Her most recent book was *Deaf Players in Major League Baseball: A History, 1883 to the Present* (McFarland, 2020). It was recognized with a SABR Baseball Research Award in 2021.

STEVEN M. GLASSMAN's article on the Chicago Green Sox will be his ninth *National Pastime* article. He previously wrote "Philadelphia's Other Hall of Famers" (SABR43), "The Game That Was Not—Philadelphia Phillies at Chicago Cubs (August 8, 1988)" (SABR45), "Walking it Off (Marlins Postseason Walk-Offs)" (SABR46), "A Hall of Fame Cup of Coffee in New York" (SABR47), "Padres' Near No-Hitters" (SABR49), "The Baltimore Orioles' 1971 Japan Trip" (SABR50), and "The Future of Baseball Cards" (*The Future According to Baseball*), and "The Hidden Potato Trick" (*Major Research on the Minor Leagues*). Steven has been a SABR member since 1994. He graduated with a Bachelor of Science Degree in Sport and Recreation Management from Temple University. Originally born in Philadelphia, Steven currently lives in Warminster, Pennsylvania.

MIKE HAUPERT is Professor of Economics at the University of Wisconsin-La Crosse. His teaching and research interests include economic history and the economics of the sports industry. He has written three books, and more than 100 articles on the business of baseball. He has been co-chair of SABR's Business of Baseball committee and editor of the committee newsletter "Outside the Lines" since 2012. He received the Doug Pappas Award in 2014 and the Alexander Cartwright Award in 2020.

DAN HELPINGSTINE is a freelance writer who has published seven books and two short stories. His publishing credits include five books on the Chicago White Sox, a local history book, and a political book about Dallas. He has worked as a stringer for three newspapers in Northwest Indiana. Helpingstine has a BA in Political Science from Indiana University. He is currently working on a fantasy novel. He lives with his wife, Delia, in Highland, Indiana.

JEFF HOWARD grew up on the Northwest Side of Chicago and is a frequent contributor to the SABR Games Project. Jeff attended Luther College in Decorah, Iowa, played four years of DIII College Football, had a weekly sports column and read the news for the campus radio station. On graduation, he worked in the insurance industry and recently retired from a Research Analyst position for the largest labor healthcare fund in the country. He has mentored youth and organized multiple community baseball, softball, and basketball teams as a volunteer, teaching kids to appreciate and love the games they play.

DAVID KATHMAN lives in Mount Prospect, Illinois, with his wife, stepdaughter, and three dogs, and works in Chicago as a mutual fund analyst for Morningstar. He has a doctorate in linguistics from the University of Chicago, and over the past 30 years he has written many scholarly articles on linguistics, Shakespeare, Elizabethan theater history, and nineteenth-century baseball history.

SEAN KOLODZIEJ, a SABR member since 2018, is a lifelong Cubs fan. He was born, raised, and still lives in Joliet, Illinois, with his wife, Amy. His greatest moment at Wrigley Field was watching Glenallen Hill hit a home run onto the rooftop of a building on Waveland Avenue.

HERM KRABBENHOFT, a SABR member since 1981, is a retired research chemist. Among his numerous baseball research accomplishments are: Restoring the 1912 NL Triple Crown to Heinie Zimmerman; Establishing, in collaboration with Keith Carlson, David Newman, and Dixie Tourangeau, the accurate major-league record for most runs scored in a single season by an individual player—Billy Hamilton, 196 runs for Philadelphia in 1894; Determining the longest consecutive games on base safely streak in ML history—84 games by Ted Williams in 1949; Creating, in collaboration with Jim Smith and Steve Boren, the definitive SBK Triple Play Database. Herm is the author of *Leadoff Batters* published by McFarland in 2001. Krabbenhoft has been the recipient of three SABR Baseball Research Awards (1992, 1996, 2013).

DAVID KRELL is the Chair of SABR's Elysian Fields Chapter. His books include *1962: Baseball and America in the Time of JFK* and *Do You Believe in Magic? Baseball and America in the Groundbreaking Year of 1966*. He does not understand why Charles Ebbets is not in the Baseball Hall of Fame.

STEVE KREVISKY has been a professor of mathematics at Middlesex Community College in Connecticut for many years. His students get used to him bringing baseball into classes, to make it more interesting for them! He is also President of the Smoky Joe Wood SABR chapter, which has periodic meetings, chapter breakfasts, and trips to local minor league games. He been attending the national SABR conventions for many years, going back to his first convention in Chicago in 1986. He has been a frequent presenter, and will also be presenting this year. He has published articles in the journals and has also been on seven teams that won the trivia championships over the years! He looks forward to returning to Chicago for this year's convention. He is in two simulation/fantasy leagues, and looks forward to that committee meeting as well as seeing old friends there!

BILL LAMB spent more than 30 years as a state/county prosecutor in New Jersey, retiring in 2007. He served as editor of *The Inside Game*, the quarterly newsletter of the Deadball Era Committee, from 2012 to 2022, and has contributed articles to various SABR publications including the *Baseball Research Journal*, *The National Pastime*, and the Black Sox Scandal Research Committee newsletter. Bill is also the 2019 recipient of the Bob Davids Award, SABR's highest honor. He lives with his wife Barbara in Meredith, New Hampshire, and can be contacted via wflamb12@yahoo.com.

JIM LEEKE is a former journalist, creative director, and copywriter in Columbus, Ohio. He has contributed to various SABR publications, and also writes about other areas of American history. His numerous books include *From the Dugouts to the Trenches: Baseball During the Great War*, winner of the 2018 Larry Ritter Book Award.

EMALEE NELSON is a PhD student at the University of Texas at Austin. Her research focuses on the experience of women in sport during the twentieth and twenty-first centuries, including topics of gender, sexuality, expressions of femininity, and race. She also works for Texas Athletics, enjoys cheering on the Texas Longhorns and listening to her hometown Kansas City Royals baseball games on the radio.

TIM NEWMAN is a patent attorney in Austin Texas. He has been a member of SABR since 2000.

BILL PEARCH is a lifelong Chicago Cubs fan and serves as secretary/newsletter editor for SABR's Emil Rothe Chapter (Chicago). In 2022, he helped establish SABR's Central Illinois Chapter. Bill has contributed to SABR's publications about Comiskey Park, the 1995 Atlanta Braves, and has written SABR's biographies of Dwight, Illinois' semipro team owner Col. Frank L. Smith and Deadball Era pitcher Eddie Higgins. Bill will have two game summaries in SABR's upcoming publication, *Ebbets Field: Great, Historic, and Memorable Games in Brooklyn's Lost Ballpark*. He is happily married to a Milwaukee Brewers fan. Follow him on Twitter: @billpearch

JOHN RACANELLI is a Chicago lawyer with an insatiable interest in baseball-related litigation. When not rooting for his beloved Cubs (or working), he is probably reading a baseball book or blog, planning his next baseball trip, or enjoying downtime with his wife and family. He is probably the world's foremost photographer of triple peanuts found at ballgames and likes to think he has one of the most complete collections of vintage handheld electronic baseball games known to exist. John is a member of the Emil Rothe (Chicago) SABR Chapter, founder and Co-Chair of the SABR Baseball Landmarks Research Committee, and a regular contributor to the SABR Baseball Cards Research Committee blog.

BILL SAVAGE is a longtime SABR member and has taught courses on baseball film, fiction, comic books, and poetry at Northwestern University and the Newberry Library of Chicago since 1995. He delivered an earlier version of this essay at the SABR Black Sox Scandal Centennial Symposium at the Chicago History Museum in 2019. A Chicago Cubs season ticket holder, he wrote a fan's point-of-view column during the Cubs 2016 World Series run for ESPN.Com, "The View from Section 416."

JOHN SHOREY is a history professor emeritus from Iowa Western Community College where he taught an elective course on Baseball and American Culture for 20 years. He has written articles and chapters on a variety of baseball topics for various publications, including *Baseball Digest*. He has presented his research at the Cooperstown Symposium on Baseball and American Culture along with other baseball conferences.

DR. JOSEPH L. THOMPSON is a Faculty Lecturer with the Department of Management and Leadership at the C.T. Bauer Business School at the University of Houston. He has taught International Business and American History at the University of Houston since 2013. He joined SABR in 2010 and is currently the Larry Dierker SABR Chapter President. He is the co-author of *Mexican American Baseball in Houston* and *Southeast Texas and Houston Baseball, The Early Years*. He has contributed to different SABR publications including *We Are, We Can, We Will: The 1992 World Champion Toronto Blue Jays*, *Time for Expansion Baseball*, and *Dome Sweet Dome*. He is a US Air Force Desert Storm veteran and spends what little off time he has spending time with his family, playing with his two Yorkies, and playing baseball with his grandson.

DAN VANDEMORTEL became a Giants fan in upstate New York and moved to San Francisco to follow the team more closely. He has written extensively on Northern Ireland political and legal affairs. His baseball writing has appeared in *The National Pastime*, San Francisco's *Nob Hill Gazette*, and other publications. His article "White Circles Drawn in Crayon" (featured in McFarland *Historic Ballparks 05: The Polo Grounds*, 2019) won the 2020 McFarland-SABR Baseball Research Award. Feedback is welcome at giants1971@yahoo.com.

JOSEPH WANCHO lives in Brooklyn, Ohio. He has been a SABR member since 2005. Wancho has contributed to both the Games Project and the Bio Project and is the author of the book *Hebrew Hammer: A Biography of Al Rosen, All Star Third Baseman*, published by McFarland. He is currently working on his second biography, on Hall of Fame pitcher Bob Lemon.

KEVIN WARNEKE, who earned his doctoral degree from the University of Nebraska-Lincoln, is a fund raiser based in Omaha, Nebraska. He co-wrote *The Call to the Hall*, which tells the story of when baseball's highest honor came to 31 legends of the game.

BOB WEBSTER grew up in NW Indiana and has been a Cubs fan since 1963. After moving to Portland, Oregon, in 1980, Bob spends his time working on baseball research and writing and is a contributor to quite a few SABR projects. He worked as a Stats Stringer on the MLB Gameday app for three years and is a member of the Pacific Northwest Chapter of SABR, the Oregon Sports Hall of Fame, and is on the Board of Directors of the Old-Timers Baseball Association of Portland.

NOTES/AUTOGRAPHS